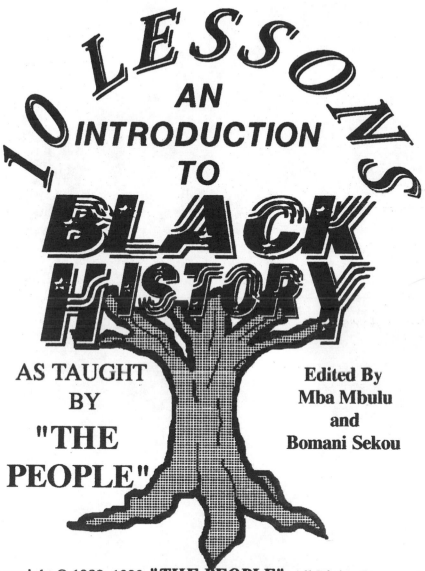

10 LESSONS

AN INTRODUCTION TO

BLACK HISTORY

AS TAUGHT BY "THE PEOPLE"

Edited By
Mba Mbulu
and
Bomani Sekou

P.O. BOX 50334   WASHINGTON, D.C. 20091-0334
Made in the U. S. of A.   ISBN 1-883885-06-X

TABLE OF CONTENTS

10 LESSONS

INTRODUCTION

This is a brief history of Black People. Its purpose is to give Us* an understanding of history. It is based on facts, but it does not relate all of those facts. It simply puts them all in perspective, makes them all part of a whole and gives Us a clear picture of what has been going on and continues to go on.

For the Black person who wants a solid foundation for understanding the history of Black People, "The People" suggests the following books as reading material. These books represent a gold mine of facts and superior scholarship, but more than anything else their value is in the conceptual framework upon which they are founded and the authors' abilities to pass on this framework as they pass on the events of history. The books include:

AFRICAN ORIGIN OF CIVILIZATION   Cheikh Anta Diop
BLACK RECONSTRUCTION IN AMERICA   W.E.B. DuBois
INTRODUCTION TO AFRICAN CIVILIZATION   John G. Jackson
THE BLACK JACOBINS   C.L.R. James
STOLEN LEGACY   George G.M. James
AFRICAN ORIGIN OF MAJOR WESTERN RELIGIONS   Yosef ben-
                                           Jochannan
BLACK MAN OF THE NILE   Yosef ben-Jochannan
THE DESTRUCTION OF BLACK CIVILIZATION   Chancellor Williams

EDITOR'S NOTE: All of the books that stated that Columbus discovered America were "scholarly" works, complete with footnotes and bibliography. But Columbus did not discover America. All of the books that said Abraham Lincoln freed the slaves were "scholarly" works, complete with footnotes and bibliography. But Lincoln did not free the slaves. All of the books that said Black People were inferior to white people were "scholarly" works, complete with footnotes and bibliography. But Black People have never been inferior to white people. All of the books that said Egypt was not a part of Black Africa were "scholarly" works, complete with footnotes and bibliography. But Egypt has always been part of Black Africa. We could continue to cite examples endlessly. The point is this: Research and honesty, not footnotes and bibliographies, are the real bases of scholarship. Don't play the fool!

---

*Throughout this Handbook [10 Lessons], and in all publications of "The People", the term Black People and all terms that refer to all of Us are capitalized. This is because Black philosophy is a philosophy of the group as opposed to a philosophy of the individual. To Us, the group, the Race, is supreme; Its identification and survival are of major concern and consideration. Therefore, whatever is referred to It is capitalized. This is in contrast to the philosophy of white people, which stresses the individual ("I") and capitalizes terms which refer to the individual while failing to capitalize terms that refer to the whole group. The difference in this particular aspect of philosophy indicates how basic the differences are between Black People and white people.

LESSON 1
LESSON OUTLINE

I. History Defined.
  A. The Story of the Past.
  B. Man (People) in Motion.
  C. Knowledge of Self (Yourself; The People You are Part of or Belong to).
    1. Knowledge of self involves knowing your enemies also.
  D. Proof of What Man (People) Will Do Under Certain Circumstances or in a Given Situation.

II. Purpose of History.
  A. To Provide Proof of a Person's Worth or a Race's Worth; therefore, To Instill Pride.
  B. To Discover What A People's Strengths Were in the Past, What Their Weaknesses were; How Each Aided and Hindered Their Development. This Enables People to Understand What Areas They Must Concentrate on NOW in Order to Progress or Succeed in an Endeavor/Aim/Goal.
  C. To Provide People With Alternative Approaches (Choices) to Solving or Eliminating Problems (So They Can Progress/Move Forward).
  D. To Psychologically and Socially Prepare People for Acceptance of an Alternative/Different Set of Values by which They can Conduct Their Lives; and to Prepare People to Defend Those Values.

III. Approaches To History.
  A. Event or Personality-Oriented Approach.
    1. Individuals and Specific Events are Viewed as Keys to Human Experiences and/or Development
      a. does not encompass the whole people-wise
      b. does not encompass the whole time-wise.
  B. Concept-Oriented Approach.
    1. Forces and Processes are Viewed as Keys to Human Experiences and/or Developments.
      a. encompasses the whole people-wise.
      b. encompasses the whole time-wise.
      c. concentrates on and makes people aware of the importance of processes and trends.

IV. Understanding History.
(People Do Things Because They Are Motivated By Something.)
  A. Human Nature Must be Understood (Human Nature will be defined as the conditioning that becomes part of a person and causes him or her to act in a certain way.).

1. As Influenced by a People's Environment and Material Needs. (This section can be used to describe why different groups of People develop dissimilar modes of practicing or expressing the same basic institution; e.g., marriage, lineage, burials, etc.).
- how people are affected by climatic conditions (as related to social development)
- how people satisfy their drive to survive (as related to economic development)
- how people satisfy their drive to be recognized by others (as related to their psychological development. Recognition is Affirmation or Confirmation of one's assumptions of value by others.)
2. As Projected in the Form of:
- Prejudice(s) (a preference or a dislike)
- Ethnocentrism (considering your group's prejudices to be inherently or naturally superior to other groups' prejudices)
- Racial Centrism (considering your race's prejudices to be inherently or naturally more valid than other races' prejudices)
-Racism (using your institutions to satisfy and validate your group's prejudices and stifle other races and their attempts to validate their prejudices)
- Their Interplay.
B. The Nature of Social Relationships (Definitely Valid Within the Realms of Private Property and Politics).
1. The Small Group
- organizes around a stated objective (and is therefore politically inclined)
- has a well-informed (knowledgeable) membership or constituency
- has a relatively quick adjustment rate or capacity
2. The Large Group (the Masses)
- reacts to plots of small group (therefore, the masses are not politically inclined)
- doesn't really understand (the intricacies or details and implications of) what is happening
- has a slow adjustment rate or capacity
- individuals in this group are not sure of the motives or intentions of others in their lot.
V. Central Motivating Force of a People (What People Base Their Social Make-up On; What Everything Else Revolves Around)
A. Religion/Ethics
(Concern for humanity the central factor)
B. Economics
(Survival/ security the central factor)

a. Individually
- what a person does in order to get what is needed to survive
- what a person does in order to get what is needed to live comfortably and securely
b. Socially
- what a group does (or a People do) in order to obtain or produce wealth (Wealth is the resources people need in order to build and maintain a Community or Nation, resources like Land, Materials, Ores, Food, etc.)
- how that group (or people) decides to divide that wealth among its members.
C. Power
(Dominating and controlling others is the central factor)
-Power is the ability to control others.

These factors are important to understanding History because they cause an individual and group psyche to develop. In effect, a man-made tendency or force is injected into each person in a given group that dictates how that person is likely to act/react in a given situation (and how that group is likely to act/react as well). And, acting, or doing (being in motion), is what History is all about.

Addendum:

I. European/White Economics and Development (European/White Economics is characterized by a conspiracy of the small group against the large group).
A. Climatic Conditions
1. Made whites anti-social and anti-human.
2. Imbedded an unusual recognition drive in them (white people).
B. Search For Material Needs (Living Necessities)
1. At Home
a. made them hoard/stockpile necessities
-affected them psychologically
b. largely determined the nature of their social structure and their social relationships.
2. Away From Home
a. caused them to search for land, resources and riches
- route to Asia/India (stumbled across America)
- exploration into Africa
- exploration into and settlement of America
C. Search For Cheap Labor (Small Group versus Large Group)
1. below subsistence (bare minimum) wages
2. Indentured servants
3. slaves
- whites

- Indians
- Africans/Black People
D. Drive for Riches/Profits/Luxuries
   1. An Outgrowth of Hoarding
   - feeling of insecurity a motivating factor
   2. Desire for Recognition
E. Economic Concentration as a Tool for Control (Small Group versus Large Group).
   1. Power (the ability to control others) and complete domination the driving forces.

I. History Defined

Before getting to Black History per se, it is important that We first get an understanding of history as a concept. In order to make this possible, the basic outline that you just read was drawn up. This basic outline can be applied to any people's history and will assist the student of history in determining if a certain version of history is slanted/prejudiced or not.

To begin with, We must get a working definition of history. There are hundreds of definitions of history. For example, it is the story of the past; every individual's past and every group's past. True history must tell what every individual did every minute of his/her life and explain the social implications of those acts. However, history told this way would be impractical. Therefore, most people/historians try to select those acts that they feel contributed a large degree to their development and revolve their version of history around those developments.

History can also be defined as the story of man, or as people in motion; that is, it is the story of man evolving and developing socially, politically and otherwise into what he is today. This involves people taking on values and developing codes of conduct. It involves people learning to communicate with each other. It involves people as they decide how to best satisfy the desires that are related to or dictated by their quest for survival. It involves people recognizing problems and attempting to solve those problems. It involves people living through one century and moving into another century, sometimes progressing, but failing to do so much too often.

History is also knowledge of self; knowledge of yourself and the people you are part of (racially, ethnically and nationally speaking). This type of knowledge is important because people in different parts of the world develop different morals and values (concepts of right and wrong) because they are challenged by different threats or obstacles to their survival. You have to understand what forces were operating that prompted your ancestors' actions and development because that is important to helping you understand yourself and what you should be about.

Understanding the different groups you come into contact with is a key to being able to act intelligently. You have to know what forces shaped other people in order to determine their capacity for acting in a certain way (humanely or inhumanely, for example). Because people/groups develop differently, their values are likely to be different and their assessment of what actions are appropriate for a particular situation is likely to be different. In order to properly prepare yourself to deal with other people and defend yourself against other people, you must know what to expect from them. Understanding their development is a key that will enable you to anticipate their actions and reactions and enable you to keep their effect on you to a minimum.

In order for Us, Black People, to act intelligently, We must know who We are and who Our enemies are. We must know who to look to for guidance and where We should not look for sincere support. One of the reasons We don't unite as We should is because We don't know who We are and We act like We don't know who Our enemies are.

History is also proof of what people will do under certain circumstances. Serious persons don't just read history; they study history and use history to help them determine what can happen if a certain set of circumstances prevails. For example, when Columbus landed on San Salvador in 1492 (when he "discovered" America according to white people), he observed the native inhabitants of that land (these inhabitants were later called Indians) and wrote to the king and queen of Spain that the Indians were a tractable and peaceful people who had the best nation in the world. They had warm and positive attitudes toward each other and life, he continued. Yet, he concluded that they, the Indians, should be made to work for white people and adapt the ways of white people. Even though Columbus recognized the supremacy of the life-style of the Indians, he still concluded that they should be made to adapt the European frame of reference (white people's values, practices and habits). When the Indians resisted white people's attempts to convert them and enslave them, they were wiped out. Since whites acted this way when they came into contact with the Indians (and history tells Us that this is definitely the case), then whites will act this way when they come into contact with any non-white people. Therefore, history is proof of what people will do under certain sets of circumstances.

Just as history is proof of what man will do under certain sets of circumstances, it implies or suggests what one group can do to prevent another group from harming it. Thus, Black People today can find probable solutions to the threat to Us posed by white people if We review history carefully and apply what We learn practically.

II. Purpose of History

People don't just read history, they read it for a serious purpose. One of the major purposes is to get proof of their worth and their race's worth. We, Black People, have not been made aware of Our worth because white persons and white-minded persons have always written the story of Black History. Such persons purposefully distort Black History (they tell lies) because they are racists and because they benefit economically from Our ignorance of Ourself. So, whites and their pitifully brainwashed lackeys tell Us that Our history was one of savages and slaves. If We accept this, then We will think We started as slaves and, as a result, We will think that Our position today represents progress for Us. But when We understand Our real history, We will discover that Our position today is shameful when compared to Our former heights. Therefore, the version of history We get is important because it will determine how We feel about Our present condition, and it will determine what steps We are likely to take to improve Our condition.

In the older cathedrals and churches in Europe, the holiest and most honored images of the Madonna and Child are Black. This proves the fact that so-called Mary and Jesus were Black. For centuries, educated whites have known this, but they have tried to tell Us otherwise because they don't want Us to be able to directly identify Ourselves (on the basis of color) with these glorified people. Whites don't want Us to know that Black People did all of those mystical things that are talked about in the Bible because such knowledge would leave Us less likely to accept their domination of Us.

We must use history to discover Our strengths and weaknesses as attested to by Our past triumphs and failures. Since we are living in a very politicized environment (under very political conditions), and since politics primarily concerns itself with the nature of conflict, We must know Our strengths and make use of them in order to survive and progress. [Politics is frequently confused with government. This is a big mistake. Government assumes that people can and will get together and create a social structure that is beneficial to the mass majority of people. Politics assumes that this is impossible. Politics assumes that conflict as a dominant factor is inevitable. Politics, therefore, involves itself with the nature of conflict. Government involves itself with the nature of harmony/agreement.]

History provides people with numerous and alternative approaches to solving and eliminating problems. It enables people to anticipate what probably will happen, and prepare accordingly. This is possible because basic principles that governed people's relations thousands of years ago also do so today. Therefore, given a certain set of circumstances, people are apt to act in essentially a certain way during any time period. History provides Us with case studies of similar circumstances that preceded Our particular circumstances, and reveals and opens up avenues to more potential solutions that We can analyze and eventually choose from.

History also serves the purpose of psychologically and socially preparing people to accept change(s). If Black People are aware of the fact that Our general circumstances have been experienced previously by other groups of people and that these other groups have succeeded in changing their condition, then We will be more apt to adjust Ourselves psychologically (mind-wise) and socially (relationship-wise) and attempt to do whatever We feel is necessary to bring about the conditions We desire to live under. Anything is possible as long as the people who want changes prepare themselves socially and psychologically for that change. As a result of social and psychological preparedness, people become willing and anxious to express their new values and defend those values. They begin to recognize that one people's values and life-style are just as valid as anyone else's, and should therefore be given the respect and recognition that any other social arrangement is given.

Additionally, history helps people understand the present. Everything (every event, person, nation, etc.) is a stage in a process. In order to understand where you are or where anyone else is, how you (or any other individual, nation or race) have developed, or how anything came to be, you must understand the past, the steps that led up to the thing or condition that exists today.

III. Approaches To History

People have developed different approaches to teaching history, depending on what their objective is. The two major approaches are (1) the event and personality oriented approach and (2) the concept-oriented approach. The event/personality-oriented approach views certain events and individuals as keys to human experiences and developments. It encourages students of history to concentrate on dates that are supposed to be particularly important because of a particular event that took place, and on individuals who have allegedly played important roles in making a country (or whatever) what it is. This approach has the effect of erasing or eliminating the mass majority of the world's people from the historical process (it makes them think that they are not important), and it destroys time as a continuity factor (since it skips from one "important" event to the next "important" event).

History should be told in a way that does not exclude any person (even though it does not explicitly mention every person) nor any span of time. The concept-oriented approach to history makes this possible. The concept-oriented approach views forces and processes as the keys to human experiences and development, and views the masses of people as playing the dominant role (by their tendency to act or fail to act) in making the present what it is. This approach encompasses the whole (by viewing everyone as a participant in the historical process and by not skipping periods of time for the purpose of highlighting outstanding events) and, in so doing, makes everyone aware of the forces and processes that led up to and made certain notable events possible and made certain individuals emerge as leaders.

IV. Understanding History

People do things (that is, act in a certain way) because they are or have been motivated by something. Thus human nature (the conditioning that becomes a part of a person or group and causes him/her to act in a certain way) must be understood in order to assess a person's or a group's tendencies. Human nature is very often overlooked by historians, but it should not be because there are no innate or inborn qualities that cause a person to act in a certain way; a person acts in a certain way because he/she has been conditioned to do so by direct and/or subtle forces. If We understand this, for example, then We should not be surprised to hear that things Black People were conditioned to do 6000 years ago affect Us (wherever We might be) today, whether We are consciously aware of them or not.

What is it that conditions a group of people? What forces push that group to function or act in a certain way (humanely as opposed to inhumanely, for example)? These are questions that relate to human nature and they must be answered if We are to understand human nature as a key to understanding history.

When we speak of human nature, we are referring to a conditioning process that has put certain values and impulses inside of people that directly and indirectly determine how those people are likely to respond under a certain set of circumstances. This conditioning process greatly affects people today, but We must understand that the process itself was most prevalent thousands of years ago, when nature played an overwhelmingly dominant role in the day-to-day affairs and activities of people. In areas where nature was cruel to people, people developed a cruel attitude toward life and survival. In areas where nature was not so cruel in critical ways, people developed attitudes toward life that were strikingly different.

White people developed in Europe. During their period of development at least three factors came into play that should be emphasized: (1) the degree to which the activities of European people were controlled and dominated by their environment, (2) the extremely cold weather and (3) the lack of economic resources and agricultural development.

European people were at the mercy of their environment at this stage of their development. They had not developed any mechanical or industrial capabilities that would reduce the effect of the cold weather, rain, snow or any of the other elements, on their life. Their only protection from the weather was a cave (which was very cold because rocks maintain a cold temperature) and an animal skin across small portions of their bodies. This extremely cold weather, coupled with the European's inability to make the necessary adjustments, forced European people to remain in their caves an overwhelming amount of time. In effect, Europeans were generally secluded from each other (not in constant contact). Only when it was entirely necessary did Europeans leave their cave. Most of the time they left in order to search for food.

Thus, in the European world, contact with others was generally an outgrowth or by-product of searches for food (economic ventures). Climatic conditions did not allow European people to come into contact with one another for purely social reasons (to mingle, chat or have fun, e.g.), and forced social contact to be incidental and secondary to economic activities. A result of this was that Europeans/whites did not have the opportunity to develop an appreciation of other persons as human beings, thus humane considerations could not develop as a primary concern of theirs. They viewed other individuals, first and foremost, from an economic perspective or vantage point. In other words, other individuals were viewed as either economic assets (persons who would help me get necessities and therefore make survival easier for me), or economic liabilities (persons who would compete with me for necessities and therefore make survival more difficult for me), and not as human beings (persons who have human rights and qualities that go beyond my economic considerations and who should therefore be respected by me at all times). This perspective, beyond sexual considerations, was applied even to persons who lived in the same cave with each other. That is, they viewed each other as economic assets or as economic liabilities.

IN THE EUROPEAN WORLD, CLIMATIC CONDITIONS FORCED WHITE PEOPLE TO EMPHASIZE SURVIVAL/ECONOMICS MORE THAN ETHICS AND MORALS (HUMAN-NESS). THIS IS CRITICAL TO UNDERSTANDING WHITE PEOPLE HISTORICALLY AND PRESENTLY.

At the time when people were developing in Africa, the climate was usually harsh, but cold weather was practically unknown. As a result, African people did not remain inside their dwellings. Quite to the contrary, they intermingled often, openly and freely for the sake of socializing and being with each other. Their contact with one another was not incidental to some other activity, so they learned to relate to each other as human beings and viewed each other from the perspective of one human being to another human being. They came to understand the basic equality of all people, the right of all people to be treated morally and humanely, and the obligation of each person to treat other humans in a moralistic and humane manner. Thus, the devaluation (low regard) of humans that was characteristic of white development was foreign to Africans, who could not view another person as an object (an asset, a liability, e.g.). Thus, the cruel things that whites do to human beings as a matter of course were not imaginable among African People; Africans had developed too much concern for human life to go about spreading pain and destruction to other people simply because they might compete with Africans for necessities.

Thus, differing climatic conditions affected the nature of Black humans and white humans in radically different ways. The results were that Black humans grew to develop a high regard for human life and a repugnance for human suffering, while white people regarded human beings in primarily economic rather than humane terms and therefore developed a capacity and willingness to mercilessly destroy humans and cause humans to suffer if economics demanded that either be done.

Climatic conditions were not the only forces that were affecting people during their early development. What people had to do to satisfy their drive to survive planted a tendency (mode of probable conduct) in them also. White people developed in an area where foodstuffs and availability of food were somewhat limited. Because of the extremely cold weather and the cold, rock-filled ground, agricultural development was not feasible at this stage of white people's development. Thus, whites had to depend almost solely on animal life for food and clothing. They had to hunt in order to survive and hoarded (kept for themselves) what they caught and killed because there was no guarantee that they would catch anything the next time they went out. Therefore, economic self-preservation and economic individualism (the forerunners of capitalism, monopoly and profiteering) became a part of white people's nature. There was always a mad scramble for the little that was available, and a fear of not having enough to avoid starvation (or some other economic curse) in the future. This mad scramble and fear of privation (not having enough) became a part of white people's psychological make-up and determined how they were going to act when they came into contact with other people (white and non-white. Thus, wherever white people are or where their presence is felt there is conflict due to attempts by whites to take economic valuables from non-whites and other whites).

Once again we observe a difference in Africa and African People. There, in spite of the harsh environment, it was receptive to the development of agriculture and the availability of foodstuffs was adequate in numerous localities. Though many areas were unproductive, many others were "gardens of eden" that were so fertile they did not have to be tended to grow. Plants, fruit, berries and nuts, etc., that could be eaten grew wild, and a further degree of security developed after African women discovered/invented agriculture and made it the basis of African economics. The products that were produced in gardens guaranteed a reliable supply of food, which made the hunting and fishing expeditions of African men less than life and death (or even necessary) activities.

With such a variety of foodstuffs and food sources in adequate quantities,

10 LESSONS

coupled with the African Peoples' humane considerations toward persons, the tendency to hoard and scramble for necessities was not a dominant one. Instead, the tendency to share was internalized. Communalism (community-orientation) evolved as an economic interpretation of life, and survival was not linked to one's ability to dominate others (physically nor militarily) and take valuables and necessities from others. As a result, conflicts of an economic nature rarely went beyond the realm of petty arguments and sham fights.

We have seen that environmental conditions and economic conditions planted certain tendencies in persons and affected certain "drives" (internalized motivating factors) that seem to be common to all human beings. One of these drives, the recognition drive, is a key to understanding history because it commands a mode of conduct that varies as we study different groups or races of people. The recognition drive itself is a quest for psychological security. It is the quest for a calm frame of mind, and that calm is gained when one realizes that his "claims" about himself or his group have been accepted as valid by others. As long as others who are considered significant do not accept these claims, a feeling of psychological insecurity persists, and the person or group feels pressured to bring himself a degree of internal peace by either getting others to change their response to the claims or by changing his mode of conduct in a manner that will make his claims valid.

Recognition became an obsession among those people who developed in areas where climatic conditions reduced social contact to an absolute minimum. Where the cold confined people to their particular cave until it was necessary that they leave for economic reasons, there were few opportunities for individuals to get the feeling that they were liked, accepted, well-thought of or valued by others. This lack of exposure to others, and the fact that they were all in competition with one another for survival necessities when they did get exposed to each other, greatly reduced the chances that they would view each other in a positive or well meaning-light. It made them paranoid and uncomfortable in the presence of others and resulted in them developing inferiority complexes. These people therefore, as a personal defense mechanism (a behavior manner that would preserve their conscious self-concept), developed the habit of attempting to impose their self-concepts and group-concepts onto others. Their chances of coming into contact with others were so limited that they developed the habit of attempting to force others to accept their "claims" of worth, and proved the validity of their claims to those who rejected them by attempting to dominate them in some manner. In other words, their recognition drive took on the following procedural characteristics:

(1) Here are my "claims". (2) Either accept them as valid and give me a feeling of psychological sure-ness/security or (3) Insult me by rejecting my assertions. If I am insulted I will feel forced to give validity to my claims by dominating you in some manner because I refuse to accept the possibility

that I have made a mistake in assessing myself/group/race/nation.

The recognition drives that characterized these individuals became characteristic of any group that they became a part of. Therefore, they are characteristic of the race that developed under those conditions and the national structures they established hundreds of years later. The manner in which they have been conditioned to seek psychological security also helps to explain why they refuse to seriously consider the assertions of people who reject their "claims"; it helps to explain why they refuse to seriously question the factual bases of their claims, and why they attempt to force themselves and their concepts onto other people and force other people to adapt their mannerisms and overall way of life. Finally, it helps explain why it is necessary for them to attempt to destroy those individuals and groups of people that totally reject them.

We can contrast this recognition attitude with the attitude that developed in areas where climatic and survival conditions allowed people to be in social contact with one another frequently, and for an assortment of reasons. Where the weather was warm, people intermingled freely and became somewhat socially involved with a large number of individuals. It is important to note that this contact was not competitive. This, combined with the extent of exposure, increased the chances that a person would have contact with some individuals that would accept them, value them and view them in a well-meaning light. Thus, the drive to be recognized was casually pacified and did not become an obsession. No inferiority complex developed. Instead of feeling the need to impose their self-concepts on others, they accepted the right of others to question the basis of their claims and were prepared, when necessary, to make changes in their conduct that others felt were suitable or appropriate. They were accustomed to receiving recognition, and their psychological balance could not be upset by the refusal of foreigners to accept their "claims" as valid. Therefore, they did not feel the need to attempt to force themselves onto others.

We can begin to see, then, that the recognition drive is an element of human nature that helps bring clarity to why people act in a certain manner. Therefore it must be understood and given just consideration if we are to get a complete concept of historical developments.

[It should be clearly stated at this time that none of what has been said indicates or even suggests that one group of people is naturally better than or superior to another group of people. We have simply revealed that different groups of people were affected by different environmental, climatic and survival conditions as they developed, and that they therefore either took on entirely different values or took on basically the same values but emphasized them in radically different degrees of priority. They developed different attitudes toward the things around them and the world in general, and took on different psychological qualities. The types of tools, implements and weapons that were to be produced were dictated by those conditions as well. When the different groups of people (specifically speaking, Black People and white people) came into contact with one another, the different attitudes, etc., met also and directed the actions of the particular persons they were a part of. In cases of misunderstanding and/or serious conflict, those whose conditions had forced them to view other human beings as either assets or liabilities found it relatively easy to de-humanize people (in this case, members of a different race) and treat them cruelly and inhumanely, while those whose conditions had geared them toward humane considerations sought, at practically all costs, to treat members of other groups like human beings should be treated. Likewise, those whose conditions had forced them to develop more sophisticated and damaging implements and weapons had the advantage because they could use those tools against people whose conditions had not made it necessary for them to develop weapons or implements that were designed for their destructive potential. Thus, environmental conditions and economic/survival necessities had prepared one group of people for a conflict-oriented or warlike mode of conduct, while different necessities and economic/survival conditions had molded a different group of people toward harmonious modes of conduct. In cases of dispute, the outcome was always predictable: those with the advanced weapons would militarily overcome those without advanced weapons.

[Note— Even today, and for a long time to come, people will be responding in accordance with how they were molded thousands of years ago!!!]

Human nature, to our knowledge, has no material substance. By that, we mean to say that the elements that go into making up a person's nature cannot be touched, seen, smelled nor tasted; therefore they cannot be scientifically examined and investigated, and it cannot be scientifically "proved". However, these elements, and human nature, do exist. All we need to do to confirm their existence is take note of the effects of human nature, those mannerisms and other external evidence that indicate what one's tendencies are and what probably goes on inside a person. These mannerisms and effects can be studied and have been called, among other things, prejudice, ethnocentrism, racial centrism and racism. We will briefly characterize each and show how they can function within the realm of history.

A prejudice, simply defined, is a preference or dislike. Such a preference or dislike is dictated by a force that is so deep-rooted that it is almost inherent, and it is therefore very powerful. Given the fact that different groups of people developed under radically different conditions, it is only natural that each would become accustomed to particular ideas, a certain environment and particular modes of conduct, and develop a feeling of familiarity with these particularities. It is also to be expected that they would like some of these particularities and dislike others. However, when presented with a choice between something they are familiar with and something that is completely new to them, their tendency would be to choose the thing they are completely familiar with (or that which more closely resembles that which they are familiar with). Thus, different groups of people from different areas would seek to band together or avoid each other based on observable likes and dislikes that they have in common. The more the conditions under which they developed were similar, the more likely they were (and are) to gravitate or move toward one another and develop substantial ties with one another.

[We will add, at this point, that people should not be blamed for being prejudiced or for having prejudices. All people are prejudiced. All people are conditioned to pre-judge certain things, and in the absence of any subsequent or follow-up analysis and understanding, they are apt to accept or reject things on the .basis of that pre-judgement alone.

Additionally, people will continue to have prejudices. Education cannot eliminate prejudice as a projection of human nature. All education can do is give people a more universal (or less restricted) basis for their prejudices. Undoubtedly, such an expanded basis for developing prejudices would benefit mankind and enable all people to communicate more effectively. Yet, the fact would remain and (subconscious) prejudices would still be the basis of a lot of choices and decisions.]

As people or groups of people with similar prejudices form ties, they evolve into ethnic communities. Ethnic as a term refers to large groups of people who have common traits and customs. These groups of people have somewhat similar mannerisms, similar tendencies and similar values. If this group of people is ethnocentric its members are under the impression that their customs, traits, mannerisms and values are inherently more valid than those of other groups. Ethnocentrism, then, can be defined as the tendency to consider your group's prejudices as inherently more valid than the prejudices of other groups. It is an attitude, a condition, that makes it easy for some groups to come together and defend themselves against attack on the one hand, and the cause of much discord among dissimilar groups of people on the other. It is important to note that members of a tribe and members of a nation-state can be equally ethnocentric.

Racial centrism is the result of exposure to groups who developed under conditions that were radically different from those that your group developed under. Not only do the mannerisms, customs and values, etc., of the other group differ from yours, but there are differences in appearance and biological effects as well. Thus, a process of comparison follows. The differences in appearance and biological effects will lead, for example, to the question of which group is more beautiful, which group has better taste in clothes, or which group smells better. The racially centric person will assert, regardless of circumstances, that his group represents beauty, good taste and inoffensive body odors. Likewise, he will feel that his group is, overall, more intelligent, more civilized or less barbaric, and more culturally and politically developed than the other group. Whenever there is a comparison of the two groups, the racially centric person or group will declare that it is superior. Thus, racial centrism is similar to ethnocentrism, with the critical difference being that race, not customs, values or mannerisms, is viewed as the determining factor when it comes to deciding the relative quality of this or that group.

Finally, human nature is projected in the form of racism. Racism is different from the projections we have already mentioned in two radical ways. First of all, racism is a conscious defense mechanism. It is spurred by an inferiority complex that developed as a result of one group being aesthetically, artistically and intellectually overwhelmed by a different group. Secondly, racism not only seeks to validate the prejudices of a particular group, but also attempts to systematically stifle other groups that attempt to validate their own prejudices. Racism, therefore, involves the attempted destruction, in some critical manner (culturally, politically, physically, psychologically) of other groups/races. Its basis is institutionalized power; the ability to force most people to adapt certain ideas and attitudes and the ability to eliminate or incapacitate those who refuse to do so. Though racism was not, in early times, a part of any person's nature, it was later introduced and ground into the minds and consciousness of a large number of people, so much so that those people have developed a subconscious tendency to respond/react in a racist manner whenever they are confronted by or in contact with a member of a different race. Because of racism, knowledge has been destroyed, hidden and distorted that could have been used to benefit people all over the world (knowledge that answers many questions that people are unable to answer today). Because of racism, entire nations and entire ethnic groups have been mutilated (billions of people have been killed because of their race alone). Because of racism, human beings today cannot take a sane and logical approach to solving or easing the problems that confront mankind, nor can they develop social contracts that are just and sincerely worked at. And because of racism, large numbers of people are yet to be destroyed because their destruction seems necessary if humankind is to even begin taking measures that will get people back into harmony with themselves and the other elements of the universe. Racism is inhumane, it is insane, it is totally illogical and it doesn't even have a real basis, but it drives some people, and We (Black People) must be aware of this fact when We deal with those people if We expect to deal with them progressively, effectively and in a manner that will be beneficial to Us.

All of the projections mentioned play on one another, are stirred by certain emotions, thoughts and events, and many times attempt to exert themselves at the same time. This results in people acting without knowledge of why they acted. We must be aware of this if We are to get a proper understanding of the trends and concepts that reveal the essence of history to Us.

In addition to understanding human nature (as a key to understanding history), We must understand the nature of social relationships. We will try to briefly explain or illustrate what we mean when we say "the nature of social relationships".

The social relationships we are referring to are those that split a group of people into what have become known as "classes". For our purposes, we will recognize at this point only two such classes. One of these is the privileged class, or small group; the other is the masses, or large group. In order to adequately understand history, We must understand the nature of the manner in which these two groups came about and developed, and how they relate to one another. We must not forget that the conditioning process each people had experienced would determine the character of the small group and the factor (see central motivating factors below) around which the activities of these two groups revolved.

The small group emerged; wherever it existed it has emerged. Here and there (within a given area) certain individuals distinguished themselves by taking a scientific approach to economic survival and/or social intercourse and social relationships. These individuals, because they took a scientific approach to the forces that were most influential in their day-to-day affairs, put themselves in a position to lead or take advantage of those persons who had not taken a scientific approach to life, survival, relating, etc. In the white world the small group applied this scientific approach first and foremost to economics since economics (getting what was needed to keep from starving to death) was the central motivating factor in their lives. In the Black world, where the environment allowed the people to take a relatively casual attitude toward economic survival while fostering humane considerations as a priority, religion, with its basic emphasis being the harmonious relationship of the people to themselves and the universe, emerged as the central motivating factor. Thus, in the Black world the small group applied a scientific approach to religion (as the central motivating factor) and all that it implied.

Whether the small group emerged to take advantage of the masses or work for the benefit of the masses, it had certain advantages. As was stated earlier, it took a scientific approach toward human intercourse, emphasizing economics, in one area, and humanity (religion) in another area. As such the small group, that is its individuals, had organized around a very clear objective. As time passed, this small group was to organize itself in order to better realize its objectives. Each person who took a scientific approach to human intercourse knew what he or she was about, so the small group was composed of a well-informed "membership". Because they were so well-informed and clear as to what their objectives were, they had the ability to make adjustments when events failed to materialize as they had planned. In short , the individuals who composed the small group had placed themselves in a position to either serve

10 LESSONS

or take advantage of those who had not taken a similar approach to human intercourse. That group which had failed to take such an approach, that group which remained after certain individuals distinguished themselves is the group we refer to as "the masses" (in this Handbook).

Because the small group had an objective that would affect the masses, and because the masses had no scientifically directed objectives of its own, the masses were doomed to react to the small group's plans and plots. Those who made up the masses randomly did what they had to do to survive and make the best of life; initially, in response to the dictates of nature and later in response to the dictates of the small group. In either case, for a long period of time the masses asked no questions and made no investigations. Thus, they failed to get a detailed understanding of what was really going on or what was controlling their lives. Therefore, when things happened that made it more difficult for the masses to be about doing whatever they wanted or needed to be about doing, they were generally unable to act in a manner that would change the course of events or eliminate an element of misfortune from their lives.

Thus, the masses can be characterized as a group that was not politically inclined (politics involves seeking control of the forces that are critical to your survival/existence). Because it was not politically inclined, because it did not see the necessity of taking a scientific approach to human intercourse, and because another group (the small group) did see this necessity, the masses of people found themselves reacting to the ideas and organized efforts of the small group. They reacted continually because they failed to get a detailed understanding of what was actually happening. They knew their life-style, their day-to-day activities (both economic and social) , was being affected in essential/basic ways that were not due to natural occurrences, and they knew that certain individuals could be somewhat linked to these changes, but they did not investigate or try to understand the depth of these changes. This general lack of research and understanding made adjusting difficult for them, to the extent that by the time they caught on to how they were being manipulated in one specific way by the small group, either the damage had already been done or the small group had anticipated a response and changed its manner of manipulating the masses. If the small group aimed at taking advantage of the masses, they kept the masses in a state of confusion and disorganization, so much so that the masses generally distrusted or felt suspect of anyone who attempted to champion the cause of the masses or attempted to bring about conditions that the masses desired (in basic terms, these conditions consisted of adequate food, shelter and other necessities). Because they were not properly informed and were disorganized, the masses did not have the capacity to recognize nor adequately support the persons among them who were capable and most concerned about their welfare.

An understanding of these social relationships is a key to getting a clear view of people in motion (history). Recognizing that nothing just happens, that every effect (outcome) has a cause, and that there are groups that concern themselves with making things happen while other groups concern themselves with "making do"; recognizing constants such as these will enable Us to tie events and incidents together that might otherwise seem entirely independent of one another. It will provide Us with the insight We need to get an in-depth understanding of history, and thereby enable Us to make the most of (learn from and act according to) that understanding.

V. Central Motivating Force of a People

The final factor we will mention that is critical to an understanding of historical processes is the "central motivating force" of a people. The central motivating force among people in a given area is that factor around which everything else revolves. It is the pivot point of a social structure (a social structure includes economic, political, moral, etc., institutions and practices), the thing the people in a given area base their social activities on.

Generally speaking, there are three such motivating factors. The first of these we will refer to as religion (remember that ethical codes have a religious or humanistic basis). The second and unquestionably the most critical motivating factor is economics, since it aims to satisfy a person's or group's survival needs. And, closely allied to either of the above is power. We will discuss each separately, beginning with religion.

The basis of religion as a central motivating factor is concern for mankind. If religion is the central motivating factor of a people, then it is a force which is supposed to bring all of nature's parts (especially people) toward spiritual and physical harmony. Its purpose is to make people freer, more loving, more humane; and it alone determines how people in a given area act toward one another on social,' economic and governmental levels. Since religion can only emerge as the central motivating factor after a people's basic survival needs have been met and somewhat secured, it is not probable that it would emerge as such in any part of the white world. It was able to emerge as such in the Black world (because of suitable environmental conditions and availability of foodstuffs), where it served as the impetus for extensive and intensive scientific research and for an advanced, civilized way-of-life. In fact, religion was such a dominant force in the lives of early Black People that they were able to lay the foundation for all of the holy books and formal religious ceremonies and beliefs that were to be practiced thousands of years later (including those that are practiced today in all the different parts of the white world).

[Note: To say that Black People laid the foundations for all of the holy books and formal religious ceremonies and beliefs is not to say that white people did not have a "religion" or worship certain "gods" before they came into contact with Black People. They did, but their type of worship was not the basis of a way-of-life. It was an outgrowth of white people's need to look to something supernatural for assistance during critical times (all people probably have this need). What Black People had developed was on an entirely different level; it was civilized, sophisticated yet simple, mature.

Where religion is not the central motivating factor of a people; where it revolves around a much more dominant factor, religion becomes at best an ethical guide to or interpretation of life based upon a people's responses to certain challenges to their survival. Whether this ethical guide is observed or not is determined by the people's response to some other more dominant factor. This means that, in such cases, religion has been robbed of its essence (because religion must be the dominant force in order to function as it should function); it becomes an ideology that represents a certain culture or a weapon that is used to help control people who are being abused or exploited. Under such conditions, religion becomes a sinister crutch and an instrument of oppression. In fact, it becomes everything but religion and would not even be called a religion by the Black People who laid down the basic principles of religious thought and actions. Thus, the dominant "religions" in the world today (Christianity, Islam, Judaism) are not religions at all; they are religious ideologies. They are the products of people who have studied religion; they studied religion and decided that it would not allow them to do the things they wanted to do, so they interpreted the religion and adjusted it (made an ideology out of it) in a manner that suited their purposes.

Nowadays, for the overwhelming majority of peoples in the world, religion is a non-dominating force. It is almost a joke, in fact. For that reason, We should not expect people who are not Black to treat Us in a humane fashion. We, Black People, should not allow any people's religion (except Ours, which is known to only a handful of Us) to become a dominant force in Our personal lives (or otherwise), because it will be used to enslave Us and take advantage of Us in a variety of other ways.

Economics is the major factor that motivates people nowadays. Initially, in all social structures, economics is what drives people. People have to solve the problem of surviving before they can start thinking about the nature of the universe and the nature of being (religion) and the systematic domination of or control of other people (power).

Wealth is the aim of any economic system or activity. Wealth can be defined as that which is needed to survive and, at a later stage, also that which is needed to live comfortably. Economics, then, from this perspective, is the sum total of the activities people go through in order to get what is needed to survive/live comfortably.

From a social standpoint, wealth is what a people need in order to build a community or nation. Wealth is based on land (which is the source of everything of economic value because the land holds resources and produces food and all other ingredients people need in order to survive), and people (who make the land as productive as possible and convert what is produced into something of value). Economics, then, from a social perspective, is what a group/people does in order to get or produce wealth, and how that group/people decides to divide that wealth among the members of its nation.

How the accumulated wealth is divided is one of the keys to explaining the disharmony that exists between the different "classes" (the small group and the large group) of a nation. The wealth is always collected and produced by the entire nation, but because of tactics, conspiracies and plots of the small group, the entire nation rarely if ever benefits equally from the wealth that is collected and produced. The wealth can be equally divided (from each according to his/her ability to produce, to each according to his/her need) and was done among early Black People in Africa, but such is not the case today among any people. However, it can be the case if people really want it to be the case.

Economics, then, concerns itself with survival and comfort. It concerns itself with the collection, production and distribution of wealth. To the early cave man in Europe, economics meant sharing a rabbit or finding an adequate supply of water. To the early white people in Arabia, economics meant following sheep from one grazing ground to the next. To the early African, economics meant collective hunts, the discovery of agriculture, and/or picking a fruit off of a tree on a regular basis. From these types of economic activities (which include sharing or hoarding the actual wealth that was produced or collected) evolved an economic system based on labor and wages. This type of economic system introduced astronomical profits (a lot of the wealth) for a few (the small group) and chump change (only a little bit of the wealth) for the large group, the masses, those who actually did the work. As the desire to live comfortably and hoard (stockpile goods and riches) replaced the drive to survive as the objective of the economic activities of the small group, those who had failed to take a scientific approach to social intercourse experienced a harder and harder time getting what they needed to survive and became increasingly poverty stricken. Even with advanced machines and technological progress which make it possible for mankind to produce enough wealth to meet the needs of all the people in the world, the condition of poverty continues to afflict more and more people. And, the masses of the people will continue to experience privation and poverty for as long as they fail to understand the nature of social relationships and allow a group of organized thieves to develop an economic structure (call it capitalism or whatever they please) that is intended to make a lot of people work but only a few people rich or comfortable.

Power is the third and final central motivating factor we will mention. The motivation in this case is acquiring or gaining the ability to control others, to dominate others against their will, to force others to do whatever you deem is necessary. Power is might. From an individual standpoint, it is the ability to overwhelm those who compete with you for goods, concessions, etc. From a social standpoint, power is the ability to determine what the priorities of a community or nation are, and the ability to force, when necessary, the citizens of the community or nation to act in a manner that will make it easier to realize those priorities.

We should not fail to stress that power is an ability. Power does not of necessity have right on its side, though more times than not those in positions of power use tactics to get laws passed that will give them the "right" or "authority" to do what they want to do. Yet, it must be remembered that power is the strong arm of politics. Since politics concerns itself primarily with conflict (ideological and physical war), it is clear that power concerns itself with disabling and eliminating the competition or enemy and enabling you to dominate others with as little inconvenience to yourself as possible. The drive for power, hand in hand with economics (the drive to hoard), is what local, national and especially international relationships are about today. Black People should be particularly aware of and sensitive to this reality.

Man (and nations) _is civilized to the degree to which he controls his excesses_ (misuse and/or unnecessary use of power) _once he has acquired power_. At one time, when the central motivating factor of Black People was religion, the social system itself discouraged and limited the incidence of excesses. However, in a social system that is dominated by greed, hoarding and taking advantage of the next person, power is virtually without restraint. Such a social system itself encourages people to take things to the extreme in attempts to secure themselves economically and psychologically (see IV). Lip service is given to "the community" or to "the common people", but reality says that the individual is supreme, particularly by the manner in which individualism is expressed by the small group. Likewise, lip service is given which encourages individuals in positions of power to not abuse that power, but the reality of the social system dictates that abuse of power is a logical follow-up to the acquisition of power. Power then, because it opens the door to legal thievery and illusions of greatness, can motivate persons and motivate nations who have satisfied a prior need to attempt to place themselves in a position that will allow them to play god with the lives and survival efforts of other persons and nations. We must understand this if We are to get a worthwhile understanding of history.

The factors mentioned throughout this outline are important because they cause a human psyche to develop. The psyche is apt to differ from area to area, but in each area a man-made tendency or force is injected into each person in a given group that dictates how that person is likely to act/react in a given situation, and how that group is likely to act/react as well.

These psyches, even though they were formed thousands of years ago, dominate the actions/reactions of various groups and races of people to this day. This fact is too important for Us to forget for even one second. We must understand that _the circumstances of a particular time are not the only factors that influence a person's or group's response or reaction_. As We begin to understand the different psyches that developed from one area to another, We can begin forming concepts about the different groups of people We have to relate to and defend Ourselves against. We will then be able to consider their psychic tendencies and their historical manner of action as well as the particulars of a given situation when We have to decide how to respond when We are approached by them or confronted by them. Considerations of this nature are too important to understress, and they can have their proper influence if We get an adequate understanding of history and historical development.

People are definitely in motion, Brothers and Sisters, and their motion has been basically the same (unchanged) for thousands and thousands of years. Understanding history enables Us to understand what people's motion is all about (what they are doing, why they are doing that thing), and places Us in a position to make motion, with the least amount of folly (foolishness) and wasted energy, in a direction that will benefit Us substantially.

Addendum to Lesson 1

In order to fully understand yourself and act intelligently, you must also understand your enemies and the people you relate to. With this knowledge you will know how you should act when We, Black People, have contact with other people.

Black People 'have what David Walker (1829) called "natural" enemies. Those natural enemies of Black People he referred to are white people. For Our benefit We should understand the psychic make-up and development of these people; that way, We will be better able to respond to them intelligently when they approach Us or confront Us.

History reveals that the central motivating force among all white people is economics. The conditions that determined what white people had to do to merely survive (at the time of their early development) instilled them with attitudes, tendencies and a manner of conduct that is individualistic and self-righteous. It instilled in them the belief that the ends justify the means, without substantial regard for those innocent persons who are victimized along the way. Survival was rough for white people during the time they were developing the attitudes, tendencies and psychological properties that have remained a part of them ever since. We should understand this, and thereby understand why they act as they do and why they will continue to act as they do.

European attempts to survive were hindered tremendously by a harsh climate and land that mainly could not be used for agricultural development. Thus, the Europeans depended mostly on animals for food. Because there was no guaranteed supply of animals and because they had to hunt animals in extremely cold weather, individuals were apt to keep all of what they had for themselves when they did manage to capture and kill an animal. This manner of acting, this overwhelming concern with "me" only, was a practical step taken by the European individual that would insure him another meal and make it unnecessary for him to face cold weather again immediately. Europeans were unable to devise a more logical solution to their economic woes, that of taking a communal or group approach to survival, because the cold weather kept them from coming into contact with one another and developing common and personal ties. It kept them from getting to know one another, and this made it easy for each individual to continue to think of the next person as someone who will compete with "me" for available food sources or as someone who might attempt to take "my" goods from me.

Thus We see, at this early stage, the tendency of Europeans to concern themselves primarily with "me". We see how hoarding and stockpiling goods was a practical step each individual took in order to insure the survival of one person or one unit (which later came to be called a family. Singular terms and phrases, as used in this section, need not be restricted to just one person. They may refer to a unit as well.). We see an individual who has had very limited contact with other human beings, and a person who has developed very few, if any, concerns for other human beings. We see a person who is primarily concerned with economic considerations, a person who will do anything necessary to get what he needs to survive. We see, at this early stage, the white person who later enslaved Black People, murdered Black People and other natives of America (the so-called "Indians"), created and monopolized a world economic system and profiteered to no end ruthlessly. If We look conceptually. We will see that, in this regard, the white person who lived thousands of years ago in caves is the same white person who lives today in apartments, houses and luxury hotels. From the beginning white people did what they felt was necessary to satisfy their economic drives, even if it called for the displacement and/or extermination of large numbers of people. And today that is still the case. More than anything else, including humane considerations, white people today are geared toward satisfying their economic drives, and they will do anything, including the most inhumane thing, to satisfy or attempt to satisfy that drive. The same forces that molded white people and conditioned white people to act in a certain manner thousands of years ago are still controlling white people today. Black People must constantly be aware of this fact.

We have already noted that the cold weather and economic attitudes made it almost impossible for white individuals to develop humane concerns for one another. This lack of social contact also imbedded an unusual recognition drive into Europeans that forced them to attempt to impose their values and assumptions of worth onto other people. Even when Europeans are able to admit that other people have a superior life-style and social organization than they do, white people still feel the need to force other people to take on their values and manners of behavior. This explains why Christopher Columbus (the person who supposedly "discovered" America in 1492), even after recognizing that "there is not in the world a better nation" than that of the Indians, still felt that the Indians should be "made to work, sow and do all that is necessary to adopt our [white people's] ways." (Dee Brown, Bury My Heart At Wounded Knee) Because of white people's development, they feel it is necessary that they impose their values, way of life and mannerisms onto other people, whether other people want them or not. Whites did this centuries ago and they still do it today, for the same basic reason and as a result of the same basic force in their make-up. White people are the only type people who developed this type of recognition incentive, and for that reason it is unusual. (For more on this, review the earlier section on recognition.)

White people, during their developmental years, were cave dwellers and shepherds (depending on the location). In either case their diet consisted of meat and meat products, and little else. The genetic ramifications of an all meat diet are yet to be fully understood and therefore will not be discussed at this time. However, we felt the need to mention it because We (Black People) must give careful thought and consideration to this factor as soon as the necessary information is made available.

Since it has been pointed out that white people were shepherds and cave dwellers during the early stages of their development, We should add that they were still shepherds and cave dwellers when they first came into contact with Black People. At the time of this contact, Black People were living a settled, agricultural type life, and were benefiting from the advantages afforded by a civilized state of existence. Since shepherds and cavemen are uncivilized and lack formal social order and social appreciation, it is definite that they had nothing to offer the Blacks they came into contact with and everything to gain from them and learn from them. We should be mindful of this fact when white people preach to Us about the benefits We have received as a result of being brought into contact with them (since the 1600s). With the knowledge we now have, we can state definitely that they learned what they know (insofar as civilization is concerned) from Us, and that they have not, even to this day, reached a fully civilized state of behavior. Because of their inability to understand a lot of what Black People had discovered and incorporated into a Black life-style, white people rejected much of Our knowledge as useless and many times attempted to destroy it. They rejected much of what civilized people made available to them then and they still do so today. Because of the rejection of this information early white people are today only a few centuries removed from barbarism. Because they are still rejecting the knowledge that civilized people are offering them today, their social practices and mores are many times more heathen than human. And they will continue to reject the wisdom of civilized people. They are not yet equipped to do otherwise! We hesitate to write such a thing because it sounds like racist propaganda, but we must reveal to Black People what the facts have revealed to those of Us who have done the necessary research and study.

European economics presently is and for several centuries has been characterized by a conspiracy of the small group against the large group. (For a review of this concept, see the section on the nature of social relationships.) In early times, because their land was so barren and unproductive, Europeans had to leave their local home base and wander here and there in search of food and other necessities. As the centuries passed, certain individuals took a scientific approach to economic survival, united among themselves and began to collectively finance the exploration of areas outside of Europe for their economic potential. The members of the small group, those who would claim "rights" to whatever was discovered, would not explore the foreign lands themselves. They would use members of the large group for this purpose and, if their exploratory efforts proved fruitful, they would use additional members of the large group to settle the area and develop the area. The only things the small group contributed to these efforts were exploration funds and a functional structure (which brought multiple numbers of large group members together under a common banner or objective). On the other hand, members of the large group lost their lives while fighting to settle the land that was "discovered" (they had to take the land by murdering the people who were already living there), sweated and broke their backs developing the area into an economically productive area (one that would produce what the small group could use to make profits), and toiled to produce what could be produced in as large quantities as possible. But the benefits received by the members of the large group were disproportionate to what they had invested; their benefits were very small when compared to the benefits received by the small group, which had invested relatively little. Indeed, it was the small group that got richer from the discovery of the land because it had "legal rights" to the land. This right meant that members of the large group were risking their lives to discover land for the small group, murdering native inhabitants so they could claim land for the small group, sweating to develop that land for the small group, and toiling to produce products that, by law, belonged to a small number of persons who had not worked at all to produce them. This conspiracy was so embryonic (at an early stage of development) and subtle that few people detected it. The validity of its premise was never even questioned. In fact, the members of the small group who got rich at the expense of someone else's labor, blood, sweat and tears were praised for their economic insight and initiative, and set up as models for all persons who wanted to "make something of themselves."

Thus, the urge of each European to "make something of himself" reenforced the immoral but popularly and legally recognized right of the small group to prosper at the expense of the large group. This individual prosperity is in fact only a phrase that describes the conditioned tendency of white people to hoard and stockpile goods that are needed by those who have been less fortunate or by those who have been used but not rewarded. Because some individuals who do not need goods hoard them, a social condition develops that is disguised by terms such as overpopulation, starvation, oil and gas shortages, unemployment, etc. These terms suggest the existence of circumstances that in fact do not exist. That is why, from an economic perspective (remember, economics is central to what white people do), all of these terms can be broken down to mean the same thing. There would be no such thing as overpopulation if the shelter and food that is available were properly divided, if the gas and oil that are available were equally accessible to everyone, and if every able body were allowed to contribute to the productive needs of the nation. But these ifs would eliminate hoarding (or whatever white people want to call it), and white people are against the elimination of each individual's right to hoard because white people have been conditioned to hoard. Black People should be aware of this fact when We run into whites who call themselves communists and socialists and who talk about a "redistribution of the wealth". They want the wealth redistributed, there is no doubt about that, but not to each according to his or her need. They want more of the wealth redistributed to them so they can hoard it and feel secure about their future survival.

We mentioned how white people had to travel outside of Europe in search of land and other representations of wealth. During the 1400s, they were hoping to find a short route to India but one of their explorers, Christopher Columbus, got lost and stumbled across what is called America today. Columbus stumbled across a small island called San Salvador, which is in the Caribbean (Columbus never knew that what is now called the United States even existed), and a huge expanse of land that he and others discovered on later trips for the small groups that had financed his trips. Columbus and his sailors sailed under the Spanish flag for the benefit of the small group in Spain, but news of his discovery got to other countries and opened a mad rush for control of America by small groups from several European countries. This mad rush signalled the end of America as "the land of the free and the home of the brave," and the beginning of an economic structure that was to make America the cotton field,

grave yard and mill of the slave and the land and home of the slaveowner.
The small group from Spain initially dominated exploratory trips into America.
At this time Spain was the most advanced country in Europe because many
Black People from Africa (called Moors) had moved into Spain. With these
Blacks came the knowledge and advanced culture of the African People, and
resulted in the establishment of large cities in Spain (of hundreds of thousands
of people) at a time when no other city in all of Europe had a population of
more than 30,000 people. These cities were characterized by shaded walkways,
public fountains and public baths, etc. As a matter of fact, before the Moors
settled in Spain, white people were not in the habit of taking baths regularly.
The Moors taught the Spanish that it was a proper and necessary thing to
do.

In 1492 the last of the Moors were expelled from Spain by the racist and
greedy small group that had gained control of the government. Less than 100
years later, Spain had sunk to near the bottom of the European totem pole
(where it remains in the 20th century). The fact of this matter cannot be
debated. When the Moors left Spain all of the intelligence, knowledge and
expertise that had made Spain develop left with them.

Not long after Columbus landed at San Salvador an extermination process
was put into motion against the native American (so-called "Indian" by
Columbus and his followers). This extermination process began as an effort
to force the Indians to deliver valuable resources (such as gold) to the white
explorers (failure to do so resulted in punishment— maybe death), it continued
as an effort to force the Indians to work themselves to death for the white
explorers, and it ended in efforts (most of which were successful) to remove
the Indians from the land altogether by killing them, pushing them to unwanted
areas and forcing them to live on special sites called reservations. This process,
began by the white Spaniards and continued by other whites, was initiated in
North America, South America, Central America and the Caribbean, and it
resulted in practically the entire removal/murder of the "Indians" in each of these
areas.

White people eliminated these people because they felt it was necessary
if they were to secure and enhance their economic status. White people are
always trying to take other people's land and resources and force other people
to work for them. If whites are resisted in either of these efforts, they attempt
to eliminate the people themselves. That way they can re-settle the land with
slaves or white people who will act in a manner that closely measures up to
what the small group considers is good for their economic welfare. Black People
should remember this. We need not even look to history for proof of this fact
because things are happening right now that bear it out quite clearly.

The drive for riches is an extension of the hoarding tendency white people
developed centuries ago. No matter how much they have accumulated, they

still feel insecure because they live in a dog-eat-dog world and no one knows what misfortune the future might bring. In case the future does hold misfortune, white people try to stock up on enough money and goods to carry them through the hard times (they do not feel that their dog-eat-dog social structure will adequately provide for them).

Luxuries are evidence of the wealth an individual has accumulated. It makes white individuals (and their imitators) feel that they are the envy of other persons and that they are respected by others. Such envy and respect from others helps the white individual feel a degree of self-respect and psychological contentment (insofar as recognition is concerned). It makes white individuals feel "equal" to the haves and better than the have-nots. In essence, the desire for luxuries is simply another expression of the white individual's ego-centric nature.

With the beginnings of capitalism as an economic order in the 1500s and the emergence of industrial capitalism as the dominant economic force in the world in the 1800s, it became crystal clear to all who looked and analyzed that economics determined the politics, worship and social structure of the white world, and that a small group existed that planned to direct and maintain control of this all-important activity, this central motivating factor. The efforts of the small group to dominate all areas of economic activity and to use the government and political processes to help it bring about this end was evidence that the small group was viewing political power as a key to unlimited and uncontrolled economic expansion. Because these individuals, insofar as business is concerned, wanted to be able to do whatever they wanted to do whenever they wanted to do it (without being hassled by rules and regulations that were not entirely tolerant of their activities), they consolidated their forces and united under the banners of trusts, syndicates, and multinational corporations, etc. This enabled them to formulate national and international business policies and objectives, to have certain individuals who would act in their interests elected to public office, and to use money, gifts and "concessions" to buy off other officials as they embarked on a mission to order the world according to their economic whims. In short, they monopolized (eliminated competition among themselves) their business forces in order to gain the power, the ability to control others, that was necessary to dictatorially rule the business world.

Such a process, if successful, would automatically eliminate much of the real power of "governments". More and more, the "government" would be the pawn of the small group. Understanding this will help Us understand why the American government does not protect the large group from the economic schemes of the small group. What We, Black People, must remember is that this type development is natural for white people and that it will be replaced by a development that is even more sinister and exclusive if white people have their way.

Much that is said later will help the reader understand this matter better.

[Note: Agriculture is a science. It is a process that involves planning and methodology. Even during its primitive (early) stages this was the case. Therefore, at the time white people were developing they had no knowledge of agriculture. This, combined with the harsh climate, rocky ground and inadequate soil, etc., dictated that agriculture would not affect their efforts to survive during this period. This is not to say that plants would not grow in Europe during this period. In some places they would, but the mere presence of plants does not necessarily prove the presence of agriculture. We should keep this in mind.]

LESSON 2
LESSON OUTLINE

I. Tidbits

A. Human Nature

(People do things for very practical or personal reasons; "noble" acts are few and far between.)

1. Fear (An emotion spurred by the natural desire to avoid pain and keep threats to your personal welfare and well-being from harming you.)

2. Sex (The natural attraction of men to women and women to men that causes events to develop in the political arena that probably would not have developed otherwise.)

3. Personal Allegiance (The tendency to act in a manner that evidences concern for only a small number of persons; e.g., an individual, his or her family, etc.)

B. Religion

(Religions are Ethnically and/or Racially-Centric)

1. Religious Wars

2. Amenhotep IV

II. White Peoples' Attacks on Other Peoples.

(No other race of people in the world has treated human beings as viciously and inhumanely as the white race has.)

III. Why the American Indians Failed to Successfully Defend Themselves Against White People.

A. Human Nature (As evidenced by their social and political, including "military", institutions and practices)

1. Started resisting too late

2. Were disunited and uncommitted

a. preferred to "get away"

3. No real leadership (in the European/white sense of the word)

4. No organized or concerted plan of action (either military or otherwise)

5. Inadequate knowledge of who the enemy was

a. they made it possible for white people to survive

b. they made military alliances with white people

6. Inadequate knowledge of what the enemy was

a. the enemy was machines/technology

b. the enemy was a product of cruel environmental conditions

IV. Why Black People Were Enslaved

A. Rationalizations (A rationalization is a "made-up" reason.)

1. We (Black People) were savages

2. We needed to be Christianized/civilized
B. Reasons
1. Human Nature
a. We could not defend Ourselves adequately
2. White people recognized that We were accustomed to the settled, civilized, agricultural way-of-life that they wanted to establish. It was therefore to the whites' advantage to enslave Us because:
a. We were able to do the work that would be needed to build the type of country white people wanted to build
b. We had the skills needed to build the type of country white people desired
c. We were a humane people; therefore the whites concluded that We were not likely to rebel viciously against them for enslaving Us.

I. Tidbits

We will begin this lesson by reiterating how important understanding human nature is to understanding historical developments (Remember: human beings make history. In a manner of speaking, historical developments are only a series of seemingly individual acts). We must understand that, because of the nature of human beings, people do things for very mundane and practical reasons. People do things because what they do will benefit them in some manner or keep them and who or what they care about from being adversely affected. Once We accept this as a very basic principle, We will have no problem accepting the proposition that "noble" acts are few and far between, if at all. We will realize that it is a rare case indeed when a person who is in a position to act in a manner that will benefit him or someone he favors fails to do so because "right" or "morality" dictates that he acts to the contrary. It is unfortunate, but people, particularly those who are in an individualistic-type social structure, just are not concerned about the welfare of the next person when they stand the chance of gaining or losing something.

We will be more direct. Persons, including those We read about in history books (so-called "great" men and women), rarely if ever do things or act in a certain way for "ethical" reasons. Careful study will reveal that noble acts are few and far between, that people do things for very personal and practical reasons, and that these actions (things people do) are motivated by factors such as fear, sex and personal considerations, among others. Persons who have been given the public's trust (officeholders, for example) often betray the public in a variety of ways because of such petty reasons and considerations. For example, Massinissa, the Black king of Numibia (an ancient kingdom in North Africa) allied with the Romans (white people) against the Khart-Haddans

(Black People who were led by Hannibal, the Black general. Khart-Haddas is called Carthage by white people) because Khart-Haddas was partly responsible for him not marrying the woman he wanted to marry. The result of this alliance was the defeat and destruction of Khart-Haddas and the control of all North Africa (including Massinissa's kingdom) by white people, and the eventual enslavement of the Black Race. If Massinissa had done as he should have done and allied with Black People in the interest of Black People, Numibia (his own land) would have survived as a kingdom and the course of African History might have been considerably different. But, partly because of Massinissa's petty narrow-mindedness and selfishness, millions upon millions of Black People have suffered.

We can see this just as clearly in American history. Thomas Jefferson, the early white American rebel and President, knew that slavery was immoral, but he lived off the sweat and blood of slaves without feeling regretful, and refused to free most of them even as he laid on his dying bed. Where were his morals when this immoral issue confronted him? The same holds true for Abraham Lincoln, who refused to use his powers as President to free Black People, even though he knew we were human beings who deserved to be treated accordingly, and even though the Americans who held most of the slaves had rebelled against the United States government. Abraham Lincoln's concern was not with morals, but with what he could do to benefit the nation he cared about and the people he cared about (all of whom were white).

Check into the "noble" acts of most persons. You will discover that they were not so noble after all, but were human responses to circumstances that got somewhat out of hand.

Thomas Jefferson and Abraham Lincoln (and thousands of other "great" persons) demonstrated quite clearly that they were not ethical when they stood to gain or lose something. Massinissa demonstrated that sex (see outline definition), if not properly monitored, can cause persons to act as if they have never been influenced by common sense.

Sex has played a political role in other cases as well. The story of Cleopatra and Mark Antony bears this out. Mark Antony, a white Roman military leader, renounced his Roman citizenship and planned to invade Rome for Egypt simply because of his love for Cleopatra VII, an Egyptian queen. Cleopatra encouraged Antony to do this because it would better her chances of keeping Egypt independent of Roman rule. While the acts by Antony were not responsible for the fall of the Roman Empire, they certainly sped up its disintegration because of the internal conflicts that erupted as a result.

Fear is one of the most natural of emotions. Therefore, no one can be blamed or ridiculed (made fun of) for responding to a threatening situation in a fearful manner. However, there are times when it is necessary to control your response to fear; to analyze what is causing the fear and determine if the risk to your health or security (or whatever) is worth enduring. Just a little bit of control at a critical time in history can determine if an event that could have broad and lasting ramifications "comes off" or not.

For example, two revolts planned by Black People that could have affected historical developments and the course of history in this country (the United States of America) did not come off because some scared Negroes snitched to the whites. In 1800, a revolt that was led by Gabriel Prosser that involved between 2000 and 5000 slaves never got off the ground because of two tomming Negroes. Twenty-two years later, the rebellious desires of 9000 Blacks (led by Denmark Vesey and Peter Poyas) were frustrated by the fear of one or two Negroes who spilled information about the plot to the whites. If either of these rebellions (involving as many resentful, determined and bloodthirsty Blacks as they did) had come off, it probably would have brought about the end of slavery in this country long before 1863, or inspired fear-stricken whites to demand that slavery be abolished and the slaves repatriated (sent to another land), or affected the economic development of America in a manner that would have made it nearly impossible for this country to dominate the world economic order (as she has done). But, because the fears of three or four Blacks were not controlled, 14000 Black rebellers did not get the opportunity to change the course of history. Nor did they get the opportunity to set examples of Black attempts at self-determination that later generations of Black People could look to and analyze.

It is critical that Black People begin to do as much as We possibly can to control Our responses to fear. If We don't control Our responses to fear, We end up keeping white people's feet pressed against Our collective neck. If We don't let fear control Us, We run the risk of catching hell, suffering or dying immediately, but We also open up the possibility that We will eliminate all of the unnecessary suffering and dying by eliminating white people as a controlling and threatening element in Our lives. One thing is for sure (history is quite clear on this point): as long as white people dominate Black People, Black People will catch hell, suffer and die quickly. If We use just a little bit of common sense while We are thinking, We will realize that, since We are going to suffer anyway, it might as well come as a result of Us attempting to become free and self-determining People.

In the first lesson we mentioned religion as one of the central motivating factors that can dominate the life-style and manner of behavior of a given group of people. It was mentioned that one of the purposes of religion is to bring out the best in each person and make each person function in a humane manner, particularly when relating to other human beings. However, it has been stressed that environmental conditions and economic factors dominated the overall development of people in all areas, so much so that different groups of people could practice similar institutions (such as religion), but in extremely different contexts and with different understandings of what "humane" might be, for example. Additionally, how much they depended on or believed in their Almighty One was determined by the extremities of their particular struggle for survival. In the white world, where survival necessitated overcoming the most extreme environmental conditions, the people's dependence on or confidence in the Almighty One did not stretch very far; they called on the Almighty One to provide for them, but if they had waited for the Almighty One to provide for them they probably would have starved or frozen to death. Thus, they developed the habit of not waiting for the Almighty One and of taking matters into their own hands (as best they could). In the Black world conditions were not as harsh, so the Almighty One was not called upon to deliver such basic material needs. What Black People sought from the Almighty One was a type of long-term spiritual salvation. Such a salvation was too far from the here and now for white people to seriously concern themselves with. Thus, the nature of what was expected from the Almighty One in the Black world and white world was different, and these expectations (outgrowths of reality) determined how "religious" each group of people was. It determined what was actually practiced and how sincere or serious people were when they "preached".

From this information, it should be clear that religions are ethnically and/or racially centric. This is not to say that they cannot have a universal message (almost all of them do, because their origin is in African religious philosophy), but that they reflect a certain view of the world based on a people's responses to their environment and their development. Since Black People and white people developed under largely different conditions and took on different attitudes toward nature and humankind, it is only natural that the "religious" beliefs of one, when practically applied, would not satisfy the "religious" needs of the other. Because Black People are being victimized today more than any other race of people, We should be particularly sensitive to this fact; otherwise, religious prostitutes of Islam, Christianity, Judaism, etc., will continue to use their religion to disarm Us socially, politically, culturally and psychologically.

The major "religions" in the world today, Christianity, Islam and Judaism, even though they are theoretically adhered to by different races of people all over the globe, are ethnic-centered and racist institutions. They are ethnic-centered because they have been distorted and are being dominated, manipulated and controlled by a particular group of people, white people. Because they are ethnic-centered and because the ethnic group they center around is white, these religions are primarily concerned with the forces that are of primary concern to white people. The most important force to white people, as we have already mentioned, is economics. White people's aim is economic salvation, therefore white people's religion, even though it preaches otherwise, is practically and primarily concerned with helping white people get the material goods they need to make life bearable and as comfortable as possible. White people's religion, therefore, is about acquiring goods, services, resources, land, etc. Because of this, persons who listen to white people or brainwashed people talk, or read what white people or brainwashed people have written, are apt to hear about such an impossibility as a "religious" war. There can be no such thing as "religious" war because the two terms mutually exclude each other, they cannot be spoken of in the same vein, they cannot go together. But white people, in all sincere hypocrisy, will insist that they have attacked other people and brutally murdered other people in order to spread the good word of their religion to those people. This is as ridiculous as ridiculous can get.

No one fights over religion; religions are not bloodthirsty for converts. Religions do not need to be forced onto people. People either accept a religion or reject a religion based on its relative merits; that is, they accept it or reject it based on what a religion has to offer a particular person or group. As was said earlier, religions are aimed at bringing out the best in a person. You cannot expect to bring out the best in anyone by attacking him or her. You can, however, expect to take something that belongs to someone else by attacking them. This is what a so-called "religious" war is about. It is about taking somebody else's resources, land or something else of value. A "religious" war is then, in fact, an economic and/or political move of aggression. It is an act that will better enable white people to satisfy what they feel are their material/economic needs.

We must remember: Religions are not acquisitive. Their purpose is not to gain something of value, but to give something of benefit, and we all know that no one has to attack or murder anyone else in order to give him or her anything of value. When someone (or group or race) wants to take something, then it becomes necessary to attack or murder the next person. But taking is not what religion is all about, so religion is not the issue when there is a fight (war) going on. Don't let anyone tell you otherwise.

It was stated that western (white) religions are racist institutions. They concern themselves with white supremacy and white superiority, and believe in their superiority to everything else so much that they have a god complex. They think the world spins because of them and "their" inventions and discoveries (they can't really prove that they invented or discovered most of what they make a claim to). They feel that they can do anything they want to whenever they want to, regardless of how their acts affect other people. In order to best realize the ends sought by white people, their religions and their governments function hand in hand. Thus, history reveals that the white religion (Islam) and white governments (Arab states) got together in North Africa and took Black People's land while ruthlessly murdering some of them and enslaving others of them. History reveals that the white religion (Christianity) and the white governments (European states/countries) got together in West Africa in order to systematically murder and enslave Black People. History also reveals that another white religion (Judaism) and white states (European/American governments) got together and decided to take some land that could be called the homeland of Jewish (white) people. These three examples are just three of many. The point is this: If you are Black and you call yourself a Christian, a Jew or a Muslim, then you are also calling yourself a white racist. You can't sensibly be a Black person and identify with white racism too. You have to choose either one or the other, definitely not both.

White people use their "holy books" to justify white racism. They use their Bible to justify the exclusion of Black People from certain schools all over the United States of America. They use their Koran (Qur'an) to justify the senseless slaughter of Black teenagers (see the Washington Afro-American, July 1, 1980, for example). Black People, therefore, should put no faith in either of these "holy" books because the people who wrote them distorted the messages of some earlier writings and had nothing but ill will for Black People. For instance, We read the King James version of the Bible, but who is King James to put out a version (note that term "version") of a holy book? Just think, King James, a white man, a mere human being who lived a few centuries ago, wrote something that has Black People today concerned about life after death. He has Us worried about something that might happen to Us after We are dead (when We won't even be able to feel anything). Meanwhile, King James' people, white people, are concerned about getting as much heaven as they can while they are living on earth. If King James' people don't put any faith in his version of their holy book, why should Black People?

Black People are vulnerable to religious rhetoric (talk) and religious manipulation because We have traditionally and historically practiced religion as if it were a central motivating factor in Our lives. We practice religion as such because, in early times, We attained a state of civilized development that made it possible for Us to understand the spiritual essence of religion. Therefore, if We review the history of Black People, We are likely to detect examples of how a truly religious person functions. Such an example is found in the person of the African Pharaoh/King, Amenhotep IV.

Amenhotep IV, also known as Ikhnaten, used the resources available to him as King of Egypt to spread the gospel and make all people aware of their obligations as human beings. When Amenhotep IV's empire was attacked by white shepherds (called Hyksos), he prayed to his Almighty One for salvation instead of calling out the military (which could have easily defeated the invaders). Amenhotep, like any religious person would do, put matters into the hands of Aten (the African God) because he knew that Aten would take care of everything, even if it was in a manner that only Aten could understand. Amenhotep was willing to put matters into the hands of his God during this

10 LESSONS

critical period because he was truly a religious person. Any religious person would have done likewise. Any person who would have failed to do likewise would have been saying, in so many words, that his religious beliefs and obligations are okay for as long as they don't cause him or her any personal or social inconvenience. These type "religious" persons should not be trusted, and these are the only type "religious" persons produced by the white world. Thus, Black People should leave white "religious" persons and their "religions" alone. They will not help Us in the least. In fact, they will hinder Us and harm Us in the worst way because they will brainwash Us into passively accepting inhumane living conditions, and they will have Us looking for a pie in the sky after We die instead of a way to consistently and nutritionally fill Our stomachs while we live.

(Incidentally, because of Amenhotep's response to the invasion of the white shepherds, the white shepherds took control of Egypt. They were driven out after only a few years, but we have a lesson to learn from the results brought on by Amenhotep's religious ways. The lesson is this: No matter how religious you are, if the people who are abusing you or inhumanely relating to you are not religious in the same way, then your religious efforts will only serve to handicap you. Be religious, if you desire, but also be practical. If someone puts a rope around your neck and intends to hang you, don't think theAlmighty One is going to take that rope off of your neck. Don't even take the time to pray or ask the Almighty One to do that because the Almighty One is not going to respond. You take on the responsibility of getting that rope off of your neck yourself or, better still, do things (like organize) beforehand that will keep anyone from even trying to put a rope around your neck. Remember, Our Ancestors believed in the Almighty One who knows all, sees all, created all and is responsible for everything. However, Our ancestors made it quite clear that, in spite of all that, the Almighty One is not actively involved in the affairs of man. Amenhotep IV apparently forgot that teaching! The Almighty One is too remote to deal with the affairs of man. Black People today who are religious should keep this in mind.)

II. White People's Attacks on Other People

When it comes to the subject of human brutality and cruelty, no other race of people can match the record that white people have made. In fact, no other race of people can come close to matching their record. For thousands of years white people have been slaughtering people by the hundreds of thousands and millions. They needlessly slaughtered millions of Khart-Haddans (Black People who started and built the empire called Carthage today), millions of Africans on the African continent, millions of other Africans in North America, South America and Central America, almost all of the native North Americans (so-called Indians), and probably a larger number of so-called Indians who were living in South America, Central America and the Caribbean. They even killed six million of their white brothers, the Jews (this figure, however, does not compare with the hundreds of millions of Black People who have been slaughtered by whites). White people have gone all over the world and ruthlessly enslaved people in all parts of Africa,.in India and China, and wherever else they could. When people resisted whites' attempts to take advantage of them, white people took the most inhumane measures imaginable. They dropped two atomic bombs on the Japanese people, waged biological and chemical warfare against the Korean and Vietnamese people, and *are preparing later generations of white people to do the same types of things*. History reveals that for thousands of years white people have been satisfying what seems to be an unquenchable thirst for human blood and suffering, and all indications are that they will continue to do the same. Is it logical to think that people who have been nursed on violence toward others and fed on the sufferings of others for over two thousand years are going to suddenly stop being violent because they develop a guilty feeling? Definitely not!!! White people will continue to murder, maim and take advantage of other people until other people stop white people from doing so. Since white people feed on violence, it will take violence on Our part to get them off of Our back and keep them off of Our back. Violence is the only thing they understand and respect. All other attempts at getting them to leave Us alone will fail. History is very clear on this point.

For oh so many years, Black People have been praying that white people would "see the light" and act right. We are always saying, "Forgive them Lord for they know not what they do." However, We should have realized by now what Malcolm X realized, that "for as long as they've been doing it, they're experts at it." White people are very much aware of what they have been doing to people all over the world. They have not done so (and do not do so) accidentally. They sat down and planned each massacre, and each massacre (whether it succeeded as planned or fell short of the objective) made them more and more expert in their later planning and operational procedures. These experts that Negroes are praying for are planning to eliminate Black People in this country right now. They are planning to wipe Us out if possible. They are already sitting down, talking amongst themselves and trying to figure out how they can most effectively, efficiently and economically eliminate large numbers of Black People. They are doing this because of economic reasons and because they think We are planning to get them for what they have done to Us. Whether We are actually planning to get them or not is not important. What is important is that they think We are, and they are planning an operation against Us and picking their time based on what they think. Therefore, We, each and every one of Us, should be planning to defend Ourselves against these people. We should not act silly and disregard such talk as "unreal". White people have massacred Black People in the 1600s, the 1700s and the 1800s. They will do the same in the 1900s and 2000s if We do not prepare to defend Ourselves.

Every Black person should know exactly where he/she stands in the world today (and historically as well). Every Black individual who realizes where he/she stands, if intelligent, will prepare himself/herself to defend himself/herself and his/her loved ones.

III. Why The American Indians Failed to Successfully Defend Themselves Against White People

Since Black People in this country (U.S. of A.) are confronted by the threat of white people, and since Indians were confronted and subdued/overcome by that same threat at an earlier period, it can not be to Our disadvantage to study the response of the Indians to the white threat. Hopefully, through such a study (which will only be touched on in this section), We can detect the major shortcomings demonstrated by the Indians (they were almost completely exterminated/wiped out), determine if similar shortcomings are being demonstrated by Us and, if so, seek to eliminate or control those shortcomings.

When white people first began to settle on a regular basis on land that was "home" to the so-called Indians, the response of the Indians was a casual one. Their philosophy on life was very humane, so they tended to share what they had with each other and with foreigners as well. Once white people, through the way they acted, began to reveal that their true intentions were to take over possession of the land, disrupt the Indians life-style and culture and enslave them or kill them, the Indians began to resist them. However, the capacity or ability of the Indians to resist were dictated by the conditions under which they had developed and lived, and these conditions did not prepare them to effectively deal with a people as cruel and inhumane as white people. The Indians, even though they had run-ins and conflicts with each other, did not feel the need to compete with each other or attempt to dominate each other like white people did. The Indians did not develop the dog-eat-dog attitude toward each other that white people had developed. Instead of assuming (as white people did) that conflict and disharmony would be the dominant factors in their day-to-day contact with each other and foreigners, the Indians assumed that harmony or the tendency of civilized human beings to seek harmony would be that dominant factor. These tendencies toward humaneness and peaceful co-existence were reflected in the institutions and inventions of the Indian people. Unfortunately, such institutions and inventions proved to be not adequate enough to protect them against the institutions and anti-human inventions (especially in the form of weapons) that had emerged in the white world.

Thus, nature herself was largely responsible for the inability of the Indians to adequately defend themselves against white people. The conditions under which Indians developed fostered a humane nature in them that caused them to expect the best out of people. As a result, they were not adequately equipped to effectively deal with a people as aggressive, war-like and materialistic (greedy) as white people. Whereas white people's institutions sprang from a generally chaotic and insecure condition, and were therefore military in nature, the Indians' institutions sprang from a condition or state of living that was relatively calm and peaceful. Whereas white people took a deadly and calculated approach to every aspect of life, the Indians took a casual and humanistic approach. The white people, those who were insecure, greedy, warlike and uncultured (which is typical of all barbarians), developed tools and weapons which were designed to make it less difficult for them to attack others and defend themselves against others. The Indians, on the other hand, because they were civilized and had been in contact with other civilized beings, developed tools and weapons that were geared toward providing them with basic survival needs more than anything else. They were not concerned about dominating or destroying another group of people, did not expect another group of people to attempt to dominate or destroy them, and functioned accordingly. As a result, when their way-of-life was challenged and attacked by white people, their chances of successfully defending themselves were slim. They, unfortunately, found themselves in a position where they had to either submit or pit their peace-oriented attitude and weapons against the war-oriented attitudes and weapons of white people. They were too proud and had too much integrity to submit, so they attempted to defend themselves. They soon discovered that they did not have the attitudes nor weapons they needed to do so adequate'y.

If it had no been for their humane nature and attitudes, the Indians might have guaranteed their own survival by attacking and killing white people as soon as they got off the ship. Even though whites had advanced weapons at this time, they still would have been at a decided disadvantage and could have been so discouraged by financial losses, loss of lives and the fear of being massacred that they (particularly the "small group") might have given up on their plans for taking control of the "new land" (America). Instead of doing this, however, instead of killing white people from day one, the Indians helped them to survive. In effect, the Indians, because of their humane nature, helped white people get the footing they needed to carry out their devilish plans and, in so doing, doomed themselves to virtual extermination.

By the time the Indians did decide to seriously resist the white invaders, it was too late. By then the whites had established several settlements in this country that were well-armed and in constant contact with one another. Even more importantly, all of the whites had the same objective (to take the "Indian's" land) and were able to unify amongst themselves rather easily for attack and defense purposes as a result. The Indians, meanwhile, were victimized more and more by the civilized nature of their development (they could not adapt the barbaric attitudes and methods that were necessary to protect themselves against the white barbarians) and proved themselves to be less and less capable of adequately defending their way-of-life and their homeland.

We will be more specific. Even when the Indians did begin to seriously resist the white invaders, many of their shortcomings became crystal clear. It must be stressed at this point, however, that those shortcomings were not due to any inferiority of the Indians. In fact, they were due to the fact that the Indians had developed a way-of-life that was geared toward interaction among civilized people who had sincere concerns about the general welfare of human beings and who were not inclined toward mutilating and murdering their fellow men and women.

White people did not fall into this class of people. Their way-of-life was characterized by an inhumane, dog-eat-dog approach to all aspects of life. They did not seek harmony, agreement and peaceful co-existence, and did not respect the rights of other people. They instead assumed that power and force were the keys to human intercourse, so they developed institutions that were machine-like and detached from the people, and they developed tools that were capable of wiping out large numbers of living things (including people) in a few days, hours or minutes. From the standpoint of civilized development, white people were lower on the ladder than Indians. However, the confrontation of Indians and white people was not a civilized confrontation; it was not a moral confrontation. It was a political/military confrontation that was brought on by white people for the purpose of benefiting white people only, particularly the white "small group". The terms of this confrontation were dictated by white people, and the Indians came up with much less than what they needed to compete effectively.

Thus, the capacity of the Indians to even conceive of measures they would have to take to effectively repel the white invaders is questionable. Their capacity to even conceive of the number of human beings they would have to ruthlessly murder, maim and mutilate is also questionable. And, their capacity to even conceive of the length of time they would have to consistently and uninterruptedly (day-in and day-out) defend themselves and attack their invaders is just as questionable. To the Indians, a war was a curse and an inconvenience; it was something they hoped to avoid, if possible, or be done with quickly otherwise. War, to them, was the unfortunate result of a misunderstanding, and they usually meant to end it, with as little harm as possible, just about as quickly as it had begun. War was not a profession to the Indians, it was not pressed into their psyche (see Lesson #1), it was not noticeable in their attitudes and it was not intended to take up much of their time. Even when it persisted, it was not generally continuous and uninterrupted-it was not an everyday thing. But with the Europeans it was, and that difference, more than anything else (including the weaponry), guaranteed what the eventual outcome of any unfriendly confrontation between the two would be.

War and conflict were so much a part of the European way-of-life that they had found it necessary to analyze war and reduce it to a science (a calculated manner of proceeding that is most likely to bring about the results that are desired). In so doing, they realized that time (getting the jump on your opponent and persevering/outlasting your opponent) and timing (the clocklike regulation of factors; the clocklike regulation of different components of a military mission) were critical factors. They realized that a combined or centralized leadership was more efficient than a leadership that was not centralized, and therefore recognized the necessity of overcoming obstacles (if only temporarily) to establishing this type of leadership among their different tribes. They realized that commitment to the war effort is essential, and that the war effort is facilitated (made less difficult) by organized and concerted plans of action. Europeans (white people) also realized that superior weapons were advantageous. They realized this because they made a profession of forcefully dominating other people and taking other peoples' possessions. In order to dominate and take from others effectively, they had to reduce war to a science, and they had to invent and develop weapons that would make them (white people) more militarily powerful than their victims. In the beginning of their history, white groups matched their military sciences and weapons against each other. Later, as they ventured outside of Europe, they "discovered" other lands and peoples and began to use their military concepts and inventions against those other peoples. Because most of those other people had different concepts of the military and the use of weapons, they were not able to war against (defend themselves against) white people to any effective degree. We can see this clearly when We review the war efforts put forth by the native American, the so-called "Indian".

Because the Indians did not recognize the true intentions of the Europeans (they had no reason to, based on their development and contact with others, to suspect that human beings would attempt to do such things - that is, take other people's land, viciously murder other people, deny other people the right to survive, etc.), and because they did not have a war-infested psyche, the Indians failed to kill or make war on the Europeans as soon as they stepped off the ship. In doing this they lost their only real chance to maintain their way-of-life. From that point on their demise was just a matter of time.

When conditions worsened and the Indians decided that something had to be done, what they did indicated that they were uncommitted to or unprepared to challenge the white man militarily. For instance, some sought to "get away"; to resettle in parts of the country where there were no whites and where it was thought the whites would not move to. These efforts proved fruitless and only delayed the confrontation because whites were not going to stop claiming additional land until there was none left to be claimed. As such, only a short time would pass after the Indians had run when the whites would want to search them out, kill them and claim the area the Indians had run to. Others decided to fight back, but failed to do so as effectively as they could have. For one thing, they did not fight as if they were one nation. Additionally, they only planned a series of skirmishes against the whites, seemingly to convince the whites that they had taken their invasion too far. The Indians who fought back did not develop a war plan which recognized that a long, drawn out conflict was inevitable. They should have.

But they couldn't. The reasons for this are understandable. First, the various Indian groups represented hundreds of Indian nations, some of which were historically hostile to each other and all of which were accustomed to self-government and inter-group or inter-tribal leadership. It is, therefore, unrealistic to suppose that they should have been able to quickly unite amongst themselves against the whites who were invading the land they had shared for so long. Secondly, to repeat what has been said earlier, the Indians did not take the approach to war that whites took. This means that, in addition to not having an efficient military leadership (when judged by European standards) and no concerted plan of military action, the Indians did not go beyond surface considerations and therefore failed to adequately determine who their enemy was. Instead of doing the necessary military analysis and coming to the conclusion that all white people were their enemies, the Indians would conclude that only the white people who were in direct conflict with their group or tribe were their enemies. This resulted in two unfortunate trends and gave the whites an additional advantage in a contest that was already lopsided in their favor.

Unfortunate trend number one was the tendency of Indians to befriend or help white people, enabling them to survive and many times helping to protect them against hostile Indian groups. History reveals far too many cases of Indians teaching the early white settlers to plant various crops and snare various animals. Without such assistance, the white settlers might not have been able to survive once their initial supply of staples (necessary food items) and ammunition ran out, particularly since it took so long to get additional supplies from Europe.

Unfortunate trend number two was the tendency of Indians to form military alliances with one group of whites (the British, for example) against a different group of whites (the French, for example). Such military alliances meant that Indians in one section of the colonies were "friends" with the very white people who were massacring Indians and taking land from Indians in another section of the colonies. Such military alliances also gave the whites the opportunity to betray their Indian allies at critical times when battles were being fought. Such betrayals usually resulted in the deaths of many brave and tactical Indian warriors.

The additional advantage these two unfortunate trends gave to the whites is that it allowed "friendly" whites the opportunity to physically and mentally disarm the Indians who trusted them, and thereby left them less prepared to defend themselves and kill their enemies. Whereas the Indians were only on guard against certain whites, the white settlers were on guard against every Indian because they recognized that, regardless of how a few Indians acted in certain situations, all Indians were their enemies. If the Indians had taken the same type attitude toward all white people, much of what was to unfold in their relations with whites might have been different.

Finally, the Indians had inadequate knowledge of what their enemy was. To be sure, white people were their enemy, but beyond this is the fact that the white frame of mind was their enemy. In spite of everything else, their enemy was a frame of mind that had a superiority complex, that was unbelievably materialistic and acquisitive, cruelly calculating and ever-insecure. The superiority complex dictated that, regardless of all evidence to the contrary, white people would view Indians as less than their equal, and would therefore forever seek to dominate them and put them "in their place". Because they were so materialistic and acquisitive, they would always be taking or attempting to take other peoples' land and valuables. Because of this, they would always be robbing and stealing, and would feel inadequate if they failed to constantly seek more than what they already had. Because they were cruelly calculating, they would scheme for days, years, even centuries, in order to get what they wanted or what they felt they needed. Day-in and day-out they would be straining their brains trying to figure out ways to get the upper hand on other people and then ruthlessly take advantage of them. And because they were ever-insecure, they could never trust anyone else, not even another white person, but particularly not a non-white person. Anyone who did not understand them and act like they act, have their values and look like them was never to be trusted. Therefore, even if the Indians had been imitation white men, it would have only been a matter of time before the whites would have attempted to wipe them out. Because whites are so insecure, they feel that everyone else is a threat to them, is out to get them and take what they have. And, because they are so insecure, they are driven to attempt to eliminate any and all things that seem to be a threat to them.

There was no way the Indians could have imagined that they would be dealing with a mind and group personality as warped and inhumane as that of the white race. They could not have known that these people were being driven by a force stronger than logic and common sense and more destructive and reactionary than obsessive emotions. They could not have known that they were being invaded by the thought processes of the devil himself. If they had known, they undoubtedly would have fought like mad to kill each and every one of them just as soon as they stepped off the ship.

White people are the product of a very, very cruel environment. If the Indians had recognized that and recognized the implications of that, it might have changed the course of American History.

There was another enemy of the Indians that came with the white invaders. That enemy was the white people's knowledge of and use of explosives, most notably in the form of weapons (this cannot be overstressed). Such weapons were a big advantage for whites because the Indians, at first, did not have them, and throughout because the Indians did not have the capacity to make them. Thus, when Indians and white men met in battle, it was not a battle of men against men, but one of advanced warfare against pre-historic warfare, and of guns and bullets against bows and arrows. It was not a war of tactics, bravery and skills, but one of brute force (where brute force would be the decisive element). It was such a war because white people had advanced to the point where they could conduct war in that manner; and the inability of the Indians to fight likewise only encouraged the whites to do so with more and more arrogance, confidence and belief in the ultimate success of their mission.

White people's mastery of explosives for destructive purposes, and their discovery that other people had failed to make similar advances made white people more daring militarily (they recognized that their chances of getting killed or injured in battle were comparatively small) and more politically arrogant than they would otherwise have been, and gave white people the impression that they were invincible (could not be defeated) as a race. Their attitudes among non-white peoples were a reflection of that impression. They became, so to speak, drunk with the feeling of power, and that feeling went to their heads bigtime. As a result they tended to be even more disrespectful and unobserving of the rights of others, and more destructive than they needed to be when hostilities did break out. They had something to prove to the world (their supposed "superiority", which was really a reaction to their inferiority complex), and because they had guns (and nobody else did), they knew they could do it — regardless of the cost in human lives, human suffering and human development.

Thus, a cruel attitude bolstered by explosive power is what the Indians were up against. A people who loved to kill and destroy life so much that they had to invent weapons that would help them do it is what the Indians were up against. A people who placed no large amount of value on ideas like love, peace, humanity and human rights, etc., is what the Indians were up against. A people who had a relatively warped psyche is what the Indians were up against. They were up against this attitude, this explosive power, this warped psyche and a person carrying all three of them. Partly because they did not recognize what a driving force each of these factors was, the Indians were overrun by all of them.

Today, Black People will be overrun by those very same forces, each more deadly and developed than ever, if We do not forget about integrating with white people and peacefully co-existing with them and start functioning in a manner that will get Us away from them. Presently, far too many of Us are expecting concessions from white people that white people are not equipped to give. (We will repeat: white people are not equipped to grant Us certain concessions, like human rights, equality, economic and political self-determination, etc.) Too many of Us are expecting white people to act in a manner that is beyond their functional capability. We must realize that white people still have the warped psyche, that distorted psychological make-up, that was typical of them when they invaded the home of the Indians. We must realize that white people still have the superiority complex that was typical of them when they invaded the home of the Indians. We must realize that white people still have the jump on non-white peoples inasmuch as destructive capabilities are concerned (their abuse of technology has embedded a god complex in them), and this advantage is ever-present in their attitude toward non-white people, Black People in particular. We must also realize that white people are just as economically insecure now as they were when they invaded the home of the Indians. Thus, they still seek economic stability for themselves by consistently and bloodthirstily robbing and stealing from weaker people. We must realize, in effect, that We, Black People in 1980, are being confronted by the very same white people who almost exterminated the native population of this land; and under circumstances that are similar in many respects to those that prevailed when white people resolved to wipe the Indians out. Surely, We have enough sense to realize that if white people murdered and abused the Indians almost to the point of extermination, they will attempt to do the same to Us just as soon as they feel that the time is right.

In order to adequately oppose them, their attitudes, their superiority complex, their destructive tendencies and their feelings of economic and psychological insecurity— in order to adequately oppose all of these forces, We must avoid as many of the shortcomings demonstrated by the Indians as We possibly can. We must, first and foremost, control Our tendency (which is part of Our human nature) to expect the best out of white people, and not expect them to act like We think human beings should act. We should expect only the worst, the most barbaric, from them, and never feel sympathetic toward them. We must recognize that they are going to keep on trying to impose their way-of-life and their insanity on Us, at whatever cost to Ourselves, and that We can not escape their impositions by trying to hide from them or by treating them kindly

10 LESSONS

(as civilized people should treat other human beings). If We treat them humanely, they will be more diligently about the business of abusing Us. We must realize that We are going to have to oppose them by developing a power base of Our own (a Black Nation), and by functioning for and within that power base in a manner that makes it clear to them that they will suffer if they do not respect Our right to life, liberty and self-determination. We must make it crystal clear— militantly clear— that We are committed to Our (Black) survival and the perpetuation/continuation of a Black way-of-life, and that We will struggle long and hard for those ends. We must establish a list of Black priorities, and use that list to organize among Ourselves, to adapt Ourselves to different concepts of time and leadership, to define what leadership entails and to unite among Ourselves. We must plan Our future as a Black future, understand who the enemies are that will attempt to deny Us that future, understand what particular elements are critical to the make-up and capabilities of those enemies, and consciously guard against them until their threat to Us has been completely eliminated. It sounds like a lot, but it is the least We, Black People, can afford to do if We do not want to be continually dominated and threatened by white people. It is the least We can do if We want to avoid being manhandled and practically exterminated the way the native American was manhandled and exterminated.

IV. Why Black People Were Enslaved

After beginning the process of massacring and murdering the Indians and taking control of their land, white people, urged on and financed by the small group of whites which was to benefit most, began to determine how they could make this newly stolen world of theirs as profitable and prosperous as possible. In every direction they explored they saw land, the real basis of wealth and prosperity. At first the small group began to plot a scheme which would make this land produce goods, services and profits that would benefit mostly the small group of white people in Europe, particularly Great Britain (England). As time passed a small group emerged in the newly stolen world itself, and this group was intent on keeping most of the riches of America for a small percentage of the white people who settled in the colonies. As more time passed, it became quite apparent that these two "small groups" would clash with one another, but that should not concern Us at this point. What We should be concerned about is that both groups, first the white small group in Great Britain and later the white small group in the colonies themselves, recognized that an abundant supply of cheap labor was essential if they were to maximize their profits. The small group in England experimented and explored in search of this cheap labor supply. They experimented with white people who "agreed" to settle the area (many had no choice), white criminals and prostitutes who were considered unproductive in England and other European countries, white indentured servants (persons who were under a contract to work for a certain number of years, after which they would be free to do as they pleased) and white people who were disenchanted with their future in Europe who were looking for another chance to "make something" of themselves. These experiments succeeded in populating and "stabilizing" the colonies, but they failed to make the colonies prosper.

White people also experimented with the Indians, but discovered that the Indians were not equipped to function adequately in the settled type structure white people were attempting to build. The Indians, whites quickly discovered, would die off like flies if they were not allowed to roam or if they were forced to work from sun-up until sundown. But white people worked them anyway because a more suitable source of labor was not yet available and because such work contributed to white people's efforts to exterminate the native American. Another source had to be made available, and was found when white people began to pay serious attention to the African continent, the homeland of all Black People.

The 1400s and 1500s were centuries when white people did a lot of exploring. The main purpose of these exploratory trips was to discover new sources of resources that could be used to make survival a little less of a struggle for white people. In the course of these explorations, Columbus got lost and "discovered" America for Spain and the Portuguese whites set up forts in Africa. These two events turned out to be disastrous for Black People because the Spanish discovered that the Indians were not able to work for them in the manner desired and the Portuguese discovered that Black People were able to do so. Because it was profitable for each of these two white nations, the Portuguese began supplying the Spanish colonies with the workers they needed. As time passed and the power relationships of white people went through some changes, the Portuguese and the Spanish lost out to the French and the British, but the process of forcefully taking Black People from the African continent, shipping them to the Americas and forcing them to do slave labor continued.

Why were Black People enslaved? Why were white people willing to cover the expenses required to constantly make trips all the way from Europe to Africa in order to capture Black People, and then take Black People from Africa all the way to the Americas? What was it about Black People that impressed white people so much; that made white people feel that a steady supply of Black People at whatever cost was the key to their labor problems? It could not have been because we, Black People, were savages, as white people claim, nor could it have been because We needed to be exposed to the Christian way-of-life. If We had been savages, then We would not have been able to do the type labor white people felt was needed to make their newly found world as profitable as possible, and We would have been an economic liability to white people as well. Instead of them making money from Our labor, they would have lost money because We would have been incapable of acting like socially responsible human beings. We would therefore have been destroying things (possibly anything within Our reach), We would have been uncooperative and We would have been unproductive as workers— and white people would have stopped investing in Us very quickly. As far as the Christian thing goes, there were a lot of white people who had not been Christianized. Why didn't the Christian whites invest in Christianizing their white brothers and sisters who were right down the street from them? Even more to the point, We must remember that white people, particularly the white small group, were about making a big profit. They were about putting some forces in motion that would bring them some monetary returns. They were not about spending money to help other people experience a more civilized form of existence. If white people were concerned about Christianizing Black People at all, it was because the Christianizing process tended to make Black People more receptive to being enslaved.

What then, are the real reasons Black People were enslaved? Let's put the lies that white people have told Us aside and reveal what it was about Black People that impressed white people so much that they were willing to go through all of that travelling and transporting in order to get Us to their newly discovered world.

When whites from Europe landed on the African continent and observed the African People, they saw a people who could not defend themselves against the arms and ammunition of white people. Partly as a result of a process that had begun more than 4000 years earlier, Black People were at a point in their history where they were generally disunited and somewhat isolated from the rest of the world. Though there were large Black empires in several parts of the continent, most of the people belonged to small groups or tribes that, for all intents and purposes, had no practical means of defending themselves against any group of people who used more than bows, arrows and spears as military weapons.

What these mostly small, scattered groups of Black People did possess though was a settled, agricultural way-of-life that had the trademarks of a very high and established culture. This quality appealed to the whites who were observing them because whites wanted to establish a way-of-life in the new world that was based on a settled, agriculture-oriented system of production. Since Black People were already living in this manner, it was safe for whites to conclude that Black People had the attitudes, discipline and skills that would make them ideal workers and builders. It followed then, as far as white people were concerned, that Black People should be made to apply their skills and workmanship to the building of the new world.

10 LESSONS   49

But, let's say a little bit more about the "attitudes, discipline and skills" that white people thought would make Black People ideal workers. What did white people see in the attitudes of Black People during this period that would make them "ideal workers and builders?" What did white people see in the discipline of Black People during this period that would make them "ideal workers and builders?" And, what skills did Black People possess during this period that would make them "ideal workers and builders?"

White people knew enough in order to realize that, in order to accumulate as much wealth as possible, they would have to enslave their work force. They also knew that no group of people would voluntarily agree to become slaves. As a result, they, white people, knew that they would have to use force to get their workers and keep them. They knew, because of the military primitiveness ("backwardness") of Black People, that they would have relatively little problem getting Black People. With their advanced weapons, they would defeat the Blacks easily. And, after observing Black People for a while, they concluded that they would have relatively little trouble keeping Black People enslaved because Black People had a humane attitude that rendered them less likely to viciously and indiscriminately rebel against their enslavers. Certainly white people expected some Black persons to rebel at times, but because Black People were not inclined toward the wholesale destruction of property nor toward the indiscriminate slaughter of people, they were not expected to be as much a risk to life and property as other groups of people would be expected to be.

If Black People had pulled off two or three ruthless slave revolts in this country, it is possible that slavery would have ended much sooner than it did. If BlackPeople had said, for example, that all property and every white man, woman and child are to be attacked and destroyed, and followed through on that statement as best as possible, it is certain that slavery would have ended in this country much sooner than it did. But Black People rarely planned such a rebellion; and when they did rebel they aimed their rebellion at particular white persons instead of all white people. Blacks did this because they did not want to harm what they thought were innocent whites. This attitude of justice was a positive human trait, but it was a weakness in this particular time and setting, and white people counted on it in order to help keep them in control of Black People and in a position to benefit from the blood, sweat and tears of Black People.

In order to accumulate as much wealth as possible white people also needed a work force that was disciplined; a work force that understood that a work schedule (routine) was necessary if a settled type community were to survive and prosper. Because Black People had been living a settled type existence for thousands of years, they knew that work, a lot of consistent work, was necessary at particular times, and they therefore revolved their production efforts around a work schedule. Because Black People were accustomed to working on a schedule, white people recognized that they would not have to do much to make Black People adjust to the rigid work schedule that white people had developed. All they needed to do was eliminate the "free time" Black People were accustomed to (the slave driver and his whip served this purpose), and Black People would soon grow accustomed to working on a rigid schedule day-in and day-out. Thus, Black People's disciplined approach to working made them appealing to white slave seekers.

The final factor we will mention that made Black People ideal slave prospects was that Black People had the skills that were needed to build the type of country white people wanted to build. The white people who observed the African tribes and empires saw structures and regular functions or manners of operation which indicated that Black People had mastered mathematics, the physical sciences, architecture, the smelting of iron and other ores and metals, blacksmithing, etc. White people saw that Black People had established primary, secondary and advanced systems of education, had built libraries, made clothes and, above all, had mastered an agriculture-based economic system. All of these skills and knowledge, white people recognized, would contribute immensely to the establishment of the "new world" as a model of white progress and white achievement.

LESSON 3
LESSON OUTLINE

I. Black History Summary
  A. Fourth Glacial Epoch
  B. Zaara (the Sahara) 20,000 B.C.E. - 10,000 B.C.E.
  C. 11,542 B.C.E.
  D. Itiopi
  E. Egypt
  F. Comparative Development of Known Cities in Black and White Worlds
   1. Nowe   Prehistory
   2. Memphis   3100 B.C.E.
   3. Rome (town)   250 B.C.E.
   4. Athens (city)   360 B.C.E.
   5. Antioch   400 B.C.E.
   6. Jerusalem 1400 B.C.E.
   7. Babylon   2100 B.C.E.
  G. The "Two Lands"
  H. Political Unification (King Menes)
  I. First Dynastic Cycle (1st - 6th Dynasties)
  J. Second Dynastic cycle (6th - 20th Dynasties)
  K. Third Dynastic Cycle (20th -)
  L. Foreign Domination, 660 B.C.E. - Present
   1. Assyrians
   2. Persians
   3. Greeks
   4. Romans
   5. Arabs
  M. Khart-Haddas (Carthage) 1000 B.C.E.
   1. 262 B.C.E. 1st "Punic" War
   2. 220 - 217 B.C.E.   2nd "Punic" War
   3. 217 B.C.E. Hannibal Barca
   4. 207 B.C.E. Black Control Broken
   5. 146 B.C.E. Last "Punic" War
    a. symbolized end of Black domination of North Africa and parts of Europe.
  N. Development of Later Black Empires
   1. Examples
   -Nobadae, Makuria, Alwa, Funj, Ghana, Mali, Songhay, Mossi, Kanem-Bornu, Kuba, Kongo-Angola, Monomotapa, Zimbabwe, Zulu, etc.

O. Further Arab Penetration (see "L" above)
   1. Withdrawal of Rome
   2. Islam
     a. slavery-slavetrading
     b. destruction of empires/manipulation and murder of rulers
     c. killing of Black People and Blackness
     d. the migrations speed up
     e. Africa unable to defend Herself
P. The European Incursion
Q. Enslavement by Europeans and Resistance
   1. Queen Nzingha
   2. Rebellion/Subversion During Middle Passage
   3. Rebellion/Subversion After Arrival in the "New World"
II. Some Black Accomplishments (Prior to contact with and domination by non-Black peoples).
   A. Examples
   1. Governmental and Political Organization 2. Political Concentration 3. Expanded International Travels and Contacts 4. Internal Stability 5. Rise and Expansion of Crafts 6. Stone Buildings 7. Public Baths 8. Writing 9. Medical Discoveries and Excellence 10. Architectural Discoveries, Originality and Excellence 11. Mathematical Frontrunners (for example, Black People determined the exact value of "pi" and made extensive use of the "Pythagorean theory" thousands of years before Pythagoras was even born) 12. Organized Religion and Priesthood 13. Scientists and Scholars 15. Public Schools 16. Engineers 17. Scribes/Professional Writers 18. Carpenters 19. Artists and Sculptors 20. Astronomers 21. the 1st Calendar 22. Agriculture and Irrigation Systems 23. Clothmakers 24. Silversmiths, Goldsmiths, Blacksmiths, etc. 25. Urban Planners 26. etc., etc., etc.
III. Effects of Enslavement on Africa
   A. Population Decimated (Greatly Reduced)
   1. Leaders and Potential Leaders Were Eliminated/Not Born
     a. the best were captured and brought to the "New World"
   B. Cultural Disruption
   1. Institutions Shattered
     a. educational
     b. administrative/organizational
     c. social
     d. religious
   2. Black People Retrogress (Go Backward)
   C. Instability and Suspicions Become Dominant
   1. Disunity Increases

2. Mutual Distrust of Blacks for Blacks Dominates the Interrelations of Black Groups/Tribes/Empires
D. Africa Almost Completely Dominated by non-Africans

I. Black History Summary

All serious scientists and archaeologists generally agree that Black People were the first people to inhabit earth. Evidence has continually indicated almost beyond doubt that during the 4th Glacial Epoch (supposedly near the end of the Cenozoic Period. The Cenozoic Period generally includes the last 65 million years of earthly time.), more than two and one half million years ago, the evolution of human beings came about; and these early human beings, who were Black in color, evolved on the African continent.

This is not a surprising discovery. During the Cenozoic Period the earth, insofar as geography and climate are concerned, took on characteristics that have remained basically unchanged to this day. Thus, in that period, as now, Africa was the place where conditions existed that were most conducive (favorable) to the development and perpetuation of humankind. After developing in Africa and multiplying, some Black People began roaming to and settling in different areas within the African continent. As time passed, Black People roamed outside of the African continent as well. For nearly two million years, curious and adventuresome Black People left their homes and discovered and explored new lands all over the planet. Many, for various reasons, either chose to or were forced by conditions to remain outside of their original homeland. Black People thereby settled on all parts of the planet, including Europe, where, due to a colder and harsher climate, lack of exposure to the sun, different environmental factors and different requisites (needs) for survival (such as types of foods available), Black People went through biological changes for tens of thousands of years that eventually resulted in them becoming what are called white people today. The major physical differences between Black People and white people, such as skin, eyes and hair color, hair texture and sizes of lips and noses, are due to changes brought on by continued exposure to the aforementioned conditions by Black People who had roamed outside of Africa and settled in Europe.

How long it took Black People to develop a civilized state of life in Africa is questionable. It is certain though that the Europeans never developed to that state of existence, and that Africans were so prior to the year 20,000 B.C.E. (Before the Common Era, a.k.a. B.C.), and that many civilized groups such as the Tasians, Badarians and Amratians settled in what is now known as the Sahara Desert which, during this period, was a very fertile area. Probably during this time, agriculture was discovered and became the economic basis of the

54   10 LESSONS

African's life. Certainly by the year 11,542 B.C.E. this was the case. Proof of this is the fact that a calendar was in use at this time, presumably to regulate some of the economic activities of the Black People who created it (calendars always serve such a purpose).

We need only to use logical inferences to assume that, by 11,542 B.C.E., African People had advanced to a level of civilized existence that necessitated or desired consistent contacts among groups on various areas of the continent; and that these contacts had resulted in the political unification of large portions of the continent. In fact, it is not unrealistic to suppose that this date represents the formation of the first dynastic period in Africa, and set in motion a form of political organization that was to remain basically unchanged and under the control of Black People for nearly 12,000 years.

Black political unity and grandeur reached its heights during the time period spanning approximately the years 3500 B.C.E. and 1000 B.C.E. During this period of 2500 years, the accumulated knowledge and genius of the African People created and expanded the empire that is called Itiopi by many historians. This empire, whose boundaries covered North Africa, the so-called Middle East, the present area of Sudan and much of West Africa, developed in the Sudan and spread northward to what is called Egypt today. It was in Egypt that this Black civilization flourished and became the center of the world's economic, political and cultural advancement. Because it flourished so it drew the attention of groups of eastern whites, who settled along Egypt's coastal area, schemed against the highly developed Black People and moved inland (took over control of land) during periods of Black dis-unity and weak leadership. Over a period of nearly two thousand years, these whites gained so much of the coastal area that their descendants, the white people of modern times, have claimed that the civilization that flourished in that area was a white civilization. Any such claim is sheer nonsense. It is an attempt on the part of white people to keep Black People from recognizing how much We have contributed to the development of the world, and it demonstrates what ridiculous claims these white people will make in order to support their claims of racial superiority. It is a known fact that the Itiopian Empire flourished at a time when white people were still living in caves and following behind sheep for survival purposes. Being nomads (wanderers) and cave dwellers, there is no way they could have built an empire that had agriculture as its economic basis and living accommodations that were not much different from those experienced by many "developed" people today.

White people were slow to develop a settled way-of-life. A comparison of development of ancient cities proves this point clearly. Known African cities go so far back into history that dates cannot be accurately applied to them. Other cities, such as Memphis, date back more than 5100 years. White cities, by comparison, only began appearing immediately before modern times (the

Common Era, a.k.a. A.D.). Thus, the oldest white city that could possibly exist could not be more than 2500 years old. The fact that they were able to develop even then is a result of white people coming into contact with Black People, learning from Black People and adapting what they learned to their racist objectives. Otherwise, white people would probably be overwhelmingly nomadic (shepherd-like) today; even the most advanced of them would probably be at most only two or three centuries (200 to 300 years) removed from barbarism.

To support their racist claims, white people declared that Egypt was divided into Two Lands; one white, one Black— both politically independent of the other or entirely controlled by whites. Once again, these whites have allowed their desires to take them away from reality. Whites, as we have already stated, did gain much of the coastal area of Egypt, but this area remained under the political control of the Black People who had developed it. Proof of this lies in the inarguable fact that a Black king, Menes (also called Narmer), initiated measures to control the spread of the whites by damming the Nile River and building the city of Memphis in about 3100 B.C.E. Memphis became the capital city of the Empire, but it was mainly a military base that monitored the movement of the white settlers. (The real capital of the Empire remained much further south, in the holy city of Thebes.) Memphis, as a symbol, stated beyond contradiction that there was only one land on the African continent, and that that land was under the political and economic control of Black People.

As we stated earlier, white people settled on the coast of the Itiopian Empire and moved inland during periods of weak leadership and disunity among Black People. During these periods of weak leadership and Black disunity, white people were able to activate their schemes of gradually invading the Empire by, among other things, marrying into the royal families and planting seeds of distrust among various self-centered and petty-minded Black "leaders". Under no other circumstances could the whites have advanced. In fact, what they achieved was not as much an accomplishment of theirs as it was a forfeit of Ours (Black People).

During periods of Black unity and capable leadership, Black People made advances that demonstrate beyond a doubt that We are capable of accomplishing anything We set Our minds and energies to. After Menes established the city of Memphis and started what many historians call the 1st Dynasty (which is probably not accurate. The 1st dynasty probably occurred long before the time of Menes.), Black People enjoyed a reign of prosperity and social and cultural achievement that continued almost uninterrupted for nearly 800 years. During this 800 year period, six different dynasties ruled Egypt (a dynasty is made up of a series of rulers from a common line of descent). The fact that their system of rule was beneficial to the Black masses is evidenced by the fact that, during this entire period, there was never a rebellion of the type that is common among white people. The Black masses were unsatisfied at times and rebelled accordingly, but not because the system was unjust. When they did rebel it was because the individual leader was unjustly applying the laws of the land or failing to respond adequately to the dictates of the people.

After this nearly 800 years period, disunity and weak Black leaders began to be the dominant factors in Black political life. For nearly four dynasties, covering a period of nearly 150 years, Black "leaders" bickered with one another and fought each other over who would control the empire. Neither of these leaders or groups they represented was strong enough to overcome the opposition and guide Black People in a single direction, and they were not intelligent enough to downplay their differences and rule jointly, so the Empire that had been united and moving in a single direction (one that was beneficial to Black People) began to split into factions that practically went to war with one another. Because of such rivalries and the disharmony that came with them, Black People were not able to carry out the affairs of the government efficiently enough to accomplish national goals nor effectively carry out or follow through on accepted national policies. One unfortunate outcome of this is that the whites who had been restricted to the seacoasts were not watched closely during this period. Thus, they were able to enhance their position both politically and economically.

Politically, they could present themselves as friends of the rival leaders, and thereby gain the favor of these leaders and open up the doors to greater political involvement by whites later on. Such contact with Black leaders led to increased contact with Black families in positions of power, so there developed a greater chance that intimate politicking on a social and sexual level would take hold and influence the objectives and policies of the national government. And, since they were not being watched adequately, the whites could more effectively scheme among themselves and plant further seeds of distrust among the Blacks. With such political forces operating in the favor of white people for nearly 150 years, they were able to overcome the restrictions established by the earlier dynasties, to solidify their position and establish themselves as a permanent (non-removable) political force in the Black Empire.

Economically, during this period of Black instability white people were able to move further inland and take control of land that was no longer occupied by Black People or properly guarded by the agents of the Black government. Since land was the basis of all economic wealth at that time (and still is so to an overwhelming degree today), this gain in territory almost speaks for itself. It served to eliminate much of Black People's direct trade with the outside world because the ports and other accesses to the sea were left in the hands of white people. This gain in territory also made white people feel more economically and militarily secure, and served to solidify the foundation that would be later used by whites to move even further inland in the years to come. These inland movements during various periods of Black dis-unity and weak leadership were to eventually result in white people controlling practically all of North Africa. However, it must be stressed that Our weaknesses (particularly the lack of unity among Black People for brief periods of time), and NOT white strengths, were the keys to what the whites gained. What was true then is still true today. If We overcome Our weaknesses, particularly Our lack of unity, We will have no problem overcoming white people and establishing real Black Power/Black Nationhood.

Strong leadership and unity returned with the 11th Dynasty and lasted for nearly 400 years. During this period, stability returned, prosperity increased, the bickering stopped and the whites who had been moving inland were controlled. As a matter of fact, the 11th Dynasty is very notable because of the analysis, understanding and actions of perhaps the greatest ruler of this period, Mentuhotep II. Mentuhotep II recognized what white people were really trying to do (take over the entire Empire) and recognized that they posed more of a future threat to Black People than an immediate one. The only way, he concluded, to definitely eliminate this future threat to the well-being of Black People was by exterminating the white people who occupied Black lands. Thus, Mentuhotep II initiated a national policy of exterminating white people. However, by this time white people were too much involved with the Black world genetically and socially. In other words, there was no way of definitely identifying every white person, and there was probably opposition from Black persons who were intimately involved in the lives and affairs of various white individuals. These considerations, added to the high number of white people living there and the expansive stretches of land which they occupied (not to mention the probability that some whites lived right in the midst of Black settlements or communities), dictated beforehand that the objective would not be reached. Nonetheless, Mentuhotep II tried, and it is a testament to his supreme love and concern for Black People that he did. If more of Us were willing to take on seemingly impossible tasks if such were necessary, We would not be controlled by the forces that control Us today.

The measures that Mentuhotep II and his immediate successors to the throne took to control the whites were rendered useless once weak leaders again came to power. As before, a long period of Black Power was followed by a relatively short but extremely destructive period of Black disunity and squabbling that allowed the whites to take control of even more land and make themselves even more of a political force in the Black Empire. Again, as if history were repeating itself, 150 years of Black bickering and disunity, and the governmental inefficiency that accompanied it, left the Black Empire open to invasion (of military and non-military natures). The whites, as usual, took advantage of that opening and, in so doing, made the task of future generations of Black People much more difficult.

As difficult as it was, it could not discourage the Blacks who moved into power near the end of the 17th Dynasty and laid the foundation for the 18th Dynasty, probably the most glorious of all the periods of Black rule. It was during the 18th and 19th Dynasties that such well-known figures as Queen Hatshepsut (the greatest female ruler the world has ever known), King Amenhotep IV (the religious ruler), Queen Nefertiti (the celebrated wife of Amenhotep IV), King Tutankhamon (who has received so much publicity in modern times), and King Ramses (the military genius) lived. It was during this time, or immediately thereafter, that Moses (the Biblical character) roamed through the Black Empire, was educated by the Black priests and used what he had learned to preach to his people about one god and lead them to self-government and nationhood. During this time, the Itiopian Empire re-emerged as the dominant force in the world. Politically, militarily and, as always, culturally, Black People reigned supreme during the 18th and 19th Dynasties, a period that covered slightly less than 400 years.

It was probably during the 19th Dynasty, under the leadership of a series of kings called Ramses, that Black People began to adapt military techniques that were not entirely defensive by nature. Up to this time, including the reigns of Menes (1st Dynasty) and Mentuhotep II (11th Dynasty), Black People had made use of their military (if that term is proper) or army only to defend themselves against their enemies (white people) and to contain their enemies. After centuries of using containment efforts and defensive measures against white people, Black People came to the realization that such efforts could not effectively deter white people, so Black People began to use their armies for attack and conquest purposes as well. As long as Black People maintained contact with the rest of the world, Black People remained up-to-date militarily and often dominated their enemies outside of the African continent. But, because they always migrated into the interior of the continent, Black People in time left control of the seacoasts (which were the keys to outside contact) in the hands of the whites who were slowly but surely becoming dominant in North Africa. Once these whites became powerful enough to actually declare that that region belonged to them (which is what happened soon after the 20th Dynasty), Black People became closed off from the rest of the world. From that point onward they competed only with themselves. One result of this is that Black People stood still militarily while their enemies outside of the continent continued to compete with each other and felt the need to develop better and better weapons (as a means toward getting the upper hand). These weapons were to give them a decided advantage in later centuries, when whites from outside the African continent began to invade that continent, enslave its Black inhabitants and colonize it economically and politically. To some extent, then, it explains why Black People are dominated politically, militarily and economically today.

Near the end of the 19th Dynasty and through the beginning of the 20th Dynasty, conditions again began to emerge that would leave Black People even less in control of the area of Itiopi called Egypt today. As a matter of fact, a Black person was not to be indisputably recognized as Pharaoh again until the 25th Dynasty, when Piankhi, a 25 year old general, and his successors militarily dominated the entire area and proclaimed it as part of the Black Empire in around 730 B.C.E. But this was little more than a claim. It is true that the leadership of Piankhi and Shabaka, his successor, was not violently challenged, but the fact is that it was too late for Black People to actually dictate and enforce policy in the area. Developments that took place for the 2500 years before Piankhi's arrival had made too much of an impression, had left white people and the white way-of-life too much ingrained, and had removed too many Black People to the interior of the African continent for this to be true. What Piankhi's victory signalled was that Black People still recognized this section of North Africa as theirs, and that they would fight to regain control of this area whenever conditions seemed favorable. The efforts of Piankhi and his soldiers is a warning to the Arabs (whites) who dominate North Africa today that their domination will end as soon as Black People get Our thing together again. The struggle for Our land has not ended. Black People have not settled for the present results of this confrontation. Quite to the contrary, Piankhi's actions indicate that Black People of the present time will attempt to take back all that has been taken from Us just as soon as We feel capable of doing so. We are down now, but this clash of the races is far from being completed. We will be back on top before it is.

The Blacks who followed Piankhi maintained their control for nearly 50 years. After that time period they were forced to withdraw and that section of Africa came under the control of foreign whites, white people who had not lived on the African continent. These foreign whites dominated the whites who had lived on the seacoasts and gradually moved inland during the periods of Black disunity and weak leadership. First the foreign whites came from Assyria, then Persia (present-day Iran), then Greece and then Rome. This period of foreign rule lasted from around 656 B.C.E. until 642 C.E. (almost 1200 years in all). When the Romans had to move out, the Arabs moved in. Their control of North Africa has lasted until this day.

With the end of Black Power in Egypt and the break-up of the Itiopian Empire into several small kingdoms, Our interest shifts from the Egyptian section of North Africa to Khart-Haddas (popularly called Carthage by white people). The Khart-Haddan Empire, located in the area of present-day Algeria and Tunisia, had developed much earlier that 1000 B.C.E. and, in addition to its indigenous native population, was populated by some of the descendants of those Blacks who had migrated from Egypt when that section of the Itiopian Empire was being taken over by white people (more correctly, it was being given to white people). In time, the Khart-Haddan Empire emerged and controlled much of North Africa and parts of southern Europe as well. Because of this, and because of the advanced level of cultural achievement in the Empire, many historians (whites) claim that white people (the Phoenicians) were responsible for the building of this Empire. Such a claim is ridiculous and proves once again to what extremes white people will go to create a lie and support it.

The most famous person associated with the Khart-Haddan Empire is Hannibal Barca, the Black general who may well be the greatest military tactician of all time. Under Hannibal Barca's father, Khart-Haddas continued to expand as a world power. During the later years of the development of Khart-Haddas, Rome began to develop and expand militarily. Since Khart-Haddas and Rome (which is white) were so close together, and since they were attempting to influence and take control of the same general area, it was clear that they would sooner or later have to go to war with one another. By 262 B.C.E. this war could no longer be avoided. In that year Khart-Haddas and Rome engaged in the first of a series of wars which are wrongly called the Punic Wars (historians who are white— and their Negro associates— call it that because the term Punic refers to the Phoenician people, who are white. However, Khart-Haddas was a Black Empire, so the term Punic should not be used. When it is used in that manner it confuses Black People and keeps Us from realizing what was really at stake). In the beginning the war went Rome's way, but by its end the Khart-Haddans had proven themselves the dominant power. But, even though Rome had been defeated, its will to destroy Khart-Haddas had not been broken, so the Romans immediately engaged wholeheartedly in making preparations for another war with their Black conquerors. This second war officially began in around 220 B.C.E. and is especially remembered because Hannibal Barca decided to end the Roman threat to Khart-Haddas once and for all by invading Rome itself. He led his best soldiers across the Alps (a mountain chain in southern Europe) and laid a siege on Rome, correctly thinking that the Romans would either have to fight and be slaughtered, starve to death or surrender. However, by laying siege on Rome with his best soldiers, Hannibal had left Khart-Haddas unprotected. After several years, a young Black general in the Roman army (his name was Scipio Nasica) came along, recognized this weakness, led some Roman troops into Khart-Haddas and effectively broke the control these Black People had held in North Africa and southern Europe. The final war between Khart-Haddas and Rome, at about 146 B.C.E., was nothing less than an attempt by Rome to totally destroy the defenseless Blacks of Khart-Haddas. It symbolized, finally, the end of Black domination of northern Africa (with the exception of present-day Ethiopia) and parts of Europe.

Noticeable in the defeat of Khart-Haddas were the roles of Scipio Nasica and King Massinissa of Numibia. Both of these were Black Africans. As we just stated, Scipio Nasica, who was born and trained in Khart-Haddas, forgot who he was and devised the military strategy for Rome that crippled Hannibal Barca's efforts to end the Roman threat. Massinissa, whose kingdom was strategically located, sided with the Romans (white people) instead of the Khart-Haddans (Black People). This helped shift the balance of power in favor of the Romans and, in time, contributed to the destruction of the Khart-Haddan Empire and the wholesale slaughter and enslavement of Black People all over Africa. The message is clear. Black People must become very conscious of color and race if We are to compete effectively. If We fail in this regard, then those who are and have been color conscious (particularly white people, at this time) will continue to take advantage of Us and dominate Us.

The defeat of Khart-Haddas made it possible for the Romans to move into many parts of Africa with relative ease. With the Romans came systematic discrimination against Black People and the speeding up of the destruction of Black civilization. African culture was systematically undermined and disrupted. When the Roman Empire began crumbling, this process of disruption sped up because the Romans attempted to save their empire by getting white people to unify around religion. Christianity as a white religion (and political tool) emerged, and laws were passed that forbade Black People to practice their own religion. The Black gods and goddesses were outlawed, free thought on religious and related matters was suppressed and Black People found themselves worshipping a god who had colorless-blue eyes, pale skin and blond hair. The damage caused by this development is too great to be estimated.

While crumbling, the Roman empire took away much of the cultural orientation of Black People. The vacuum it created in the African People was cruelly filled by the Arabs who moved in as conquerors once the Romans finally had to give up their African possessions. We will go more into this Arabic invasion/incursion shortly.

Black Empires that were to emerge and/or expand later on were, like Khart-Haddas, grand but small reproductions of the Itiopian Empire. It is difficult to imagine how numerous they were, since many existed at different times in different places. We will name a few though, but not for the purpose of drawing attention to these at the exclusion of those not mentioned. We will mention these only for the purpose of those readers who might use this information as a basis for further research.

We will begin by mentioning Nobadae and Makuria, the two major segments of the Itiopian Empire to emerge after the disruption of the dynastic kingdom. Alwa was a third such empire. Ghana, which was probably an outpost of the Itiopian Kingdom, emerged as a power in West Africa as early as 500 B.C.E., but was overcome by the Mandinka Empire (Mali) many years later. Mali itself was later overcome by Songhay, which also wanted to bring the Mossi States under its domain. The Mossi though, being fiercely independent and militaristic, maintained its independence. The Mossi are particularly noted for their opposition to Islam and their refusal to allow white people to enter the boundaries of their empire. They were so anti-white, as a matter of fact, that their motto for hundreds of years was, "When the first white man appears in the land the nation will die." The Mossi States were a power as late as 1800 C.E.

Also powerful was the kingdom of Kanem-Bornu in the Sudan. The kingdom of Kuba flourished moderately in central Africa. Monomotapa, generally dated at around 1000 B.C.E., might have been established in southern Africa as early as the Itiopian Empire. Zimbabwe is another early established empire in this region of Africa, whereas the Zulu Empire, known for its warriors, was subdued by the Europeans (white people) only a little more than a century ago (the mid-1800s).

We stated earlier that we had more to say about the Arabic penetration. With the Arabs came Islam, which like Christianity, was forced upon the African People. With the Arabs came the systematic destruction of many of the Black empires that had managed to survive earlier invasions by white people and the systematic manipulation of African rulers, the systematic and wholesale slaughter of African People and African institutions, the systematic enslavement of African People and the systematic transport of African People to other parts of the world for slave labor purposes. Islam was the banner behind which the Arabs marched, and it justified the systematic and unrelenting hunt for Black human bodies that was carried out by the Arabic people. For the first time, Black People were forced to be steadily on the move, steadily migrating for the purpose of merely maintaining their survival. This steady motion kept them from settling down and building as their ancestors had done, and kept them from accumulating further knowledge and recognizing the cumulative value of that knowledge. In fact, this steady movement of Black People, this return to nomadism caused by the hunt of Muslim slave hunters/catchers caused the African People to lose knowledge of much that they had known. It caused them to go backwards; so far backwards, in fact, that white historians could use their condition as "proof" that Black People were not capable of achieving anything of note at an earlier time.

But, We must remember that the present alone is not an adequate indication of past accomplishments nor future potential, and have this in mind when We are forced to listen to the racist ranting and racist "logic" of white historians, researchers and ideologists. We must remember that *the present is simply a reflection of conditions, fortunate or otherwise, that have persisted for an extended period of time*. These persisting conditions, if unfortunate, can cause even the most advanced people to gradually move back toward barbarism and, if fortunate, can cause the most uncivilized and barbaric people to move toward an advanced state of life. For that reason, Black People today need not be concerned about *whether* We can change Our present condition; We can, there is no doubt about that. Even now, as We play the role of the human floor mat, We exhibit the intelligence, expertise (know-how) and functional capacity to elevate Ourselves quickly. The only question is will We do so; will We actually attempt to use Our intelligence and expertise to change the condition of Black People and catapult Ourselves back into the forefront of human activity and development? The answer to that question will be provided, in more than a small degree, by the person who is reading this Handbook.

As the Arabic invasion was made easy by the devastation caused by Rome, the European invasion was made easier as the result of the devastation caused by the Arabs. By the time the Europeans (white people) began to explore the world in search of resources and means of economic survival, the African People had been forced to retrogress (go backwards) to the point where they could not adequately defend themselves against any non-African foe. The Portuguese recognized this as early as 1442 and conceived of establishing a Portuguese empire in Africa as a result. Later, other European countries would come to the same conclusion. However, they were not to satisfy themselves with non-Arabic sections of Africa like the Portuguese did. These European whites, particularly the small groups, planned to make all of Africa their garden of Eden. By the 1500s (C.E.) their plans were in full force.

The discovery of America by white people (in 1492) was a serious blow to the development of Black People. White people were to fully exploit or take advantage of this discovery by initially enslaving Black People for labor purposes and later by taking control of Black People's land for its mineral and productive capacities. The task of enslaving Black People was relatively easy because of the lack of military resistance Black People could put up. White people established forts (which were also human storage areas) along the African seacoasts and conducted inland missions in search of small groups or tribes that could be devastated and captured, and in search of larger groups that could be threatened and bribed into attacking other groups for the purpose of obtaining prisoners who could be turned over to the whites as slaves. The groups that were threatened were faced with the option of either providing white slave hunters with slaves from other tribes or of being enslaved themselves. Those groups that were bribed were led by individuals who had gone backwards to such an extent that they had little, if any, concept of racial pride and placed more emphasis on selfish concerns and petty material considerations (like the trinkets the whites rewarded them with) than they placed on human life, particularly Black human life. Such individuals were not representative of Black People on the whole. What they indicated was how low some Black persons had been forced to descend, and to what low and despicable depths white people had planned to force all Black People to descend.

Generally speaking though, Black People resisted the enslavement efforts of white people but, as we stated earlier, their resistance was greatly handicapped by their lack of advanced weaponry. When they knew slave hunters were in the area, Black People, particularly small tribes, stayed on the move. If they were tracked down, they fought as best they could, but their chances of successfully repelling the whites were slim. Larger groups of Blacks often engaged the whites in combat, but more of the intelligently led groups of Black People employed (made use of) guerilla-type measures, Black alliances and psychological warfare to confuse and ward off the white slave seekers as best they could.

One such intelligent leader was Queen Nzingha, whose 17th century empire covered much of the area called Angola today. Queen Nzingha despised the slave traders and ordered her troops to employ "hit and run" tactics against them whenever they trespassed into her kingdom, if for no other reason than to cause them moments of fear and anxiety. Queen Nzingha also trained many of her soldiers in the Portuguese manner and had them infiltrate the Portuguese camps (since the Portuguese employed Black soldiers), where they caused unrest and attempted to convince other Black soldiers to be disloyal to the Portuguese. Queen Nzingha also declared herself the enemy of all the African kings and queens who refused to resist the white invaders, thereby forcing them to take a stand on the slave issue, and declared that any Black person on any territory governed by her was free. This caused the white enslavers many problems, particularly if they captured slaves and had to cross Queen Nzingha's territory in order to make it to their forts (human storage centers). The Blacks who were captured, once made aware of the fact that the Queen's territory was free territory and that they could expect to receive assistance from the people of her empire, were more prone to attempt to escape. As a matter of fact, the Portuguese were so much hindered by the policies and efforts of Queen Nzingha that they waged an extensive war against her. They were not able to defeat her, however, and only got a semblance of relief when she died in the middle 1600s. Her spirit lived on, and is evidenced by the struggle of the Angolan people that resulted in freedom for them in the 1970s.

The Blacks who were captured and enslaved did what any intelligent human being would do— they rebelled and attempted to undermine the efforts of their enslavers. Such Blacks fought to keep from being captured, they fought after they were captured, and attempted to escape, kill themselves and kill the enslavers, they fought after they arrived at the fort, and rebelled during the trip from the African continent to wherever they were going (usually somewhere in North, Central or South America), and often jumped overboard, where they drowned or were eaten by sharks, rather than face a life of certain hell. And, the captured Blacks rebelled after they arrived at their point of destination. We will go into several of these rebellions later on. It is only important at this point that We (Blacks People) understand that the Black People who were forced to come to this land (the Americas) were not interested in integrating with the white people who had enslaved them. They were interested in obtaining freedom, which meant self-government and self-determination. They wanted these things because they were self-valuing and self-respecting human beings. They had not been convinced that they were anything less. When Black People today begin to value Ourselves and respect Ourselves, We will begin to appreciate the actions of the Blacks who were brought here in chains, and will accordingly begin to seek the things that self-valuing and self-respecting human beings seek.

II. Some Black Accomplishments
(Prior to contact with and domination by non-Black People)

In summary, it is important that We recognize that, before Black People had had any contact with white people, Black People had developed economically, politically, socially and culturally to very advanced degrees. Economically, Black People had learned to revolve their basic activities around agriculture, and had developed a calendar which made it possible for them to plan their agricultural activities in a manner that would most enable them to reach their objectives. In order to develop an accurate calendar (as they had done) they had to have scientific (not random or guessing) knowledge and a scientific understanding of the laws and principles of the universe, particularly as they related to weather conditions/cycles and forecasts. It is clear then that Black People were intensively studying the planets, the stars, the sun, the moon, the systems of outer space, their functions and their effects on the earth for thousands of years prior to Black contact with white people. In short, Black People recognized the value of a planned economy more than 7000 years ago and developed the first calendar, and became the first astronomers as a result.

Proof of Black People's political concentration are our previous references to the dynastic eras. The ones we discussed covered the period from around 3100 B.C.E. until around 660 B.C.E. It is probable, however, that the 1st Dynasty was established as early as 11,542 B.C.E., which indicates that Black People in their right mind have recognized the value of political consolidation and unification for more than 13,000 years. The idea of political concentration, then, had its origin and development in Africa, and not among white people.

Socially and culturally, for thousands of years before Black contact with white people, Black People had advanced to a degree that has not been matched even to this day. The major social accomplishment, which was largely the result of conditions under which Black People developed (see Lesson #1), was the maintenance of the humane attitude Black People held for each other. These attitudes were reflected in the social institutions that were developed to cater to the needs of the people in general. Governmental policy helped also, since it promoted internal stability (a feeling of security on the part of individuals and groups), general education by way of a public school system, and practical conveniences such as public bathrooms. The cultural achievement of the African People was apparent in at least two advanced systems of writing (one alphabetic, the other pictorial or hieroglyphic), an abundance of artists and sculptures, and arts and crafts that have been imitated and sought by people all over the world.

The known architectural accomplishments and philosophical pondering and revelations of Black People are evidence of their/Our degree of development at this early time in human history, a time when white people were so backward that they were not even recording their development (if "development" is the proper term). Yet, Black People had an organized religion as early as 4500 B.C.E., and had an advanced educational system (the Mysteries System) just as early. By the 20th Dynasty, branches of the Mysteries System had been established in several places outside of Africa, and foreigners who could pay the price and assumed the proper attitudes preferred to be educated there than anywhere else. As early as 3100 B.C.E., Black People had dammed the longest river (the Nile) in the world and established the military city of Memphis, and within 400 years had built the Great Pyramids, the Sphinx and marvelous tombs that captivate and puzzle the most knowledgeable onlookers today. During this same period Imhotep, a Black man, was acknowledged (recognized) as the father of medicine, and it was not to be long before Black People were performing surgical operations on such delicate organs as the human eye. Colors that have refused to fade after more than 5000 years and embalming techniques that mystify today's morticians are proof of Black People's understanding of chemistry during this period. The presence of engineers, scribes, libraries and goldsmiths, etc., indicate an advanced form of living and the mastery of various smelting processes. It is unmistakably clear, then, that Black People had to have mastered the sciences, particularly mathematics, at an early date, a very early date. This cannot be debated by any logical thinking person with an unbiased mind.

Black People accomplished so very much before We came into contact with white people. After that contact, the condition of white people gradually improved and the condition of Black People gradually deteriorated (got worse). This indicates that white people were learning from Us while attempting to undermine Our civilization. They had not developed themselves, therefore they had nothing to offer or contribute to the development of any group as highly developed as the Black Race. We must remember this!! That way, We will no longer be tricked into feeling grateful for what white people have supposedly done for Us. They haven't contributed anything to Our development but hell, and We need express no feelings of appreciation for that.

III. Effects of Enslavement on Africa

What Black People's contact with white people has really meant to Us is clear to anyone who has seriously attempted to analyze the effects of enslavement on Africa. Such an analysis will reveal that white people are responsible for the senseless slaughter of untold millions of Black People, and that slave-related murders alone account for the death of more than 100 million Black minds, spirits and bodies. Many that were not killed in combat on the African continent were removed from their homeland and forced to support the living habits of white hustlers and flesh seekers. The obvious political result of this is the destruction and disruption of Black empires and Black leaders. A much more sinister and long-term political result of this is that many of the Black leaders-to-be were either killed, enslaved or not even born. Many of the men and women who would have been most capable of directing the resistance efforts and modern development efforts of Black People were never in a position to do so, and many of the able minds that would have come along if Black People had not been tampered with were not even born. Thus, leadership on the African continent today is less than adequate, and the consequences have been and continue to be painfully endured by Black People. That is because mental pygmies are attempting to play a role that they would not be allowed or expected to play if the African continent had not been invaded by that catastrophe We call white people.

Contact with white people has also resulted in the cultural disruption of African/Black People. The institutions that had kept Us progressive and moving in a unified direction were shattered by the persistent destructive efforts of white people. The general system of public education was interfered with. The Mysteries System was outlawed and all its teachings were banned. The administrative and organizational abilities of Black People were stifled, and the accumulated knowledge of Black People was rendered null and void (and was therefore not used to the benefit of mankind) by the barbaric and ignorant white invaders. Black People were not allowed to practice their own religion or worship their own gods, and had to overcome attempts to keep them from speaking their own languages. We were brainwashed and psychologically motivated to think that anything Black is useless or evil while anything white is good. All that We had done to interpret the world order and the natural laws, all of the ideas that had enabled Us to function according to a central code of conduct, were stripped from Us and replaced with self-hatred and self-doubt. Over a period of time We went from being very sure and proud of Ourselves to being very uncomfortable with Ourselves and anyone who resembled Us.

In short, We began to distrust Black People and lack confidence in Black People. These tendencies are still clearly evident today.

As a Race of People We went backwards. From being politically organized and concentrated, We had to split into small groups that were later to be derogatorily called tribes. After a while this physical split-up became psychological as well, so that We began to think of Ourselves as different from other groups of Black People. This thought became more dominant when white people forced and bribed Us into hunting one another for slave labor purposes. A constant feeling of insecurity kept Us from establishing any real roots in any single place, kept Us on the move— hopefully one step ahead of the slave hunter, and pushed Us in the direction of barbarism. We did not retrogress to that condition, however, though·We did retrogress a lot. From makers and weavers of cloth and fine things to wear, We retrogressed to a state of semi-nakedness. From a People who had developed at least two advanced systems of writing, We retrogressed to a People who could no longer recognize the written word. From a People who had grown accustomed to living in steady (sometimes grand) structures, We retrogressed to a People who satisfied Ourselves with an easily assembled hut. From a People who had grown to appreciate the finer things in life (both practically and intellectually), We retrogressed to a People who found solace in merely surviving. The damage white people have inflicted or caused to be inflicted on Black People is overwhelming to say the least. There is no way, absolutely no way any person can begin to accurately estimate how much Black People have suffered as a consequence of Us coming into contact with white people.

The more white people became a factor in the lives of Black People, the more Black People became detached from each other. The more Black People were hunted and enslaved, the more unstable Black People became, socially and psychologically; and the more Black People were hunted by other Black People, the more Black People began to distrust and be suspicious of other Black People. From being a People who were receptive to strange faces, particularly if they were Black, We became a People who were fearful of anyone who was not a member of Our particular tribe. The fear of being betrayed and/or captured by strangers forced attitudes and suspicions into Black People that have persisted and make it difficult for Us to get together even today. As a matter of fact, We have become so obsessed with keeping Our eyes and ears open for the misdeeds of other Blacks that We frequently let Our real human enemies, white people, do Us harm without even the slightest risk to themselves. Our inability to unify, even in a crisis situation such as the one that exists today, can therefore be traced to the disruption in Our being caused by white people.

The final effect of enslavement on Africa that will be mentioned at this time is that Africa came to be (and still is) dominated by non-African people. This is true economically, socially and politically. The riches of the African continent serve to satisfy the desires and needs of white people, not Black People. The codes of conduct on the African continent more and more reflect the priorities of white people, not Black People. And the governments established on the African continent are either white or white-controlled, not Black. Across North Africa, We find white Arabic governments in the United Arab Republic (Egypt), Libya, Tunisia, Algeria, Morocco, Mauritania, Mali and the Sudan. In South Africa We find European whites governing Azania (Union of South Africa), Southwest Africa and, until recently, Zimbabwe (Rhodesia). Of the countries that are left, only a few are intelligently governed by Black People for the benefit of Black People. The overwhelming majority are ruled by "toms" (as in Zaire, Chad, Central African Republic, Liberia, Ivory Coast, Kenya, etc.) or mental pygmies (as in Botswana, Nigeria, Uganda, Ghana, etc.). Consistent with this is the fact that the major continent-wide political organizations, such as the Organization of African Unity, are dominated by non-Black ideologies and ideologists. Practically no individuals in positions of authority concern themselves with sincere attempts to improve the lot of the masses of the African People. One of the reasons for this is that such individuals do not identify with the masses of the African People. They consider themselves superior to the masses of African People and feel quite at peace with themselves as they cause Black People to starve and labor in mines for the benefit of non-Africans. Such Africans/Blacks have descended, as white people wanted all of Us to, to the lowest level possible.

Europeans were such a dominant force on the African continent that they felt at ease carving Africa up and dividing it among themselves. This happened in the 1880s, and led to the imposition of territorial boundaries that were totally out of touch with the reality and the limits recognized by the African People themselves. Curiously though, African People have fought each other over these white imposed territorial boundaries (witness Somalia and Ethiopia, and Tanzania and Uganda, for examples), while Europeans have fought each other in two world wars in order to get a larger slice of the African pie. They consider the Blacks to be such a small threat that they felt comfortable offering an African country (Uganda) to the Jews in the late 1940s (to be settled as the Jewish homeland, now called Israel). The fact that these type things are done without regard for the rights of the African People or the ability of Black People to retaliate against whites is proof of their domination. Only recently, since the late 1950s, have Black People began to reclaim Our territory. So far, the results have been more cosmetic than real. Africa today is still unquestionably dominated by non-Black people, but steps are being made that will change this condition in the years to come. Black People all over the planet Earth must struggle diligently and speed this process along. The salvation of millions of African People depends on it.

LESSON 4
LESSON OUTLINE

I. White People in the Americas (1492-1619)
  A. Began to Establish Colonies/Settlements
  B. Began to Wipe Out Native Population
II. Types of Colonies Established
  A. Those That Were to be Populated by Large Numbers of White People
  B. Those That Were Not to be Populated by Large Numbers of White People
III. Development of Colonies (1619-1700): North America, A Case Study
  A. By 1700, Four Things Were Perfectly Clear
    1. A small number of persons had set the main patterns of government and society.
    2. Only a small number of persons were intended to benefit from the development and exploitation of the colonies (to become known as the United States of America).
    3. The basic character of the colonies had been acquired and was not to change (In fact, it had been established in the "mother country"/Great Britain).
    4. Racism and Racial Inequality were entrenched parts of that basic character.
IV. Black People In White History (1492 -)
  A. As A Human Force
    1. We were slaves, less than human beings (whether "free" or not).
  B. As an Economic Force
    1. We provided the genius and labor that made the white world thrive.
    2. Because of Our presence, white people who would otherwise have been idle were gainfully employed.
    3. We made white individuals and white countries rich.
    4. Because of Our presence, European industries developed and European cities grew and thrived.
  C. As A Political Force
    1. Whites fought among themselves over control of the slave trade.
    2. Whites fought among themselves over control of slavery.
    3. Whites fought among themselves over slavery itself.
    4. Whites fought among themselves over control of Africa
      -World War I
      -World War II
    5. Whites are fighting over control of Africa today.
V. Black People in American History (1492-1865)

A. The Work and Genius of Slaves Made America Prosper
B. Slavery Made the Revolutionary War Inevitable
C. Slaves Helped Make America Free
D. Slaves Helped Keep America Free
  1. San Domingo
  2. War of 1812
E. Slavery Forced America to Expand in Order to Satisfy the Demands of Labor/Small Farmers/Industry
F. Slaves Fought and Kept the North and South One Country.

I. White People in the Americas (1492-1619)

In this lesson, Black People arrive in the Americas. Based on what was discussed in the last lesson, all of Us should have a clear understanding of Black History prior to this event; of Our days of greatness and achievement, of Our gradual decline, of Our domination by eastern and western whites, of Our capture and enslavement by white slave hunters on the African continent and of Our removal, in chains, from that continent to the continents of North and South America (including Central America and the Caribbean). Thus, by now We should have a fairly clear picture of Our history as Black People, and We should have a substantial/strong connection that ties Black People in this part of the world (the U.S. of A., the Caribbean, etc.) unmistakably to the African continent and the African People who still reside there. We have historical proof now that the Black People in the Americas are African People, and We have enough knowledge of Our past to know that being African/Black is something to be very, very proud of.

Before We actually get into the activities or history of Black People in the Americas, We will get an idea of what white people in the west (Europeans) were doing on these continents at about the same time they were spreading havoc across the African continent (from around 1492 on). Careful analysis will reveal that their activities revolved around two basic processes: (1) that of searching for a suitable supply and type of labor and (2) that of settling white people in the Americas.

Earlier it was stated that after white people "discovered" America, they set out to make it as profitable to white people (particularly the "small group") as possible. One of the factors that would most contribute to the profitability of America was a supply of labor that was both cheap and readily available. Columbus quickly seized upon the idea of having the native American (so-called Indians) satisfy this labor need of white people. However, Columbus and his followers quickly discovered that the Indians would not adapt themselves to the type of work schedule or work requirements which whites felt were most desirable. Therefore, alternate sources had to be explored.

In the meantime, though, the work of developing America and supporting the whites who had settled here had to be done, and undesirable and not adequately productive laborers who did not have to be paid were better than no laborers at all. Because of this understanding, white people set out on a mission that would make it possible for white people to profit from the labor of the Indian and eliminate the Indian at the same time. In other words, white people decided to force the Indian to work for white people because this forced labor would enable whites to accumulate a degree of wealth and provide the whites with a means of killing off the people who were the rightful owners of the land. White people were aware of the fact that Black People would soon be forced to replace the Indians as a source of free labor, and they were also aware of the fact that, as long as the Indians remained in America in substantial numbers, they would be a threat to the white people who were taking over the Indians' land. Since the Indians' labor would soon be unnecessary, and since their presence was undesirable, the only practical thing to do, white people reasoned, was to wipe the Indians out.

As a result (and because of factors mentioned in Lesson #1), in less than 50 years after Columbus "discovered" America in 1492, nearly every one of the Indians in the Caribbean areas had been wiped out. Before the Caribs (original natives of the Caribbean) had been completely eliminated, the Spanish whites had set about attacking the Indian population in South America, and at least three Indian empires, the Aztec, the Inca and the Chibcha, were destroyed. Not long afterwards, the French and British whites began settling in North America (which includes the United States of America). As early as 1607, with the settling of whites at Jamestown, Virginia, these whites began their attack on the Indian population. This process developed into a government operated project and continued until 1890 when, symbolically at least, the threat of the Indian presence was erased with the senseless massacre of Indians at Wounded Knee, South Dakota. In between these years, the Indian population in what is called America today was hunted down, poisoned, lynched and legally executed by the millions by white people. Today there are so few Indians left that, politically speaking, they are practically negligible. Their extermination is a testament to the morality of white people and white people's regards for the rights of others.

As was stated earlier, the second basic process initiated by white people at this time was the settling of white people in the Americas. This process, which began at the end of Columbus' first trip in 1492, sometimes called for the establishment of a permanent white population and at other times called for the establishment of a temporary or transitory (constantly changing) white population. The basis for the first white settlement was laid by Columbus when he left some of his men at the colony of Navidad, in the Caribbean (the colony itself did not survive; it did start the process though). The next year an attempt was made to colonize Hispaniola (presently called the countries of Haiti and the Dominican Republic). As time passed and more white government sponsored exploratory trips were made into the area, additional colonies were established in the Caribbean and in South America and North America as well. Wherever a colony was established, white people settled the land in large or small numbers; some times temporarily, other times permanently, took control of the productive powers of the land and imposed white rule on (or wiped out) the native inhabitants. Essentially speaking, this is what colonization has always been about.

II. Types of Colonies Established

Most history books will inform Us that there were different types of colonies established in the Americas. We agree, but the way we distinguish the types of colonies will not be appreciated by champions of white scholarship and brainwashed victims of white history/propaganda. To get a clear understanding of the political and economic implications and realities of the colonial system, and to avoid introducing factors that will only confuse most persons, We must define only two types of colonies: (1) those that were to be populated by large numbers of white people and (2) those that were not to be populated by large numbers of white people.

In colonies that were to be populated by large numbers of whites, the white settlers, over a period of years, had the tendency to think of themselves and their settlement as a model of European standards, values and practices. These settlers went about the business of making their settlement as much like the mother country (the country from which they came) as possible. They thought in terms of permanently remaining where they were and of establishing institutions that would insure their survival and preserve their particular way-of-life. In other words, they established a way-of-life (modeled after that of the mother country) and instituted measures that would safeguard their way-of-life and keep it from being over-influenced by non-European intangibles (ideas, customs, etc.). Not long after the white settlers took on such a frame of mind (particularly if their settlement showed signs of prospering), they would begin to view their settlements as white cultural centers that should be politically independent of the mother country. Of course, this political independence would mean that the economic activities of the settlement would be re-directed, changed or adjusted in order to benefit mostly the whites in the settlement instead of the whites (mostly the small group) in the mother country. (Remember: The primary purpose of a colony is to provide goods and services that will benefit those in the mother country. The economic support of the colony itself is not of primary importance or concern.)

But the important factor to note about this for the time being is that whites in these type settlements were about the business of establishing institutions that would leave their permanent stamp on the settlement and of institutionalizing measures (laws, agencies, etc.) that would protect their way-of-life and keep their settlement from being overinfluenced by non-Europeans. The whites in these areas were largely concerned about embedding and increasing the white (European) influence and keeping those who represented a non-European influence under strict control. This meant that the Black People who were forced to come to these settlements for labor purposes would be strictly restricted by two basic fears of white settlers. The first of these was the fear of the slaves rebelling and destroying white people and their property. The second of these was the fear of Black People introducing Black standards, Black ideas and Black values that would somehow take root within the settlement, destroy the "purity" of the white way-of-life and eventually destroy the settlement itself by turning it into a center of human activity that revolved around a fusion of Black and white politics, culture and society. Even at this early stage such a fusion was not acceptable to white people who were serious about establishing a permanent settlement in the New World. What was acceptable to white people, and what they sought, was the establishment of a white settlement that was militarily and internally secure, prosperous and safe from the ideological, cultural and social influence of non-Europeans.

This was not the case in colonies that were not to be populated by large numbers of white people. This was not the case in colonies that had a European population that was transitory as opposed to permanent. In colonies like these, the whites were not concerned about transforming the colony into a model of Europe because they had no plans of establishing any roots in the colony. Their intention was to remain in the colony only so long as it took them to accumulate a desired degree of wealth, and not one day longer. They had no plans of making the colony home, so they did not initiate measures that were intended to go beyond safeguarding the economic interests and investments of themselves and the small group they represented.

What do these factors indicate? They indicate that, contrary to what historians usually assert, religion was not a factor in the treatment of the slaves in the various colonies. Economics and politics were the factors because they determined the de facto (actual) treatment of the slaves. The Catholic (Portuguese, Spanish, etc.) masters might have had more laws on the books regarding the "humane" treatment of the slaves than did the Protestant (English) masters, but the slaves in the Catholic colonies generally caught as much hell as the slaves in the Protestant colonies. This was true because the law in the Catholic colonies did not represent the will of those in power to actually improve the condition of the slaves, nor did it represent the attitude white people held toward Black People. White people in these colonies knew they could ignore the law without fear of being punished, so their general treatment of the slaves (Black People) was not noticeably influenced by the law. The law was just words on paper; it merely represented the best treatment the slaves could hope to receive. The treatment they actually received, whether in Catholic or Protestant settlements, was determined by whether the white population was transitory or permanent; that is, by whether it was the intent of white people to make that colony a model of Europe or not.

Where the whites had political and economic objectives that necessitated a permanent white settlement, laws regarding the "humane" treatment of Black People were not even put on the books. This indicated that the Black People in these areas could not even hope to receive the treatment or achieve the status that Black People in other type settlements could hope to achieve. The laws in these type settlements were meant to safeguard a way-of-life that did not allow for political, economic or social equality for all races. In transitory type settlements, settlements where it was not necessary to safeguard a way-of-life, laws were passed which made it possible for a non-European type social and political environment to evolve. The whites in these colonies were not overly concerned about keeping the slaves from getting married or allowing a free Black person to vote as long as these possibilities did not interfere with white people's efforts to amass the economic rewards they sought. What did these whites care if laws were passed that made it possible for a Black person to take a white person to court or refuse to call a white man "Mister"? After all, the colony was not meant to be a model of white values and priorities anyway, and the possibilities were always made impossible when white people wanted them to be so. And, if the possibility became a reality after white people had amassed their fortunes and left the colony, it would not affect them anyway.

Even today, the treatment received by Black People in all of the colonies (now countries) that were settled and dominated by white people is determined not by religious or moral considerations but by economic and political considerations (see Lesson #1— Central Motivating Factors). What exist today are only later stages of processes that existed and were developing 100, 200, 300 years ago. This type continuity is characteristic of all historical processes.

III. Development of Colonies (1619-1700): North America, A Case Study

At this time we will review the development of the North American colonies between the years 1619 and 1700. 1619 is the year historians say Black People were first brought to the English colonies as slaves, and the 81 years between that year and 1700 represent the period of resettlement, adjustment and establishment of a new way-of-life for the whites who had chosen or been forced to leave Europe. During these years the whites experienced the fears and insecurities associated with moving to an unknown locality, benefited from the civilized nature of the native American (so-called Indian), explored and realized how the colony could be used to enrich the small group in Europe, and molded a "small group" of its own that developed a sense of economic self-control and political self-determination that would, in time, cause them to declare themselves free and independent of Europe. Thus it was during these years that the secondary motivators that were to consciously or subconsciously govern white people in America were embedded/re-enforced in them and institutionalized by them; such that, by the year 1700, four things had become perfectly clear.

(1) A small number of persons had set the main patterns of government and society. This small group of persons, at this early date, took control of every facet of American life. With them came a cultural concept, which they called the Puritan Ethic, an economic concept, which they called free enterprise (self-preservation), and a religious concept, which they called Christianity. Upon arriving on America's shores they established a political concept based upon the controlling of the masses (the majority) by a select few for the benefit of that select few (called democracy and symbolized by the Mayflower Compact of 1620). This political concept was called a democracy because it broke with the European practice of one person rule (usually in the form of a prince or a king) by giving more persons a controlling role in government. In fact, it is only a poorly disguised version of one person rule since it fails to include the mass of the people in the governmental process and since it is based on the assumption that a small portion of mankind should benefit at the expense of the masses.

Thus, We can see that the institutions, practices and beliefs upon which this country is founded have been embedded into white Americans and their systems of government and economics since before 1607. The ideas of government and society which dominate America have dominated white people, with minor and non-essential exceptions, since before the trips of Christopher Columbus (pre-1492). The ideas on economics and survival, where their concept of free enterprise naturally evolved into profiteering, monopolizing and capitalizing, is just as embedded. Therefore, it is not likely that Black People can raise issues and arouse emotions that will bring about basic changes in white people or their system. For Black People to talk about changing "the system" and making it possible for the masses to control themselves, benefit from their own labors and receive the goods and services they need to survive because they are human beings is something that white people will not even seriously consider. Six hundred years of believing in something entirely different will not allow white people to seriously consider anything that radically differs from what they have come to believe.

This system, as it presently exists, has at least 600 years of history and development behind it, and it has white people behind it who believe in it to no end. To white people, the idea that the masses must suffer for the benefit of the few is so sacred that it is not even open to serious debate. As a matter of fact, white people believe in that idea more than they believe in Jesus. Additionally, it is the role of the individual, they wholeheartedly believe, to do whatever he has to do in order to become part of the small group. At that time, at the time he becomes a member of the small group, he can consider himself a success in life and enjoy the fruits of success (meaning he can benefit from the labor of the masses economically, politically and as a matter of course).

So, a small group emerged early and established the system that prevails in America today. Even though the system was meant to serve only a handful of white people, it almost perfectly represented the preferences of all white people. Most of them will verbally admit that it is wrong to allow people to starve and go without necessities when necessities are available, but this admission by them carries no weight because they all strongly desire to benefit at the expense of someone else. They all desire to obtain status and recognition, and to turn their noses up at those who are unable to do likewise. Black People should remember this. That way, among other things, it will be less likely that We will waste time uniting or allying Ourselves with whites who call themselves "laborers", "liberals" and/or "communists", etc. White people are white people!! If they want to organize to form a new government or if they advocate "revolution", it is because they want to be in a position of power and convenience— and organizing a new government or advocating revolution is their means of so doing. If they mumble or grumble about unemployment or minimum wages, it is not because they think the system that champions the exploitation of the masses is bad; it is simply because they (as individuals) are not satisfied being part of the abused group (the masses). Whereas Black People be sincerely concerned about making basic changes, changes that will benefit the masses, the whites who call them "comrade" and stand among the demonstration crowds with them are only concerned about changing their particular circumstances. White persons, regardless of what they call themselves, are not concerned about the welfare of the group; they are not concerned with changing the condition of the masses. White persons are concerned about white individuals ("me"), and their activities are designed with the object of changing the position of certain individuals within the system. Black People should know and accept this by now. Those who fail to do so will probably learn when it is too late for them to undo the harm that uniting with white people will cause Black People.

So, we will repeat. White people believe in the role that is now reserved for the small group in the white scheme of things. White people are filled with respect for those who make it (at the expense of the masses) and disdain or scorn for those who fail to succeed. Therefore, if you are holding hands with them you are not going to go beyond this concept. If you stand with some of them against "the system" in America, your efforts will not result in a single basic change. You might go to a different form of the concept or become able to present this concept in a different costume, but white people will make sure that their concept of government, economics and society in general is not effectively tampered with.

(2) Only a small number of persons were intended to benefit from the exploits of this country. This goes in with what was just said, but it focuses in on the economic aspect of American life. Black People in this country talk as if the wealth of this country was meant to be spread out among all of the people of this country, when that has never been the intention of the white people who grabbed control of this land. What We Black People have to understand is that America was explored and settled in order to enrich the small groups in different European countries. There was no intent whatsoever to make life less strenuous or less uncomfortable for the majority of the people. As a matter of fact, this majority was viewed as tools of the small group who would either work in Europe for the small group, or come to America and work while the small group in Europe got the rewards, or come to America and stay, thereby removing themselves as a poverty stricken threat to the wealth that the small group in Europe had accumulated. Under no circumstances was it even imagined that all of the colonists (people) should share in the wealth created or generated by the colony.

By 1700, a small group within the colony had developed and emerged. This group did not appreciate the fact that America's wealth was going to the small group in Europe. They felt, instead, that that wealth should be spread out among the small group in America. As slavery made America more and more prosperous, and as more and more of America's wealth was being sent to the small group in Europe, the developing small group in America became more and more determined to keep the wealth that was being produced over here for themselves. They stopped playing the game with the small group in England completely in 1776, when they declared that the colonies were independent states under one federal union (the United States of America).

Since 1776, nothing has changed. Free enterprise, white people's style, naturally evolved into profiteering, monopolizing and capitalizing at the expense of the large group. All over America, in the North, South, West and East, a handful of Americans got rich while the rest got used and/or abused. Some of those who got used (lackeys) also got comfortable, but this was incidental, not intentional. This was true of the plantation system in the South, the industrial system in the North and the capitalistic system of the North and East that began to dominate all sections of the country during the late 1840s. Capitalism used the discoveries of the Industrial Revolution, which was supposed to make it possible to produce enough goods and services to take care of the needs of everybody, to expand the profit making capabilities of those who controlled the machines of production, but instead of working to the advantage of the whole, worked to the advantage of the Rockefellers, Vanderbilts and other members of the small group (they got richer). In the same manner, technological discoveries have made it possible for everyone to get adequate food, shelter and clothing today (and other necessities as well), but the fact of the matter is something different. Only the small group has intentionally benefited from the discoveries of technology, and some lackeys have unintentionally benefited. Nonetheless, the story has not changed from the beginning of America until now. The theme of the story repeatedly tells Us that if Black People are concerned about developing a system that provides adequate goods and services to the masses, We have no reason whatsoever to expect white people to sincerely assist Us. No economic activity in America has ever been intended to make the masses comfortable; and such a thought is not even consistent with any economic activity held dear by white people. America (white people) is simply not about that.

(3) By 1700, the basic character of the colonies had been acquired and was not to change. In fact, as previous information reveals, this basic character had been established in the mother country (England) and was transferred to America without basic alteration by European dissidents (unsatisfied white people). This in itself indicates that even the abused whites were not against the basic environment or principles of exploitation that prevailed in Europe, they were simply dissatisfied with their position in it.

But, what do we mean when we use the term "character" in this regard? We mean, quite simply, that the American colonies took on an American personality, a white personality that has not changed in more than 300 years. We mean that America took on certain traits, certain patterns of behavior, certain attitudes and certain ways or manners of functioning that are second nature to it. We use the term "character" because it implies that this personality, the patterns of behavior, the attitudes, etc., represent the American condition (norm) as opposed to an American circumstance (unusual occurrence or divergence from the norm). It is what one should expect to confront when one has to deal with the American system or an American.

Briefly put, the American character, set since before 1700, is one of individualism, exploitation, wastefulness, hypocrisy, perversion, militarism (when confronted by a weaker body), bribery, cultural insecurity, political elitism (exclusivism) and economic greed. It lacks imagination, it is uncreative, it seeks to make people function as if they were machines, it seeks to control nature, it seeks to destroy all that it cannot control, and it is racist. America has been like this for centuries and it will continue to be like this, or die trying. Black

People in America had better get used to that fact. Any hopes We might have of changing this system or white people are hopeless hopes. We might destroy America, sure, but We will not change America. Therefore, We might as well stop wasting Our physical, emotional, spiritual and mental energies trying.

(4) By 1700, racism and racial inequality were entrenched parts of America's basic character. White people have been racist and have systematically expressed their racism since Alexander the Great conquered parts of North Africa in around 332 B.C.E. Immediately after doing so, he forbade Black People to participate in certain activities and to travel to certain parts of Alexandria, the city he established as his capital. This attitude of restricting Black People and discriminating against Black People has continued without losing any steam until this very day. It was evident when western whites first invaded Africa, it was evident when western whites established the Atlantic slave trade (from Africa across the Atlantic Ocean to America), it was evident throughout each American colony/state, it was evident when white people sliced Africa up and divided it among themselves in the 1880s, it is evident when one views employment statistics, it is evident when one visits an American jail or prison, it is evident when one analyzes American literature and it will continue to be evident in all types of ways. America and Americans are racists, and the cries of abused Black families and pleading Negro "leaders" are not going to change America or Americans to any substantial or meaningful degree. The evidence in this regard is so abundant (plentiful) and overwhelming that the facts cannot be distorted enough to keep the truth from coming through. Let's face it; racism is to America and Americans what barking is to a dog—you don't find one without the other.

Black People have been spoon-fed information about America by white people, but We generally fail to chew into that information and send it to Our mind, where it can be properly digested, sorted out and accepted or rejected based upon Our particular experiences in America and Our ability to reason and use common sense. Now though, it is time that We stopped accepting white people's lies about justice, "honest Abe", democracy and "the land of opportunity". America has been lied about so much by white people that even they have trouble recognizing America for what America really is. Instead of facing up to the rotten core of this country, white people come up with excuses for this country's wrongdoings and get Us, Black People, to spread these excuses around. Unfortunately, We don't even analyze what We are told. White people simply feed Us some information and tell Us to keep it on the tips of Our tongues. That way We can quickly call on it when We need it to defend white people and denounce those who attack white people. It is shameful but it is true, and We are dealing with the truth in this <u>Handbook</u>.

IV. Black People in White History (1492-)

At this time We will review the role of Black People in American history from around 1492 forward. We will review more white attitudes, but concentrate on Black People as a human force, an economic force and a political force in the white world and its development (particularly America).

As a human force, as far as whites were concerned, Black People were not human. They labeled Us as slaves from jump street and classed Us as chattel (movable) property, which put Us in the same wagon with their cattle, their oxen, their cows and horses, their pigs, their hoes and their wagons. By 1800 they needed to call Us 3/5 of a person (the 3/5 Compromise, which did not recognize Us as humans, but allowed each master to get 3 political votes for every 5 slaves he owned), which is saying that We are still less than a man and therefore less than a human being. By the 1850s, it had been re-emphasized that Black People had no rights that needed to be respected by a white person. Since all persons have human rights that need to be respected (the white founding fathers called them life, liberty and the pursuit of happiness), whites were saying, again, that We were not humans. Even today, in 1980, We are seeking equality, which implies equality with a human being. Thus, it is clear that We are still not viewed as human beings by white people. Our humanity is still being denied.

Historically, the terms white people have habitually used to refer to Black People would not be habitually used to refer to human beings. Whites traditionally called Black females wenches, pickaninnies, nannies and bitches. They traditionally called Black males bucks, boys and coons. All of these terms have less than human connotations. When they called Us wenches, the best they could have meant was that We were whores. More accurately, though, the term wench de-emphasized everything about Black females but the female's sexual aspect. Thus the term wench turned the Black female into a "pussy". That term is not one we prefer to use but it is the one that accurately describes what they meant when they used the term wench. Likewise, they called Our young females pickaninnies in order to keep from calling them children, which would have put Black babies on the same level with white babies. A nanny is a female goat. White women preferred to have Black women breast-feed and raise white children. Instead of calling these Black mothers women, though, which would have put Black females on the same level with white females, white people called Us goats. This term (nanny) kept Us in Our below human place. The term bitch served the same purpose. As much as we use that term (due to Our abject ignorance), We should know that a bitch is a female dog. Black bitches do not qualify as white people's best friend, however. Black bitches are too low down to play that role.

A buck is a male animal, but it is not a human being. A buck can be a he-goat, a deer, an antelope, a horse, etc. To white people, a Black buck was something that looked like a human whose function was to "knock-up" wenches (get Black females pregnant with baby slaves). The term boy does refer to a human being, but as applied to Black males by white people it was an underdeveloped human being. That explains why a 30 or 40 year old Black male could still be a "boy". All human boys develop into men, but manhood was an impossibility for a Black male. Black males did not possess enough human qualities to reach manhood. The most We could develop into was an old coon, a sneaky, low down watermelon stealer who was somehow related to rabbits, raccoons, etc.

Anyone who could check out the spots where white people made slaves sleep and stay would realize that they were not proper shelter for human beings. Anyone who knows what white people forced Black People to eat knows that that food is not fit (nutritionally nor otherwise) for human beings. Anyone who saw what white people gave the slaves to wear would know that they could not have thought that they were providing dress for human beings. Black People, slave and free, were less than human as far as whites were concerned. This is one of the reasons whites had no problem castrating or sexually crippling Black People, and why they had no problem cutting open the wombs of pregnant Black women so they could stomp the Black fetus that was soon forced to fall to the ground. No one can do that type thing to a human, or approve of it being done; but white people did that type thing to Black People, slave and free, as a matter of course— and with the approval of other whites.

History reveals quite definitively that, as far as white people are concerned, there is no such thing as a Black human being.

Before closing, we will add that Black People have been too human in Our relations with white people. While white men and women have inflicted harm on Black sons and daughters, Black mothers and fathers have cooked these white people's food, nursed these white people's children and taken care of these white people's property and goods without attempting to systematically or scientifically "get them back". All too often, Black males and females who were in a position to "get whites back", individually or collectively, have failed to do so (or even try to do so). This is unfortunate because history reveals that white people have not acted as human beings should act, therefore they do not deserve to be treated as human beings should be treated.

Economically speaking, without Black People the white world would not have developed the way it has developed. Better put, the white world would have developed very slowly if it had not been for Black People, and would probably be classified with so-called "underdeveloped" countries today. Black People made it possible for white people to colonize the Americas and reap the riches of America. Black People made it possible for cotton and tobacco to become money crops in the United States, for sugar to become a money crop in the Caribbean, for cocoa to become a money crop in Venezuela (South America), for coffee to become a money crop in Brazil (South America) and for hundreds of other money crops to emerge in hundreds of other places. Much of the land in the Americas would not have even been tilled if it had not been for Black People, and many crops would not even have been grown were it not for Black People. Because of Black People crops were produced that made people, white people, rich, and the areas where they were produced became places where white people lived and often grew into centers of European living and culture. Black People not only provided the type of physical labor in the fields that was needed, but were craftsmen as well and excelled at every major occupation, both skilled and unskilled. These skills were not new to Us because We had made extensive use of them on the African continent. We, Black People, did the necessary mining work, Black People built churches, cathedrals and other group structures, Black People cooked, cleaned and pressed clothes, raised children, functioned as nurses and midwives, built homes/houses, made discoveries (invented machines that eased work and methods that increased efficiency), did artwork on buildings, carved statues of saints, built carriages and coaches, forged iron and other ores and metals (were blacksmiths, silversmiths, etc.), played music in orchestras and on plantations, designed clothes, made shoes and clothes, provided satisfying entertainment, trained cocks (fighting roosters) and horses, etc., painted, did plumbing work and, in areas where they were allowed to do so (like Brazil), filled administrative, clerical, judicial and business positions. The major work, both skilled and unskilled, and the method by which this work was to be done or carried out, was supplied by Black People who had been forced to serve the interests of white people. Indeed We, Black People, provided the genius and labor that made the white world prosper.

We also provided white people all over the world with an income. The slave trade was a profitable business. It was not that unusual for a person who sold a slave in the 'Americas to get 25 to 30 times what it had cost him to get that slave in Africa. More regularly though, a person gained from 30% to 40% on every slave sold (after having deducted all expenses). In at least one European city (Liverpool, England), and probably more, almost everyone had a hand or share in the slave trade business.

The slave trade was not only profitable as a trading activity. It created a great deal of prosperity for persons who were not directly involved in the trade by giving rise to the development of untold numbers of industries all over Europe and part of the Americas that gave employment to white people. Hundreds of thousands of white people were needed to build ships, to make and transport guns, to make ammunition, to manufacture, smelt and sell iron, to build boats, to paint ships, homes and other structures, to make the hundreds of items that were used to bribe the Africans on the continent (Africa), including beads, basins, different types of European fabrics, etc. In this regard it can be accurately stated that each Black person that was transported from Africa provided the economic support for a small white family (4 or 5 persons) in Europe or in the Americas. This is an incredible realization, but it is true!

Yet it does not reveal the greatest economic contribution Black People made to the development of the white world. That becomes apparent when We realize that the slave trade and slavery (Black People) made the Industrial Revolution possible in Europe. The Industrial Revolution changed the conditions of life in the white world and made it possible for human beings to use mechanical power in the production of needed and desired goods and services. Nearly all of the industries in several European countries had their beginning in the slave trade, and others lived or died on the success of the slave trade. Indeed, modern industry in the white world was made possible as a result of the slave trade and slavery (Black People). If it had not been for the profits they received as a result of exploiting Black People, white people wouldn't even have been able to invest in the economic possibilities opened up by the Industrial Revolution.

Because white people were able to invest in the Industrial Revolution, Europe was able to develop at a much faster pace than other people during the last 200 years, and it was made possible for Europeans (white people) to underdevelop/overexploit Africa by taking Africa's resources and using them to the advantage or benefit of white people. It enabled white people to get an additional jump on Black People that made it possible for white people to make use of the resources that belonged to Black People. It made it possible for white people to impoverish Black People and enrich white people at the same time; in fact, as part of a single operation. When We come to understand this, We come to understand a lot about the relative conditions of Africa (and Africans) and white people today. White people, while in the process of making themselves rich and "progressive", impoverished Black People , put Us in the pitiful economic circumstances that characterize Us all over the world today, and pushed Us backwards (Please see Lesson #5).

As a political force, since 1492 Black People have been right in the middle of white history. Our presence and Our roles, however, have not been officially recognized by white historians. Instead of stating outright that Black People's presence (and development related thereto) was the cause of certain political processes or events, white historians cover Us up in a maze of economic, political and social principles and theories that account for what took place without specifically identifying the major factor involved. Nevertheless, the person who is thoughtful enough to reduce each of the given principles to its least common denominator is likely to discover Black People and/or matters related to Black People.

Politics is a system (a scientific method) of relating to those in your environment (town, country, continent, etc.) that assumes that conflict will be the dominant force in the lives of men and women (that is, human beings). It assumes, for instance, that the country or individual that seeks to be prosperous must overcome the efforts of other countries or individuals to keep it from becoming prosperous. Politics assumes that the country that seeks to become able to adequately defend itself will have to overcome efforts of other countries that will try to keep it from becoming able to adequately defend itself. Even on the domestic level (within one country) this assumption of dominant conflict reigns supreme. That is why presidents, congressmen and lobbyists assume that laws that are introduced will be opposed by those who do not stand to benefit from those laws. Politics does not assume that those who will not be harmed will not oppose, nor does it assume that those who will not be affected will be in favor of a law if that law will be beneficial to other persons who are in need. Politics assumes that other agencies, congressmen, countries, etc., will naturally oppose whatever you intend to do, so the politician prepares his or her method of approach/attack based upon this assumption of opposition.

White people, because of the nature of their development (See Lesson #1) have always taken a political posture toward everything. They assume that other white people (their near and distant neighbors) will interfere with their attempts to get basic necessities by competing with them for jobs, etc. They assume that non-white people will attempt to live off of them by making them support social programs like welfare and medicaid. They assume that the government will use their taxes to support "lazy" individuals. They assume that white people in other states will attempt to keep them from having access to certain services by competing with them for federal subsidies and private grants. And, they assume that other countries will attempt to keep them from becoming prosperous by competing with them for control of available resources and/or markets. It is within this context, the context that accurately puts politics in perspective, that We can understand the role of Black People in white history as a political force.

When the Americas were "discovered" and it became apparent that Black People/Africans would be the major source of labor for its development, a commercial activity developed and flourished into a booming industry. This activity was the slave trade. Whichever country controlled the slave trade had a certain path to prosperity, so each European country that was able to do so immediately tried to build up its own capacity to transport Black People. At the same time it tried to keep other countries from becoming capable of doing the same because the country that monopolized the slave trade would be in a position to hinder the efforts of other countries to prosper. And, with the wealth it would be receiving from the slave trade, the monopolizing country could develop culturally and militarily to such a degree that it could dominate the other countries in Europe.

The Portuguese whites had the early jump (they controlled the slave trade since the Portuguese had built forts on the African coasts as early as the 1440s. As a matter of fact, Portugal began transporting slaves to European countries during these years and gained the right to be the sole transporter of slaves from the papacy (the term papacy refers to the leadership of the Catholic Church, the Pope. For a long time during these years the Catholic Church was the sole arbiter or judge of disputes involving Catholic countries. There were no international laws or agencies like the United Nations that pretended to regulate relations between countries.). Even before the "discovery" of America, the slave trade was a lucrative business for the Portuguese, but not lucrative enough to draw the envy (jealous eye) of other countries. Thus, even as Portugal declined in the early 1500s, it maintained undisputed rights to the transport of Black People from Africa to other parts of the world for slave labor purposes.

After Columbus' "discovery" in 1492 and the following attempts by the Spanish, the English, the French and the Dutch to establish colonies there, the importance of the slave trade expanded beyond anybody's wildest expectations. The colonies settled in the Americas, if supplied with slave labor, could cause the colonizing country to become richer than rich. However, each country assumed that it would not get a proper supply of slaves unless it controlled the slave trade. Thus, the Spanish ignored the Portuguese rights and claimed that Spain had the right to transport Black People to the American colonies for slave labor purposes. The English, not bound by the Portuguese right anyway since England was not a Catholic country, challenged the Spanish and asserted that England had that right. Naturally, the French and the Dutch were to do the same. All of these white countries were arguing with each other and coming to agreements with each other (and were later to war with each other) over who would profit from the slave trade itself and over who would be responsible for making the colonies of the Americas prosper. For almost 300 years, they argued and fought with each other over who would control the slave trade. For almost 300 years their major political and military decisions revolved around who controlled the slave trade and who was going to control the slave trade. For almost 300 years their major government allocations were determined by the issue of the slave trade. Take away Black People and you take away the basis for this argument and those decisions and allocations.

But, Black People could not be taken away. As a result, the arguing continued and the fighting started. The British fought the Spanish and the French over control of the slave trade, the Spanish fought the French and the British over control of the slave trade, and the French fought the British and the Spanish over control of the slave trade. Additionally, each of them tried to keep the others from supplying their own colonies with slaves. Thus, for example, the British outlawed the slave trade in order to keep the French from supplying the colony of San Domingo with slaves. The British did not have the authority to outlaw slavery for everybody (politics does not needlessly concern itself with authority and legality, only power), but the French would have attempted to do the same thing to the British if France had been in a position to do so. Anyway, the French resisted the British efforts, all types of tension-causing activities took place and the two countries went to war with each other. White people were continually doing these type things and were continually fighting with each other because whoever controlled the slave trade controlled the destiny of every European country and the Americas. Take away Black People and you take away this possibility. Take away this possibility and you take away the dominant political and military theme of European history for nearly a 300 year period.

White people also fought over control of slavery itself. The British attempt to outlaw slavery after it was no longer considered most beneficial to the British economic scheme of things is an example of this. Once the British began to benefit substantially from the Industrial Revolution and recognized the advantages of moving toward capitalism and wage slavery, the British felt that countries that were maintaining the old type slave system were interfering with Britain's attempts to expand her production capacity and open up new markets. A way to end this interference was to outlaw slavery (specifically the slave trade) and thereby force other countries to make economic adjustments. Another example that We are all familiar with is the American Civil War (this will be discussed more in Lesson #6). The central question in that war was, "Who is going to control the labor of Black People, the southern planter and his plantation slave system or the northern businessman and his wage slave system?" Of course, Black People were not the exclusive issue at this time (the 1860s), but were it not for Black People the two sections of this country (if it would have developed into a country) would have been making use of similar type labor systems. Under such circumstances the North and South would not have been at odds with one another, the South would not have attempted to get its independence and the Civil War would not have been fought.

Just as white people fought each other over control of the slave trade prior to the 1800s, they fought each other over control of the African continent itself less than one century later. The newly developed countries of Germany, Italy, Austria, Hungary, etc., emerged during the 1870s and joined the British, French, Portuguese and other European countries in the search for economic support and prosperity. Since the slave trade, by this time, was no longer desirable, and since the Industrial Revolution had made the availability of raw materials in large quantities so critical, a source of these materials would guarantee economic stability to whichever European country that possessed it or controlled it. This source of raw materials would also create jobs for white people and support white families in much the same manner the slave trade had done. The place where these raw materials and resources were most plentiful was the African continent. Thus, white people rushed to control Africa and thereby to control their and Black People's economic destiny. (Because Africa had been kept in such turmoil by the slave hunting and slave trading activities of white people, Africa was not in a position to benefit immediately from the discoveries of the Industrial Revolution.) The white powers jockeyed for position and became so hostile toward each other's actions that they decided to sit down at a conference table and divide Africa up among themselves in order to avoid a war. By this agreement, in 1885, each European country that was powerful enough or slick enough was awarded undisputed rights to make use of the raw materials, resources and Black labor in a specified section of Africa. Other European countries got the same right in other parts of Africa. This agreement, it was hoped, would keep each European power out of the way of other European powers and preserve the peace among the white people who were literally raping the African continent.

The split of Africa into European zones was not enough to preserve the peace because it did not account for the greed and insecurity felt by white people and the small group (see Lesson #1) in each white country. Neither country that had the power to get more of Africa was satisfied with what it had (by way of the agreement). As a matter of fact, each of them wanted more, and some of them probably wanted all of Africa. They therefore began to move in on each other's zones, and the explosion that followed after this had gone on for a few years is generally referred to as World War I. World War I, then, was a war to determine which white nation was going to control the raw materials, resources and Black labor of Africa. It was a war to determine which nation of white people was going to abuse the African People and the African land. Take away this Black element and you have no World War I. In spite of all the other reasons white historians give for this world conflict, the fact remains that if you take away Black People you have no war because you have nothing to fight over.

The same is true for World War II. Adolf Hitler wanted to establish a world empire under German domination. The key to him doing so was the control of raw materials, resources and cheap sources of labor. Between 1936 and 1939, Hitler defeated or invaded several European countries without upsetting the major European powers. However, once Hitler invaded Belgium, little-bitty Belgium, the British declared war on Germany immediately. Why? Because Belgium, in 1885, had been given the right to make use of the raw materials, labor and resources of Central Africa, specifically the area called the Congo. When Germany invaded Belgium, that meant that Germany was then in a position to make use of the raw materials, resources and Black labor of the

Congo. With the wealth it would get from the Congo, Germany would be able to expand its military productions and put itself in a position to control most of Africa and possibly dominate the world. The British could not allow this to happen. The way to try to keep it from happening was to declare war on Germany and try to get other European countries to do the same. Sides were taken, and World War II moved into full motion.

Once again, though, the reason for this war revolved around the Black element. Take away the riches and labor of Mother Africa and there is no World War II. However, if you listen to the story white historians tell, you would think that World War II was all about white people trying to progress and/or stop the evil schemes of a sinister man.

The other great event of the 20th century, the Great Depression, is a tribute to white people's greed and their inability to develop an economic system that is based more on real wealth than on artificial economic theories. White people's economic philosophy stresses the importance of keeping assets and liabilities balanced on the books, but misses out on the importance of actually having the wealth that those assets and liabilities are supposed to represent. Much of the supposed wealth of this country and the rest of the white world after World War I was based on opportunities and expectations of wealth created by the developing economic exploitation of African resources by white businessmen. They were just beginning to tap a source whose resources seemed inexhaustible, and they planned, invested and produced on the basis of those expectations. The immediate result was wholesale speculation. Businessmen were mounting up liabilities (bills and obligations) against assets (wealth) that they didn't have or that could not be converted into suitable amounts of cash or currency, and little people in search of big profits invested unwisely. After this went on for a number of years, the economy, like an overinflated bicycle tire, burst with a bang. Unfortunately, it did not burst so badly that it could not be patched up by the production brought on by World War II.

White people have been revolving their economic activities around the labor, land and/or resources of Black People for so long that it is difficult for them to imagine any other major means of sustaining themselves. Thus, it is not surprising to find them, even today, molding their history and destiny around Black People. In their own way they are fighting for control of Africa right now. Sometimes they use their military to fight, sometimes they use their "intelligence/ spy agencies" (the American CIA, the Russian KGB, for example) to fight, sometimes they fight each other and sometimes they fight Black People. They use their economic powers to strangulate African rulers and African People, they use their advanced weapons to threaten the existence of Black People, they use their scientific research to keep Black People from developing an Africa for the Africans (by denying Africans access to the practical application

10 LESSONS

of scientific knowledge), they use their communications channels to propagandize in their favor and against Black People, they use their 32 tooth smiles to deceive Black People, and they use their Negroes to form an image of Blacks and whites united in approval of what America and other European countries are doing (or attempting to do). They have already planned for World War III, which they are certain will be a war among white people (in total disregard for Black People) for control of the African continent, which they have admitted is the only place left worth fighting over. But, even as all of this takes place, white historians are recording the facts as if Black People are incidental to the whole process. Today, as 200 years earlier, white people still cannot see Us or acknowledge Our presence because they have convinced themselves that Our invisibility and insignificance (lack of importance) are matters of fact. Their versions of history support those conclusions.

V. Black People in American History (1492-1865)

In American History, between 1492 and 1865, it was slavery that made the colonies rich, and it was this richness that led to the military clash between the small group over here and the small group in England that is commonly referred to as the Revolutionary War (1776). White people over here wanted their freedom, but it was more about the freedom to hold onto the profits brought in by slavery than it was about political rights. The prosperity brought on by slave labor, the labor of Black People, made the American colonies worth fighting over. Without this prosperity, it is probable that neither England nor the white settlers would have been anxious to determine the political path the colonies should follow.

In addition to making the colonies rich and thereby sowing the seeds for a Revolutionary War, Black People fought and helped make it possible for white people over here to get their independence from white people in England. Without the participation of Black People from the United States and San Domingo, it is likely that England would have won the Revolutionary War. This is true because not enough of the white settlers were willing to sincerely participate in this war. Some refused to do so because they wanted to continue to maintain contact with England and others refused to do so because they realized it would be a case of little men fighting a rich man's war. Many of the white settlers who did participate in the war deserted when times got unusually hard. This made the role of Black participants critical even though, from the white's point of view, it was undesirable. Whites did not want Black People fighting in the Revolutionary War because they felt it was a white man's war, because they knew the war was not being fought to change the condition of Black People and because they knew that, by participating, Black People would be in a better position to take their own freedom at a later time.

Nevertheless, things got so bad for the white small group in America that slaves/Black People had to be allowed to fight. The ones who fought were promised freedom, but as soon as the war was over, as soon as the whites over here had gained their freedom, the freedom promises they had made to the Black fighters were forgotten. Conditions changed for white people as a result of the war but remained the same for those of Us (Black People) who had been led to believe otherwise.

After fighting from 1776 - 1783 (the Revolutionary War years) to make white people over here free, Black People fought and kept America free. We did this in two ways, one direct and the other indirect. The direct contribution We made was by repeating the participation of 40 years earlier; We provided Our services to the American army forces because white people failed to do so in the necessary numbers and with the necessary sincerity. Our indirect contribution was just as critical. When the Black People of San Domingo fought to get their freedom they virtually destroyed the British army. If it had not been for the demolition job these Blacks had done on the British in the early 1800s, the British army would have been much stronger than it actually was when it sought to regain control of the American states in the War of 1812-1814. As weak as it was, the British army was able to rout the American forces and march to the capitol, which was burned to the ground by them. If the British had been able to keep the pressure up for just a little while longer, victory would have been assured. But it could not keep up the pressure, and the reason it could not do so was because it was not even near its regular strength. It was suffering from the effects of its encounter with the Blacks of San Domingo. Thus, the whites of America would not have thought in terms of independence if it had not been for Black People, and they would not have kept their independence if it had not been for Black People. But, to read the traditional history books, one would think that Black People were, at best, incidental to everything that took place in the development of this country.

Because of the presence of Black People, America had to expand land-wise, and because of the activities of Black People America was able to expand land-wise. The use of Black People as slaves made it possible for southern planters to exploit (make use of) huge amounts of land. This resulted in the need for more land by southern planters and the need for land by other whites who were forced to move westward as a result of being victimized by plantation expansion. Additionally, the agricultural methods used by southern planters did not preserve the fertility of the land, with the result that fertile acres had to be found to replace those that had been made waste.

Our presence led to expansion for political purposes as well. Because there were two economic forces operating within this country in the 1800s, one in the North and the other in the South, because they represented two different life-styles, and because both were expanding into new territories, it was necessary that a delicate balance be maintained between them on the federal government level. If this balance were not maintained, it would not be possible to keep the two sections part of one federal union. Since the Union was growing, it was necessary that land be available that could be used to carve "free" and "slave" states, so that when one territory qualified for admittance into the Union (as a "free" state, for example), a second territory could be carved and admitted into the Union too (as a "slave" state). By this process, a balance could be maintained in the legislative branch of the federal government that would keep each section from feeling that the federal government was stacked against it and was not likely to act in its interests.

Where was this territory that could be carved into "free" and "slave" states coming from? It was coming from the Black People in San Domingo. Let Us see why.

We mentioned earlier that the Black People of San Domingo defeated the three strongest armies in the world. One of these armies was the French army, whose emperor, Napoleon, wanted to establish a French Empire in North America. His proposed empire, if he were successful, would have restricted the United States to the 13 original states that were born with this country. However, because of his defeat by the Blacks of San Domingo, Napoleon dropped his plans of establishing a French Empire in North America and was forced to sell land in order to get money into the French treasury. He therefore sold the United States the territory of Orleans, which the United States needed for navigational purposes, for two million dollars, and he sold to the United States the rest of the area called the Louisiana Territory for less than 13 million dollars. This gave the United States 828,000 square miles of land for less than three pennies an acre (Louisiana was all the territory lying between the Mississippi River and the Rocky Mountains), it gave America control of the Mississippi River and it doubled the size of the United States. Thirteen states were carved out of the Louisiana Territory, in part or in whole. These states included Louisiana, Arkansas, Missouri, Iowa, Minnesota, North Dakota, South Dakota, Nebraska, Kansas, Oklahoma, Colorado, Wyoming and Montana. This territory, converted into states during critical periods, preserved the union of the North and South, provided land for the expansion of slavery and the maintenance of the balance between the northern and southern states in the Senate, and greatened the wealth of this country immeasurably. Without this land the essence of the Civil War (the split up of the two sections) possibly would have taken place 40 years earlier. In fact, South Carolina threatened to leave the Union in 1832. Certainly this course would have seemed inviting to other southern states at this time if they had not been able to expand and if the balance of power in the Senate had become stacked against them.

The final point we will mention is that the slaves/Black People fought and helped keep the South and North one country. We will not make much mention of this at this time because Black People's participation in the Civil War will be discussed in a later section (see Lesson #6). White people in the North, ignorantly thinking that the war was being fought to free the slaves, failed to support it to the degree necessary to "preserve the Union." Only when the North was on the brink of defeat did the Blacks see an opportunity for freedom if the North won. Once the Blacks recognized this probability they threw their wholehearted support and participation to the North, changed the course of the war and enabled the North to be victorious. Without the support of Black People, the North would have been badly defeated by the South, and two independent federal governments would now be functioning where only one presently is. Under such circumstances it is unlikely that the United States would have emerged as a world power.

This Handbook recognizes the role Black People have played in the development of the white world. It makes it quite clear to all who care to pay attention that We can function independently of white people and other people. However, if We continue to let non-Black minds transmit Our history, Black History, from one generation of Black People to another, We will lose Ourselves even more, doubt Ourselves even more and come to think of Ourselves as historical and human zeroes. To avoid this fate, We must seek knowledge of Ourselves and spread knowledge of Ourselves. We must pay attention and think analytically about all information that concerns Us. The more We do these two things, the quicker We will rid Ourselves of Our burden (white people and all things related themto).

LESSON 5
LESSON OUTLINE

I. Review: Points to Remember
  A. Slavery Gave Employment to Whites Who Would Have Been Idle Otherwise
  B. We, Black People, Provided the Genius and Labor that Made the White World Prosper
  C. In the White World, Religion Is a Fraud
  D. In the White World There Is Always Only A Short Step From Aristocracy and Money to Political Positions and Power
    1. Parliament seats are bought.
    2. Elections in America are bought.
II. Black Responses to Slavery and Inequality
  A. Analysis (Many Blacks Seriously Analyzed the Condition of the Black Race): Cases in Point
    1. David Walker
    2. Henry Highland Garnet
    3. Harriet Tubman
    4. others
  B. Rebellion/Search for Self-Determination: Cases in Point
    1. Maroons (North America, South America, the Caribbean)
    2. Palmares
    3. San Domingo
    4. 1800
    5. 1822
    6. 1831
  C. Rebellion/Search for Equality: Cases in Point
    1. Abolitionist Movement
    2. Escape (Underground Railroad)
  D. Rebellion/Search for Relief: Cases in Point
    1. Individual Escape
    2. Sabotage
      -work, poison, fire, etc.
  E. Submission
    1. Voluntary/Declared
      - accepting the superiority of the white race and the inferiority and lack of humanity of the Black Race.
    2. Involuntary/Undeclared
      - not accepting the superiority of the white race nor the inferiority and lack of humanity of the Black Race, but failing, for whatever

reason, to act in a manner that would help change the nature of white/Black relationships.

I. Review: Points to Remember

It is important that We recognize what slavery has meant to white people—to the development of white people. To adequately do this, We have to observe slavery's indirect affects as well as its direct (more obvious) affects. Additionally, it is important that We understand the mind of white people and be clear on what they are all about (review Lesson #1). It is for these purposes that we will briefly review some points from the previous lesson.

(1) Slavery gave employment to whites who would have been idle otherwise. In this regard slavery provided a degree of economic security and political stability to Europeans/whites and their governments, even in areas where slaves were not used extensively. Thus, the slaves who were shipped to the Americas in order to benefit rich white people (the small group) were also benefiting white people in Europe and the Americas who had to work for a living. The industries and by-product industries (industries and jobs that resulted from slavery even though the work itself did not necessarily involve slaves, such as the lumber industry, shipping industry, rum industry, etc.) created by slavery and expanded by slavery gave many white people a job that kept food in their stomachs and clothes on their backs. If it had not been for slavery, these same whites would have been without a job and therefore without adequate food, clothing and other necessities. They would have had nothing to do with their time but loiter and think of illegal ways to get the things they needed. As a result, crime would have increased, discontent with the government and authority in general would have increased, and a fertile ground for rebellions and revolution would have been created. Slavery eliminated much of the potential for much of this type unrest. It made white people, lots of white people, feel secure and enabled a somewhat stable set of circumstances to exist that allowed white people to adapt and develop mannerisms that are associated with "good taste" today.

We will repeat: Slavery benefited rich white people and working class white people in the Americas and Europe (it is logical to assume that all who benefited from slavery supported slavery). Slavery brought stability to American and European governments and enabled white people to develop and spread a culture that they claimed was theirs.

(2) We, Black People, provided the genius and labor that made the white world prosper. White people did not provide the brains that made Black People's sweat productive. Black People provided those brains, the intelligence and the know-how, in addition to the actual work, that made it possible for white people to accumulate wealth and invest in the Industrial Revolution, and

reap its benefits (the Industrial Revolution signalled the general use of machines in the production of goods and services. Until that time, most of the goods and services produced were the result of human labor/manpower). White people want Us to think that they provided the brains because such thoughts will have Us thinking that Black People are not smart. The logical conclusion to such thoughts is that Black People are not capable of adequately dealing with the complex problems that go into building a nation or surviving if We attempt to separate from white people. But WE can build Our own nations and WE can survive because We have the brain power and the manpower to do so. We have done so several times already. Surely We can do so again.

(3) In the white world religion is a fraud. Religion does not represent a code of ethics that white people intend to lead their lives by. Religion is just a toy to white people, something to be talked about and played with but nothing to be taken seriously. This is one fact that Black People seem to have failed to accept even to this day, and partly explains why We continue to appeal to white people's "morality". If We would only accept the facts that are as clear as day We would recognize that white people are not religious, that they are not moral nor ethical, and that appeals to their morality, etc. are wasted energy. If We would only accept the facts, We would recognize that We are being dominated by people who are only concerned about wealth and power and We would see that their "religion" is just one of the weapons they use to get the wealth and power they desire. If We would only accept the facts We would recognize that religion does not motivate white people, and it definitely does not inspire them to help their fellow human beings. Religion helps white people carry out their devastating activities without getting a substantial guilt complex. It preaches one thing but supports something entirely different and is therefore a fraudulent doctrine or ideology. Black People must stop ignoring this fact! That way We will stop adopting their fraudulent religious ideas about humility, sacrifice and turning the other cheek, and function in a manner that will rid Us of white people's destructive influence.

(4) In the white world there is always only a short step from aristocracy and money to political positions and power. Because personal wealth (as opposed to being part of the community) is so central to survival, access to services and convenience, it is not difficult to use money to get power nor influence those in positions of power. As a matter of fact, using money for this purpose is part of the fabric of the white world and helps explain the success of the small group, which constantly conspires against the large group. Because money means so much to white people, because it carries so much weight in the white scheme of things (the white world), it is easy to use money to convince those in positions of authority and affluence that the rights of the poor, politically unaware and politically unorganized can be ignored. This conspiracy, a conspiracy of those who already have and those who are seeking

to have against those who have not helps explain why large businesses can get million and billion dollar stipends and subsidies from the government (which is supposed to be concerned about everybody's welfare) while individuals have to go through all types of hassles just to get a $200.00 public assistance check. This type conspiracy has existed since white people first began to form governments and it will continue to exist for as long as whites form governments (be they called democracies, communist states or socialist states, etc.) because such is basic to the white concept of government. It is important that Black People be aware of this because such awareness will keep Us from wasting Our time, resources and energy on efforts to get white people to adjust their system so it will serve the interests of the overall community. If We desire that type system, We can only get it by establishing a system that is politically and economically independent of white people and their ways. In short, We can only get it by getting into Ourselves, into Our Blackness, and into a concept of nationhood and government that revolves around Black Power, Black priorities and Black self-determination.

II. Black Responses to Slavery and Inequality

Having re-emphasized the above points, We can now move into a summary of how Black People responded to being enslaved and de-humanized by white people. This summary will stress that all of Our responses to the slave condition involved a process of analysis, and that that process of analysis resulted in Black individuals either submitting to slavery (this is particularly the case when fear influenced the process of analysis) or rebelling against slavery.

The analysis made by most Black individuals was probably more superficial (not in-depth) than detailed. Most Black People then, as now, were probably more concerned about what their eyes saw and their ears heard than what their minds could make them understand, so their responses were based more on impressions than anything else. For example, they saw white people with guns and Black People without guns, and automatically concluded that Black People could not effectively or successfully rebel against white people. It never occurred to them that guns alone do not determine whether a rebellion will be successful or not, and it did not occur to them that, during a rebellion, Black People would get possession of guns by various methods, some planned and some unexpected. The only thing that occurred to them was what their eyes saw, and they reacted or responded accordingly (usually by submitting).

But there were other Black individuals and groups that went beyond what their eyes saw and their ears heard. Such Black persons let their minds explain the situation to them in detail, and used this explanation or analysis as the basis of their response to the condition of slavery. They began to get an in-depth understanding not only of the condition of the slaves, but of the condition of white people and the power of white people, and realized that most of white people's power over Black People was a result of Black People's (slaves and free persons) failure to assert themselves and demand their freedom. One such Black person was Henry Highland Garnet. Garnet's analysis of the situation revealed to him that whether Black People got freedom or not was up to Black People, not white people. He said that the slaves should rise up in rebellion in spite of the apparent (seeming) odds and kill as many whites as were necessary to achieve their freedom. Instead of submitting, instead of accepting slavery, Garnet said, "Let Our Motto be Resistance, Resistance, Resistance."

Another person who went beyond what her eyes saw and ears heard, analyzed the situation and decided that resistance was the best response was Harriet Tubman. Harriet Tubman was born into slavery in around 1820. Her father was a student of nature who had the ability to calculate seasonal changes, predict the weather, use roots for medicinal purposes and travel by night (using the North Star to guide him). In order to be near her father and absorb his knowledge, Harriet tricked her master into thinking that she was extremely ignorant. After learning as much as she could from her father, she convinced her master to hire her out, hoping that she could make enough money to buy her freedom. While on one of her jobs she met a rebellious slave named Jim, who told her about the Underground Railroad (a means by which slaves escaped from the South to the North). This information interested her and Inspired her and helped give substance to her dream of Black People rising up in rebellion and taking their freedom.

During one of her talks with Jim he revealed to her his plan to escape. He needed her help, and because she understood more than meets the eye, she recognized his chance of success and agreed to help him. In the process of helping him she got hit on the head with a two pound steel weight. It almost killed her but it was not enough to kill her dream of freedom for Black People. Her understanding had convinced her that Black People could take their freedom, and this understanding pushed her beyond obstacles and setbacks that would have defeated a less aware person.

On a later hired job Harriet met John Tubman, a free Black man. In 1845 she married him. Although she loved him deeply, they looked at life differently; he seemed unable to understand her passionate hatred for slavery. Given the choice between him and freedom, she left for free soil. After she reached free soil, she realized that her freedom meant nothing as long as Black People were forced to work in the fields of the South. So she decided to rebel even more. In spite of the apparent odds against her succeeding, she began making contact with anti-slavery sympathizers and worked to save money which would finance slave rescue trips into the South. It was in this capacity, as a conductor of the Underground Railroad, that she dealt a crippling blow to slavery and gained the hatred of southern slave holders.

Under Harriet's influence the Underground Railroad reached its highest stage of organization and effectiveness. She made nineteen trips into the South, led an estimated 300 slaves to freedom and convinced thousands of other Black persons that Black People could rebel successfully. As a result of these trips, Harriet became known as the "Moses of her people".

Many anti-slavery people considered the Underground Railroad a slow method to freedom and sought other methods. Harriet recognized the truth in what they said and aided their efforts in all types of ways. She really wanted to rebel in a much more substantial way herself, and had agreed to work with John Brown in setting up an active army of slaves in the Allegheny Mountain Range (these mountains are in parts of Pennsylvania, Maryland, West Virginia and Virginia). Her job would be to enlist freedmen (Black persons who were not slaves) in Canada for the army. Because of a betrayal this scheme had to be abandoned, but it was replaced by a plan to attack and temporarily take control of Harper's Ferry (an army arsenal) on July 4, 1859. The date had been picked by Harriet, and the objective of the takeover was to get weapons that could be used by Black rebellers to attack slavery and the plantation system in the South. However, Harriet had a blackout and could not play the role she wanted so desperately to play. The fact that she was willing to do so, however, indicated that her analysis of the slave system and the power of white people had convinced her that Black People could rebel and do so successfully.

The person whose analysis we will concentrate on in this lesson is David Walker. We will concentrate on David Walker's analysis because it is one of the most scientific studies of slavery and related matters that has ever been conducted. Instead of concentrating on how things looked, David Walker characterized all facets of Our condition and all facets of Our relationship to the people who enslaved Us, and stated clearly what Our response should be. Let Us review what he discovered.

In 1829 David Walker published a book entitled <u>David Walker's Appeal to the Coloured Citizens of the World</u>. This appeal was directed to the slaves, telling them that they should take matters into their own hands. The <u>Appeal</u> did not plead to the slave owners. This is very important because it indicates that David Walker realized that each people's destiny is in the hands of that group of people, and that group of people alone. This realization was accurate in David Walker's time and it is true today. Black People today, therefore, will determine the destiny of Black People. If We function in a progressive manner and take care of Our own affairs, We (Black People) will progress. If, on the other hand, We choose to sit back or follow other people, We will be victimized and dominated by other people. It is just that simple.

The object of David Walker's <u>Appeal</u> was to awaken in Black People (slave and free) a spirit of inquiry and investigation respecting Our miseries and wretchedness in this so-called republican land of liberty (America). The central points of the Appeal are:

[A] We Coloured People of these United States are the most wretched, degraded and abject set of beings that ever lived since the world began, and that Our wretchedness is a result of (1) Slavery (2) Ignorance (3) Religious Manipulation and (4) Colonization;

[B] There must be a willingness on Our part to end Our wretchedness for God will not take Us by the hairs of Our head and drag Us from Our very mean, low and abject condition; and

[C] The white slave holders (and their lackeys) are the enemies of Black People by nature, and their greatest earthly desires are to keep Us in abject ignorance and wretchedness.

Let Us carefully review each of these central points and try to understand how they relate to Black People in 1980.

In Article I of his Appeal David Walker tells Us what slavery is. It is important to point out that David Walker does not define slavery as a condition wherein a person or a group is forced to work without being paid, nor does he say a slave is a person who is forced to wear chains. No, David Walker does not say such things because such statements miss out on what slavery is at its root. A true definition of slavery must characterize slavery as a concept, and Walker fulfills this obligation by recognizing that slavery is a condition experienced by a person or group that is characterized by (1) a lack of political power (2) a lack of land and economic power and (3) a denial of humanity. Any slave, Walker suggests, by merely accepting the slave condition, subjects himself to a life of misery, wretchedness and constant victimization, and can only overcome this wretchedness and misery by attempting to eliminate his slave condition or status.

In 1829 David Walker defined a slave as a person (or group) that has no political power, no economic power and no recognized human rights. Walker did not use these exact terms but they are properly applied terms which, if used as a standard today, would undeniably suggest that Black People in 1980 are still slaves in America. Black People in 1980 have no political power because We do not have the power to make or enforce any laws that will be beneficial to Us and because this political system does not represent Our values or being. We had no say-so or input into the establishment of the United States government nor the making of the basic laws of this land (the Constitution, for example). We have no economic power because We do not have an independent Black economic base (land of Our own) and We do not have control of any economic means of producing and distributing vital goods and services within this white -dominated economic system. And We are denied Our humanity because We have no human rights that are not questioned and challenged by the power of white people, white affluence and white governments that dominate Our lives. We are slaves, pure and simple, and Our general condition is a slave condition. As long as We fail to recognize or face up to this condition, as long as We accept this condition, as long as We fail to resist this condition— other people will continue to make Us feel miserable and wretched, and other people will constantly victimize Us.

The condition of Black People, then, has not basically changed since the time of David Walker. We are still slaves, but many of Us find this hard to believe because We don't look like slaves (looks carry a great amount of weight among individuals who fail to go beyond what their eyes see and their ears hear). Looks, however, do not change reality, and the reality of Black People in America is one of powerlessness, misery, wretchedness and constant victimization.

In Article II of his Appeal Walker characterizes ignorance and explains the role it plays in Our wretchedness. He tells Us that ignorance is being unaware of what obtaining freedom and security entail, not knowing what freedom and security are really all about and therefore not taking a long range view when We seek freedom and security. Ignorance, in other words, makes Us too concerned with the here and now. It makes Us overly concerned about having access to goods and services We need and desire, and unconcerned about creating conditions and accumulating the power that will enable Us to keep what We have accumulated and pass it on to later generations of Black People.

According to Walker, Our ignorance victimizes Us (causes Us to suffer needlessly) when We attempt to deal with Our problems individually instead of dealing with them as a group or Race, when We fail to ignore differences that keep Us from unifying as a Race of People, when We do uncalled for things like helping the "authorities", when We fail to help each other in large and small ways and when we satisfy Ourselves with a job or a position instead of dignity, for example. Ignorance causes Us to "tom" and attempt to appease whites, Walker reveals, and must be controlled if we are to escape Our condition of abject misery and wretchedness.

Most of Our educated Blacks are in fact ignorant, Walker explains. They are ignorant because they are taught and talk about theories that are of no use to Black People and because they memorize and recite facts and figures that mean nothing to Black People who want to liberate themselves and get a measure of dignity. They are ignorant because the entire white educational system is designed not to benefit Black People, but to benefit white people. Therefore, Black individuals who get "educated" are actually brainwashed and subtly manipulated; they are encouraged to imitate white people and take on white values as they are being alienated (drawn away) from the masses of Black People. Ignorance, Walker continues, has many of Us thinking We are smart and free, when in fact We are not. Consequently, We remain under the domination of the people who benefit from Our sub-human condition (slavery/

wretchedness).

Black People are just as ignorant in 1980 as Black People were in the 1820s. We are still allowing differences to keep Us from uniting as a Race, We are still taking individual approaches to problems that afflict Us because of white racism, We are still "snitching" (giving the white authorities information and leads), We are still disproportionately job conscious, We are still graduating from high schools, colleges and universities without knowing who We are or how what we have learned can be applied to improve the condition of Black People, We are still failing to help each other and We still take a here and now approach to freedom and security. In fact, because We have been more exposed to white ideas as part of a formal procedure, We are undoubtedly more ignorant now than We were 160 years ago. This explains why some Negroes will cry that race is no longer an issue in this country and why other Negroes will urge the masses of Black People to vote for one white candidate instead of another when it is clear to any thinking person that neither candidate will attempt to make it possible for Black People to accumulate the power Black People need. Ignorance is definitely still afflicting Black People, causing Us to suffer misery and wretchedness that could be avoided if Black People would only start applying the knowledge We have in a manner that will contribute to the establishment of a structure that is primarily concerned about the general welfare of Black People.

In Article III, Walker analyzes religion and explains how it contributes to the miserable condition of Black People. Even though he was a very religious person, Walker recognized that religions are manipulated against Black People and condition Black People to a state of servility (submission), to accepting Our condition. It helps white people maintain control over Us by getting Us to place more emphasis on a pie in the sky after We die than on keeping Our stomachs adequately fed while We are alive. Since We have discussed religion previously, we will not go further on this subject at this time.

We must add, however, that Walker clearly states that Americans make a mockery of religion (they still do). White people who call themselves Christians hinder, injure and maliciously kill Black People and use their religion to salve their consciences. Clearly, no white religion will be of benefit to Black People, be it Christianity, Islam, Judaism or whatever. They all will help white people keep Black People in a state of slavery and abject poverty. Therefore, We should avoid them at all costs.

Article IV of Walker's Appeal explains how colonization contributed to the slave's wretched condition. Colonization is the term which refers to white people's plans to relocate free Blacks by shipping them to other parts of the world. Its importance to Walker was that colonization was a prime example of how white people attempted to control the exposure of the slaves to ideas and ways of living that differed from the model white people had set up as desirable. Thereby they attempted to control the slaves by limiting the slaves' chances of hearing about new ideas and seeing Black People who did not have to work for a white master.

The importance of Walker's article on colonization is that, even today, white people and their power structure attempt to keep Black People under control by doing all they can to keep Black People from getting exposed to ideas and modes of conduct (actions) that are not coming from a white point of view. They use their televisions, radios and newspapers, etc., to expose Us to their viewpoints, but they refuse to expose Us to viewpoints of non-white peoples for fear that We will realize that non-white values and ways of doing things are just as valid as those of whites, and that non-white systems are just as functional as white systems. More than anything else, they try to keep Us from getting into Ourselves, into Our Blackness. They realize that once We become aware of Ourselves as human beings, as mature, gifted and intelligent persons who have contributed more than any other race to the civilized way-of-life, then We certainly will express Our discontentment with their world and Our position in it. To reduce the chances of this happening, white people flood Our minds with their ideologies and brainwash Us into almost automatically rejecting ideas and ideologies that are not approved by them or publicized by them.

White people do not want Black People to realize that We can separate from them without doing Ourselves a disservice. They don't want Us to realize that We don't need them, so they keep a steady supply of integrationist ideas (such as civil rights, communism, Islam, etc.) running through Our minds, and spend a whole lot of money trying to keep Us from being exposed to non-integrationist ideas (such as Black Nationhood). As long as We place more emphasis and value on their preferences, We will be limiting Our options. As long as We limit Our options (or allow Our options to be limited) We will be less capable of eliminating this condition of disguised slavery that white people have forced on Us.

We stated that there are three central points to Walker's Appeal. The first, which we just reviewed, revolves around an analysis of Black People's wretched and miserable condition. The second central point revolves around ending this condition of wretchedness. It is here that Walker stresses the necessity of Us ending Our wretchedness. We can not rely on nor intelligently expect any other group of people to end this condition that afflicts Us, nor can We rely on or intelligently expect religion (God) to end Our wretchedness. Walker, a very religious person, nonetheless makes it quite clear that God is not going to do what needs to be done to change the quality of Black People's lives.

We should not expect other people to talk for Us or do for Us, Walker says. Other people cannot adequately express what We feel and are not willing to take the extreme measures that will be needed to free Black People. Only We can prove that We are worthy of freedom. Only We can prove Our overall worth. Only We, Black People, can disprove the negative things that are said, thought and felt about Us, and when We fail to resist those who have put Us in bondage We prove that those negative inferences are true.

Black People, like all people, have natural rights, Walker emphasizes, and We should leave no stone unturned trying to get everybody to recognize Our natural rights. We should not let numbers nor lack of education slow Us down in Our pursuit of those rights. However, Walker adds, We should organize and plan carefully before We make any move because lack of careful planning and proper organization will cause Us problems in the long run. Once We have organized though, We should not call for public demonstrations or try to work through the system. Such actions reveal that We are not mature rebellers, indicate that We are not willing to take extreme measures and allow Our enemies to identify the most rebellious among Us and either kill them or confine them. Once We have organized We should be about the business of separation, and We should not trifle, half-step or "mess around".

Before moving on, Walker makes a final point: Those who refuse to show a willingness to get their own freedom deserve to be enslaved, and deserve to suffer the misery, wretchedness and constant victimization that come hand in hand with the slave condition. He then closes by repeating the following points: (1) that no one can prove the worth of Black People but Black People, and We won't get any respect until We do so; (2) that Black People have a right to kill those who systematically victimize Us and injure Us, and that We should no longer let Our civilized nature and Our regard for human life keep Us from doing so; (3) that Black People will survive any confrontation with white people because We have a history of fighting intelligently and surviving, and because We have already survived the most genocidal attempt they could make to destroy Us; and (4) the only thing Black People need to do to end Our condition of being dominated by white people is to regain Our manhood/womanhood and assert Ourselves.

Since Black People are still experiencing the condition of slavery today (even though it is disguised), We can take note of what Walker advises, organize Ourselves and plan while avoiding unnecessary contact with non-Blacks and integrationist techniques, and end Our wretchedness— that is, if We are willing to do so. If We are not willing to do so, then We deserve to be dominated and discriminated against and don't deserve to be listened to when We cry out about racial brutalities and injustices.

The third central point Walker makes is that white people are Our enemies _by nature_, and their greatest earthly desires are to keep Us in abject ignorance and wretchedness. Whites have to keep Black People ignorant, Walker says. They don't want Us to realize how much harm they have done to Us nor how pervasive (all-inclusive/penetrating) their destructiveness has been to the lives of Black People in general. The more We know, particularly if We are self-respecting People, the more white people will be convinced that We are planning to get them back. White people fear that We are going to retaliate, so they continue to set up barriers that will keep Us in Our wretched condition for as long as possible. Additionally, because of their greed and power complexes, they don't want Us to make any gains because any gains We make will be accompanied by losses on their part. They are on one end of the see-saw and Black People are on the other end. If We move up or make a gain, white people will have to move down or take a loss, and in their efforts to keep from taking any losses white people will naturally act in a manner that will keep Black People from making any gains. Their aims are naturally opposed to the aims of Black People, therefore they are Our natural enemies.

Walker characterized whites as a race of profiteers. They have always been unjust, jealous, unmerciful, greedy and blood-thirsty, and are always seeking after power and authority. Walker uses history to support his contention, viewing white people and their behavior in Europe and wherever else they have been. Then he views them as Christians and concludes that they are even worse because their Christianity prepares them to do evil and then provides a defense or rationale (excuse) for their evildoings. Therefore, if the world is to be civilized, We cannot look to whites to lead, he adds. We have to look to Ourselves, not only as leaders of Our race but as leaders of the world. We have the civilized nature, concern for human beings and other necessary qualities to offer the world. White people have no such qualities to offer. Therefore they are not capable of leading the world to a civilized way-of-life. But, before We, Black People, can offer what We have to give to the world, We must first eliminate Our wretched condition, Our slave (disguised) condition.

David Walker writes that he is awfully afraid that white people's pride, prejudice, greed and _blood_ will lead them to ruin. What he is saying is that white people will not change because what they do is a part of them, a part of their being. They enslave, attempt to dominate and destroy other people just as naturally as they eat, sleep or have bowel movements. Therefore, We, Black People, should not expect any justice from them nor should We expect any of them to sincerely help Us free Ourselves.

In 1829 David Walker was saying white people would not change. They have not changed, and Black People in 1980 (160 years later) can testify to that fact. Since they haven't changed in the 160 years since the time of David Walker, and had not changed in the more than 350 years before the time of David Walker (when they were wiping out the Indians and abusing Black People), We have no logical reason for expecting any changes from them in the years to come. As a result, We should not expect them to be concerned about Our welfare or do anything that will substantially benefit Us.

Thus, those who analyzed the condition of Black People realized that those of Us who are willing to accept Our wretched condition are really the ones who are holding Black People back, that all of Us must be free and secure before any of Us can be so, and that Black People have nothing to be grateful to white people for. All who analyzed the situation, who went beyond the apparent revelations of their eyes and ears, recognized that resistance was the correct response of Black People to slavery. For, in the words of David Walker, "What is the use of living, when in fact [We are] dead?"

David Walker, Harriet Tubman and Henry Highland Garnet were only three of the many who critically analyzed Our condition and came to the conclusion that Our motto and Our course of action must be characterized by resistance, resistance, resistance. There were many more, but it is not the purpose of this Handbook to discuss all of them. Our purpose herein is to expose Black People to information that will inspire Us to do further reading and research on Our own (see suggested reading list in Introduction to this Handbook). What has been said so far, we are certain, will bring about that response in any person who is serious about gaining knowledge of the history of Black People.

After analyzing the situation, what most Black People did was to rebel and resist. The rebelling took on several different forms, many of which We will discuss briefly, and had many different objectives. However, there were those whose response was not to rebel or resist in any noticeable manner. Such persons submitted, and an analysis of their response is forthcoming as well.

Those Black People who rebelled did so usually with one of three general objectives in mind. Number one, some rebelled with the objective of setting up a government of their own. Number two, some rebelled with the objective of obtaining true equality within the context of the American dream (integration was not a necessary element of this objective). And number three, some rebelled in order to get a degree of personal relief. Of these, those who wanted self-government are the most impressive. An extract from a previous publication of "The People" ("The Republic of New Afrika: Its Development, Ideology and Objectives") bears this out quite clearly.

"Freedom, Independence, Self-Government and Self-Determination have been objectives sought by Black People ever since We were brought to this country as slaves. From day one, in 1526, when We were brought here by the Spanish, Black People rebelled and sought a way-of-life that was more rewarding and beneficial to Us. We did so in 1526 by rebelling against the Spaniards in South Carolina and running to the Indians, who helped Us drive the Spanish away and made it possible for Us to experience the self-governing process. Time and time again afterwards, Black People gave their lives for what was dearest to any human being— Freedom and Self-Determination.

"In 1619, Black People were forcibly brought to this land by some other white people, the English. Blacks did not like this forced migration from Our homeland (Africa), but there is no record that indicates that We got together to rebel against Our condition. Individual resistance was frequent though, and began to reach new heights in 1672 when individual rebellers started getting together and conspiring against their enslavers. Many became maroons (runaway slaves who set up their own social structure in the woods, mountains, swamps, etc.) and armed themselves, however possible, and harassed plantations in the area as they created bases from which they could operate and to which other slaves might flee. These slaves considered themselves outside the legal authority of the United States. As far as they were concerned, they were free and self-governing Black People.

"By the end of the 1720s, because of their raiding and attractiveness to other slaves, such self-governing Blacks had become important enough to attract widespread attention in Louisiana and Virginia. In Louisiana there was a maroon village called des Natanapalle, where Black People lived, governed themselves and protected themselves from recapture. Another such village was not far from des Natanapalle.

"A similar village of self-governing Blacks existed in the Blue Ridge Mountains in 1729. These Black Nationalists had guns and ammunition with them, and agricultural implements that would serve as a basis for their economic survival (along with guerilla-type attacks on plantations in the neighborhood). A similar self-governing group of runaways occupied a fort near St. Augustine, Florida, and lived there as free people. Throughout that year and the next, other slaves, some as far away as South Carolina, rebelled and headed for this base of Black Power. Most of these Blacks were attacked by white militiamen and defeated.

"In 1738 several slaves in Prince Georges County, Maryland, broke out of jail, united themselves with some maroons in the area and waged a small scale guerilla war for freedom and independence against white people. These Black People intended to destroy all the whites in the area, possess the whole county for themselves and establish their own government. Eventually these Blacks had to flee to the woods, from where they continued their guerilla war against the whites.

"Maroons, or runaway Blacks who governed themselves, were continually a lot of trouble for white Amerikkka. In 1767 one group went into action near Alexandria, Virginia. Others banded and settled in the area of the Savannah River, where they terrorized neighboring whites while in the process of plundering for necessities.

"During the Revolutionary War period, when white people were fighting to get their freedom and keep Us enslaved, Blacks assisted the British and Amerikkkans in hopes of getting freedom and a chance to share in the governmental process. They didn't get this opportunity from either of the white groups. Therefore, immediately after the end of the War, in 1783, Black People in South Carolina and Georgia fled with arms and established a village of their own where they governed themselves and carried on guerilla warfare against whites for years. During 1786 and 1787, most of these type settlements were attacked by white militiamen and destroyed, the one mentioned included. When attacked these Black Nationalists almost always resisted and fought with whatever they had until they were killed or seriously wounded. To those Blacks, self-government was a necessity; Black Nationhood was desirable and sought at the expense of death.

"Thus it was that, even in the face of well-armed white militiamen, Black People continued to run away, govern themselves and give white people hell. In the 1780s and 1790s these Black Nationalists terrorized North Carolina, South Carolina, Mississippi, Louisiana and other states.

"In 1800, between 2000 and 5000 Black People planned a rebellion near the city of Richmond, Virginia (the governor of Mississippi estimated that 50,000 Blacks were in on this plot). Gabriel Prosser, one of the leaders of this revolutionary plot, and the other Black Nationalists planned to kill most of the whites, capture key points in the city and trigger a general slave revolt throughout Virginia and the rest of the states. Virginia itself was to become a Black state. A violent storm and two toming slaves nipped this insurrection in the bud, but nothing stopped the desire of the Blacks to be free. Thus it was that two years later, a similar rebellion involving close to 10,000 Blacks was uncovered.

"During this same time period, maroons were terrorizing Elizabeth City, North Carolina, and a plot was hatched to capture the city of Savannah, Georgia. As a matter of fact, plots were so frequent in the South that the Northern states, which profited little from actual slave labor, decided to manumit (free) the Blacks in northern areas.

"In 1811, a revolt of slaves in St. Charles and St. John parishes (a parish is a county) in Louisiana took place. The Blacks here were originally armed with sugar cane knives, axes and clubs. After several killings they got a few guns, drums and a flag and started marching from plantation to plantation killing whites and getting numerous Blacks to join them in their quest for freedom and eventual self-government. It took the U.S. Army to capture them. Most were killed in battle and decapitated (their heads were cut off), and their heads were hung in different spots near New Orleans for public view.

"It was hot for whites in Cabarrus County, North Carolina also. There, in the same year, a group of runaway slaves who had been governing themselves had to be slaughtered by white troops because they refused to stop their activities. Without a doubt, scarcely a day passed when there was not an insurrection or act inflicted by Black People aimed at getting their right to freedom and self-determination.

"A fort built by the British at Appalachicola Bay, Florida, during the War of 1812 was occupied by fugitive slaves and maintained for some time after the British had left. More than 300 Blacks and some Indians took over the well-supplied fort, governed themselves and used the fort as a shelter for other runaway Blacks and as a base for carrying out guerilla warfare and raids against slave holders in the area. In 1816, U.S. troops set out to destroy this Black Nationalist stronghold. They surrounded the fort for ten days and then bombarded it with cannons until all but nearly 40 of the inhabitants were dead.

"During 1820, maroon self-governing attempts continued. However, in 1822, there was a plot led by Denmark Vesey and other Black Nationalists that sent white people all over the country into hysterics.

"The plan laid out by Peter Poyas and Denmark Vesey was masterful. It had several cells of operation, but most of the 9000 slaves who were involved knew only one commanding officer— their own. In June, the leaders of the rebellion met for the final preparations. The rebellion was supposed to begin at midnight, June 16th. The leaders reviewed the plans, which called for attacks on arsenals, guardhouses and armories, and simultaneous marches on Charleston by Blacks from several points outside the city. Many of the slaves were to operate within the city limits by camouflaging as white men, painting their faces white and wearing wigs, mustaches and false whiskers made of white men's hair. All whites in the cities and surrounding areas and all toming niggers were to be killed, and the city was to be set on fire. Simultaneous revolts were to take place outside the city, causing general hysteria among the whites which would give the Blacks a better opportunity to establish a base from which to operate. However, one of the toming niggers got wind of the plot and revealed what he knew to his master. As a result, this move for self-government never got off the ground.

"This did not save the whites in Norfolk County, Virginia, however, where in 1823 maroons were terrifying the area. These maroons governed themselves, defended themselves against attack, got what they needed to subsist (live) and attacked surrounding areas to spread fear among the whites and recruit other Blacks. The same was true near the fork of the Alabama and Tombigbee Rivers. Many Black Nationalists in this area had been self-governing for years and had made many attacks on neighboring plantations. Their government was broken up entirely by white militiamen, but not without a fight (all of the maroons were poorly armed, but they engaged in battle against the well-armed whites anyway).

"In the 1830s, similar self-governing camps existed all over North Carolina; in Wilmington, New Bern, Elizabeth City, near Dover Swamp, Gaston Island, on Price's Creek and in several other spots. These small self-governing camps were only a step toward what Black People really wanted— a country and large government of their own.

"In 1831, the nationalist sentiments of Black People were put into motion by Nat Turner and his fellow revolutionaries. In August of that year, these men began an insurrection which, it was hoped, would lead to a general slave rebellion throughout Virginia. In case they were stopped, they were to follow the example of the maroons by retreating to the swamps and carrying on guerilla warfare against the whites.

"Sixty dead white people later, Nat Turner and his comrades were close to their destination of Jerusalem (present-day Courtland) Virginia, place of the county seat. There they were stopped by their lack of preparation and federal troops. They were not regretful, however. They preferred death while attempting to get freedom and self determination to life as a slave. Two months after the Nat Turner led rebellion, another rebellion took place in Alabama. Three months after the Nat Turner led rebellion a rebellion took place in Fayetteville, Tennessee. The objective of these rebellions was to set fire to buildings and, amidst the confusion, seize guns and implements of destruction in order to massacre whites.

"Between 1835 and 1842, whites witnessed more organized struggle by the Black Nationalists. Maroons were particularly active in Georgia, South Carolina, North Carolina, Virginia, Maryland, Alabama, Louisiana and Texas. Black People in Missouri planned to murder their masters and flee to Canada. In the District of Columbia and Charles County, Maryland, a plot was hatched which had as its purpose the obtaining by Black People of 'their rights.'

"To the Black People who were forced to come to this land, Black Nationalism was not viewed lightly. Self-government was what Blacks wanted; here, in Canada or Mexico or wherever necessary. Thus it was that in 1849, about 300 slaves in the region of St. Mary's, Georgia planned to seize a boat and go to the West Indies. A delay in the arrival of the boat caught the Blacks by surprise, and their plot was uncovered.

"Between 1850 and 1860, there was more trouble than ever as Blacks became daring in their insubordination to white rule and determination to rule themselves. For 250 years they had sought to express their nationalistic desires, and had done so most effectively by rebelling against whites, terrorizing whites and establishing camps that were governed by Black People, independent of whites and in spite of white efforts to kill off such governments... These Blacks were, in effect, contributing what they could to the development of a Black self-governing Nation that would make life easier for the Black People who had been forced to come to this land by white greed and white firepower..."

Maroon activity, that is, the search for self-government, was not limited to North America. As a matter of fact, this activity probably reached its highest stage of development in South America, in the country of Brazil, where the Black Nation of Palmares was founded and maintained for nearly 70 years by Black rebellers. For more on this, we will refer to an article that appeared in Volume 6, Number 10 of "The People's Newsletter."

"During the 1620s, Black People/slaves began fleeing from towns and plantations of Brazil. They went into the forests, settled communities and established governments of their own. By 1630, these various communities had evolved into major settlements; Greater Palmares, with more than seven thousand inhabitants and Lesser Palmares, with close to five thousand. Together they demonstrated the will of Black People to rid themselves of white people and establish governments by Black People for the benefit of Black People.

"Palmares demonstrated the ability Black People naturally had to govern themselves. From a handful of fugitive slaves and communities it grew into a complex political organism of many settlements. The government was headed by a king, who was assisted by a minister of justice, guards, and military and civil servants. A system of law was devised, and such crimes as murder and robbery were punishable by death. At first, these Black nationalists solved their economic problems by attacking the plantations in nearby towns, but a more self-sufficient system soon evolved. They began to produce their own agricultural products and use them to trade for such necessities as arms and ammunition.

"Each community of Palmares was designed for defense purposes; the Black Nationalists knew they would be under attack from the whites and they wanted to protect themselves as efficiently and effectively as possible. It was good they did! In 1644, whites attempted to destroy the Black Nation and almost did so, but the Blacks were able to rebuild and re-establish themselves. In 1676 another attempt was made to destroy Palmares, but the Blacks refused to surrender. Finally, in 1696, an army of nearly 8000 white men was organized for the specific purpose of destroying Palmares. They ran up against a group of Black nationalists who were determined to either live as free men or die. After a bloody battle, the superior arms of the whites began to tell, and the white soldiers entered the Black Nation, only to see Black People jumping to their death rather than submitting to white rule. As these proud Black People jumped, the Black Nation of Palmares died; but their love for self-government and freedom were passed on to following generations of Blacks who have never ceased, to this day, to establish a New Afrikan (Black) Nation and government of Black People, by Black People and for Black People."

The white people who ruthlessly and confidently governed the island of San Domingo (in the Caribbean) will testify to the fact that Black People's love for freedom and self-government (from Palmares and elsewhere) was passed on to following generations of Black People, for it was in San Domingo that, beginning in 1789, the Black slaves rebelled, organized, met and defeated in battle the three strongest white military powers in the world at that time, and declared themselves independent and self-governing people. (The impact of this on the United States has already been discussed. See Lesson #4) Let Us briefly review this grand historical process, this testament to the beauty and power of Black People who are united and who know what they want.

When Columbus "discovered" America in 1492, he landed in what we now call the Bahamas and the West Indies. One of the islands in this chain was called Hispaniola by the Spanish, and one portion of Hispaniola became known as San Domingo. San Domingo was an agricultural paradise. San Domingo could produce high quantities of the highest quality sugar, large quantities of indigo (dye), cotton which only needed to be planted (it didn't need to be tended), molasses, cocoa, rum, coffee, tobacco and a host of other products which people could live off of and get rich off of. San Domingo also had numerous mines. Because it was so prosperous it was given priority attention by the Spanish. Workers were needed, so Columbus began satisfying this need by enslaving the native inhabitants of the island (the Arawak Indians). When, by 1517 they had been just about exterminated, the Spanish crown and the Catholic Church got together and decided that Black People from Africa should provide the labor needed to adequately exploit the island.

Slaves were transported not only to San Domingo but to other islands in the Caribbean as well. The sugar plantations which dominated the economic activities in San Domingo required a demanding and continuous manner of work. Young sugar cane had to be tended for 3 or 4 months and grew to maturity only 12 to 14 months later. Since it could be planted and grown at any time of the year, the reaping of one crop was just the sign that a new crop was to be planted. The result is that the slave was forced to work throughout the year for as many as 14 or 16 hours per day. Anyone who had observed the condition of the slaves would have believed they were defenseless against their masters, particularly after taking note of the effects of overwork and underfeeding.

The safety of the whites required that they keep the slaves in the most profound ignorance and wretchedness. All instruction, religious or otherwise, was kept away from the slaves. The control of the whites seemed so overwhelming that the slaves seemed resigned to their condition on the plantation. No talk of emancipation came from the masters and no demands of freedom were noticeable among the slaves.

With the decline of the Spanish empire, the French moved into San Domingo and replaced the Spanish whites. Their treatment of the slaves was just as inhumane and their control seemed just as overwhelming. Under the French the production of San Domingo more than doubled, so that between 1783 and 1789, it was undoubtedly the finest colony in the world. In order to keep the production at a peak, the French transported more and more slaves into the colony.

This continued flow of slaves into San Domingo was filling the colony with native Africans who were more resentful and ready for rebellion than the customary plantation slave on the island. When these Blacks began hearing about the revolutionary fervor that was taking place in France, particularly as it related to freedom for all men, they caught the freedom spirit too. Before the end of 1789, the Blacks were holding mass meetings in the forests at night. Revolutionary talk was circulating, and the Blacks soon became convinced that they should no longer be in bondage. They started rebelling.

But before We go forward, let Us go back for a moment. Long before the plantation slaves had started rebelling, maroon activity in San Domingo had been frequent. Probably before 1760, the maroons on the island were organized under the leadership of one Black man. His name was Mackandal. Mackandal and his Black companions had designed a plot aimed at uniting all of the Blacks on the island and driving all of the whites out of the colony. The major weapon they planned to use was poison. Mackandal and his comrades went from plantation to plantation recruiting Blacks and perfecting their plans. The plan was that, on a particular day the water of every house in the capital city would be poisoned, and that a general attack would be made on the whites while they were in anguish. Then, bands of Black People would leave the town and spread over the island to massacre the whites. Unfortunately, Mackandal's plot never got off the ground. Mackandal got drunk, ran his mouth too much about how the whites were going to pay for what they were doing, and was burned alive by the whites of the island.

The Blacks who started rebelling in the 1790s had learned a lot from Mackandal's misfortune of 20 years earlier. By 1791, under the leadership of a Black man named Boukman (who was a High Priest. Most Black revolutionaries were very religious persons.), the Blacks had organized and were ready to move. Their plan was massive and aimed at exterminating the whites and making the colony a Black colony. There was much more to this plan than the poison that dominated Mackandal's plot. On a given night, the slaves in the suburbs and outskirts of LeCap (the capital city) were to set the plantations on fire. Upon this signal the slaves in the towns would massacre the whites and the slaves on the plains would complete the destruction and slaughter. These Blacks were so much together that the whites had no idea that anything was in the making until this vast plot had actually broken out. This is a testimony to the solidarity of the Black People and the ignorance of the whites, who despised the slaves too much to believe them capable of organizing a mass movement against the slave condition.

On the selected night the plan was activated. For nearly three weeks, because of the fires, the people of LeCap could barely distinguish between night and day. The slaves destroyed with a passion. They knew that as long as the plantations stood they would remain slaves. As the slaves rebelled, more slaves joined them. Before their objectives were fully realized, Boukman was killed and the action began to die down. The masses, still full of revolutionary energy, needed clear and vigorous direction, but the remaining leaders did not know what to do. The leaders became confused and afraid and decided to submit to the whites if the whites would grant liberty to a few hundred of the slave leaders. This was a betrayal of the masses by the leaders. However, in this case the whites refused to bargain. The slave leaders then asked for freedom for 60 of their leaders. Once again the whites refused. Then and only then did the Black leaders decide on liberty for all or liberty for none.

(Before continuing, we will point out that the manner of the slave leaders is more typical of leaders than atypical. _Leaders frequently betray the masses_. For this reason, all Black People must understand basic principles and be on the alert for developments, etc. Additionally, because of this Black People should not get hung up on any individual leader. Our response to individual leaders must be based on what they do, not what they have done. This is not to say that We should not trust Our leaders; it is simply to say that We should not trust them beyond a certain point. Nonetheless, the key is for each person involved to get the understanding that is necessary to adequately evaluate developments and the response of leaders to those developments. Leaders, Black and non-Black, can be tempted by Our enemies in a variety of ways.)

At the point where Black leaders recognized it would have to be liberty for all or liberty for none, Toussaint L'Ouverture emerged as the leader of the revolutionary Blacks. With freedom on his mind and some knowledge of European military tactics, Toussaint organized out of the thousands of ignorant and untrained Blacks an army capable of fighting European armies. Toussaint trained the Blacks and drilled them, realizing that the Blacks' abilities on the battlefields would be the determining factor in whether they would be free of slaves.

Soon Toussaint and the Blacks were the decisive factors in whatever occurred in San Domingo. The British and the Spanish, well supplied with arms, money and men, made a united effort to take the island. They hoped that by taking the island they would destroy the power of France. Instead, the British army was practically destroyed. It was annihilated by the Black revolutionaries.

The Black army was often without food. Many times the British attempted to bribe the soldiers, but their attempts failed because the Blacks knew what they wanted— liberty and equality— and they knew this was not what the British had in mind. Supporting the Black army were the masses of the people who, during 1795 and 1796, became extremely confident in Toussaint as a man who was devoted to their interests. This support gave Toussaint the confidence he needed, on and off the battlefield, to enact measures which needed to be enacted.

Toussaint and the Blacks gained control of the entire island. However, Toussaint was reluctant to declare the island independent of France. As a result, the Blacks became inactive and began losing some of the ground they had gained. The French proposed a war of extermination against the Blacks, hoping to kill off all the Blacks on the island and then to re-populate the island with an entirely new group of slaves, slaves who had not been bit by the freedom bug. The French drowned so many persons in the Bay of LeCap that for a long time no one would eat fish. The French also brought in dogs that were fed so many Black persons that they would attack Blacks at sight. The French burned alive, hanged, drowned, tortured and buried Blacks up to their necks near nests of insects, where they died an agonizing death. The French also captured Toussaint, and much seemed lost as far as the Blacks were concerned. However, the will of the Black masses to be free was not lost, and from among them emerged Jean Jacque Dessalines, one of Toussaint's ablest generals.

Dessalines has been called a one-sided genius, but he was the man for this crisis. Recognizing what the French were trying to do, he traded blow for blow with them. When the French killed 500 Blacks at LeCap, Dessalines hanged 500 whites and left them for everybody to see. Dessalines set an example, but it was the Black People of San Domingo who won the victory. They burned San Domingo flat so that at the end of the war it was a charred island. And, far from being intimidated, they met the French terror with such courage and defiance that it frightened the white terrorists. This was even truer with the women. The French, now powerless, saw in this strength something peculiar to Black People. The muscles of the Blacks, they said, contracted with so much force as to make them insensible to pain.

Not surprisingly, the French decided to give up. The Black masses were triumphant. To emphasize their freedom, the Blacks renamed the state Haiti and Dessalines was crowned as emperor.

It is important that We, Black People, understand the San Domingo Revolution in its proper historical perspective. To help Us to do this, We should refer to the affect of the Revolution on the development of the United States (see Lesson #4), and give serious thought to the following points.

(1) The San Domingo Revolution was the only successful slave revolt in the Americas. By successful, we mean it turned the political order of things upside down. Palmares was just as successful in that it too was a Black Nation, but Palmares did not disrupt the social or political order in Brazil; it did not upset the norm, it just established an alternative way-of-life for Black People. San Domingo put the Blacks on top and removed the whites from that position. It proved that Blacks could succeed against the dominant powers just as long as they were together and just as long as they were clear as to what they wanted. As it was then, so it is now. Black People today can do whatever We want to do if We get together and if We are clear as to what Our objectives are.

(2) The San Domingo Revolution inspired the Blacks in the United States to intensify their efforts to get freedom. All of the major revolts that took place

in this country did so after the rebellion in San Domingo was in full swing. The revolt in Virginia in 1800 that was led by Gabriel Prosser was inspired by the efforts of the Blacks in San Domingo. Denmark Vesey frequently mentioned the San Domingo Revolution while he was making preparations to eliminate the whites of Charleston, South Carolina. David Walker, whom We have discussed already, repeatedly referred to the Blacks of Haiti (San Domingo was renamed Haiti by the Blacks), and his writings inspired Nat Turner and Harriet Tubman, among others. It cannot be debated; the Revolution in San Domingo had grand and grave repercussions among the inhabitants of the United States of America.

(3) The San Domingo riches led to the abolition of the African slave trade by England, which was jealous of the prosperity the island was bringing to the French. When one recognizes that England was the undisputed queen of the seas at this time, and that the slave trade was strictly over water, one can see how much this stand was likely to affect the transport of slaves from Africa to the Americas. This declaration did not stop the slave trade but it cut into it deeply and set the stage for the general acceptance of an end to the trade. If San Domingo had not been making France so wealthy, there is no telling how much longer the slave trade would have remained legal, and there is no telling how many more innocent Black People would have been killed as a result of the search for slaves.

(4) The San Domingo Revolution also made Americans more receptive to the idea of abolishing the slave trade. Up to this time, many Americans thought in terms of always having Africa as a source of slave labor. After the Revolution in San Domingo, the fear of slave rebellions in the United States increased dramatically. The willingness of the Blacks in San Domingo to kill white people and destroy property instilled fear into the hearts of many Americans and caused them to stress the importance of Americans "breeding" their own slaves and developing a domestic slave trade that would satisfy the needs of the country. Americans definitely did not want any slaves straight from Africa in this country.

(5) San Domingo is proof of how slavery was the basis of the European economy and European development. Political and economic decisions that would affect three or four *continents* rested on developments in San Domingo. San Domingo determined which European countries got rich and which ones would get in a position to attempt to control the politics of the world. In this regard, San Domingo is just representative of the role Black People and Black lands (the Caribbean, Africa, etc.) have played in the white world historically.

In San Domingo, there occurred a successful revolt of Black People against white people. Just as We have a lot to learn from it, so too We have a lot to learn from the slave revolts that were not as successful. For this reason, we will now review the slave rebellions in the United States in historical perspective.

These rebellions, mentioned earlier in this lesson, took place in 1800, 1822 and 1831, and were led by Gabriel Prosser, Denmark Vesey and Nat Turner, respectively.

(1) Each failure was due to one internal weakness— Negroes who ran to the whites. The Rebellions of 1800 and 1822, which involved more than 14,000 active Black participants, were betrayed by 2 Negroes who actually ran to the whites and told everything they knew, while the Rebellion of 1831 sacrificed proper preparation, organization and numerical involvement in order to limit the possibility of betrayal. This lack of preparation had its impact when Nat Turner's comrades came up against the temptation of pleasure and organized resistance. The message for Black People today is that Our internal weaknesses victimize Us more than any external or outside force. We need to get together and prepare properly if We are ever going to get people to recognize Our human rights. Those of Us who are not going to help Us achieve Our objective should not do anything that will hinder Our efforts.

(2) Each of the leaders of the rebellion and most of the participants had been inspired by previous revolutions or insurrections, although they knew that most of the previous insurrections had failed. These rebellers were not looking for a plan that guaranteed success, they were looking to get what they knew was theirs by right. They were serious about getting what they wanted, and serious people take chances and make their own guarantees. The message for Black People today is clear— "no risk, no chance for advancement." If you are not willing to step outside the limitations of "the system", you are not serious about bringing on a change. No risk guarantees no change for the better.

(3) None of these men and women were prompted by personal considerations. They were physically abused, psychologically brainwashed and socially disregarded not for individual reasons but because they were BLACK!! Therefore, they knew they could not go through any individual changes that would improve their condition in any basic manner. Once again, the message to Black People today is clear— you should not take a personal approach to solving a social/racial dilemma. You cannot deal with it properly or effectively that way.

(4) All of the rebellers realized the importance of articulate plans which had long range objectives. This is important to Black People today for at least two reasons. First, immediate results are not necessarily real results. Thus, the here and now is not the only thing We should be concerned about. We should also concern Ourselves with the future, because only future considerations can guarantee that what benefits Us here and now will also benefit Us in the years to come. Secondly, long range objectives recognize that the first step is only the beginning. The more difficult job is making additional progress after the initial step forward has been made. All of Us should be aware of this fact

because it will mentally prepare Us to struggle and keep on struggling even when things don't seem to be going the way We hoped they would go.

(5) None of these men and women were ignorant of the power of the established authorities. Still they acted. This tells Us today that We cannot be afraid to challenge the powers that be, regardless of how strong the state or government looks, because you have to challenge it in order to get away from the hellish conditions it has forced on you. And, you must get away from it in order to successfully establish a power base of your own.

(6) All of the Blacks who refused to participate in the Rebellions are dead today. In other words, they did not avoid death by not rebelling. They are right where those who did rebel are. The only difference is that the rebellers died for a cause— they died trying to improve their condition and the condition of later generations of Black People— while the other dead Blacks played Negro and failed to even attempt to improve their condition and that of later generations of Blacks. No one has escaped death yet, and everybody who is reading this Handbook will probably be dead 50 years later. Since you cannot escape death, there is no need to run from it. You should instead attempt to do things that will benefit people, particularly Black People, while you are living. Under no circumstances should you think you are going to live longer simply because you be a "good" person and abide by the "law". You cannot possibly do that; you cannot possibly control how long you will live, but you can do things that will improve the conditions under which you have to live (for however long or short that may be). Since Our conditions are so bad, all of Us/Black People should be about the business of improving them.

(7) All of the leaders (and most of the participants) of the Rebellions were very religious. This invites a comparison of the Black church as it was in the beginning and as it is now. Thoughts of pie in the sky did not seriously enter the minds of Our ancestors who had nothing in their stomachs. Poorly dressed Blacks at that time did not cherish the illusion that they would get clothes and shoes in heaven. Black People then were not as misdirected about religion as We are today. Simply put, We should re-examine, personally and socially, the role of religion in Our oppression and desires for liberation. We should check Our "religion" out to see if it has gone off track. If We fail to check it out and make the necessary adjustments, We will undoubtedly be betraying Our religious heritage.

(8) The Almighty is not pulling the strings of human history. Natural forces are constantly in motion; man has to adapt to these forces or pay the price sooner or later. Man-made forces are in motion which people can either adapt to or challenge. If you adapt, these man-made forces will control you and maintain the status quo (keep things the way they are). If, on the other hand, you challenge these man-made forces, you establish yourself as a force that has to be reckoned with and respected by other men/people, and thereby open

the door to changes that will benefit you/Black People. People are pulling the strings of human history, and if Black People function, Our pull is just as strong as anybody else's pull.

(9) The Black rebellers recognized the importance of establishing bases from which they and Black People could operate on a wide and generally organized scale. We have to have bases of operations; small branches that take the form of community organizations, for example, that must be supported and maintained by Black People, and the large base in the form of a structure or provisional government that functions to make the Black Nation a physical reality. It is Our responsibility to support these nationalistic community organizations and the activities of the government or structure that systematically presents Our nationalistic aspirations and justifications to the world's communities.

WE have to pay attention and WE have to think. Some of the most analytical and intelligent Black persons who have been in this country have paid attention, thought and come to the conclusion that the course for Black People in this country must be aimed at Black Nationhood. We need to be about Black Nationhood even more nowadays. If We pay attention, think and act accordingly or intelligently, We will be about the business of establishing a Black Nation, a real base of Black Power and Black Self-Determination.

At this time, we will go into a brief discussion of a second form of rebellion. This form of rebellion had equality for Black People as its main objective, and is represented most popularly by the Abolitionist Movement and the Underground Railroad. But, before we get into each particular one, We must understand what Black People in this era had in mind when they spoke of freedom and equality. Quite simply, these terms referred to Black People's desire to exercise all of the rights and privileges that other people are allowed to exercise. These include the right to make basic decisions that would affect the welfare of Black People. In effect then, what these Blacks wanted was a form of self-determination, but they were not willing to take the extreme measures to get it that the Blacks we have just discussed were willing to take. They wanted to govern themselves, but they were willing to remain under the official domain of the United States government if that government would not blatantly interfere with their efforts to take care of themselves. Whereas they would not have participated in the activities of the maroons, the Blacks who rebelled for equality would sympathize with maroon activities and definitely would not betray the maroons or willingly side with the United States government against the maroons. It could be argued that many of these Blacks just imagined that this type of equality represented the easy way out of an unfortunate set of circumstances; one that was less than what was desirable, but one that was satisfactory because it allowed Black People to maintain their respect and dignity to some degree. Whatever the case, these Black rebellers were definitely not concerned with integrating with white people. What they were concerned about was getting the same concessions from the government and other authorities that white people got.

Being separate from white people was something these Blacks were quite content with. In that respect, the Blacks of that era who took the abolitionist approach were not unlike many Black individuals today. The overwhelming number of Black persons today who speak of equality are not concerned about integrating with white people. They, like the Blacks of an earlier era, are concerned about receiving the rights that are Ours by nature and the concessions that all other people receive. This push for integration is at worst an effort spearheaded by whites and acted on by Negroes who want to be as close to white people as they can. Such Negroes are a minority, a decided minority, among Black People. At best, this integration thing represents a lack of communication between the Black masses and those individuals who say they are Our "leaders". Somehow, such leaders failed to realize that there is a difference between equality and integration, and they failed to take this difference into account when they tried to interpret the demands of the Black masses. It is up to Us (the Black masses) then, to make it crystal clear to those who propose to represent Us that they *feel* as well as hear what We are saying. If they have been so far removed from Us (through education or domestication) that they can no longer understand or interpret Our use of the language, then it is up to Us to make sure that they give up their leadership claims. Additionally, it is up to Us to accept the fact that the United States government is not going to allow a political relationship based on equality between white America and Black People in America to exist. Whites, individually and through their governments, are not going to allow Black People to partly rule Ourselves while remaining a part of the United States governmental structure. In one regard they won't do so because of their racism, and in another regard they won't do so because the government wants to manage every facet of the lives of everyone in this country. Black People have to accept the fact that if We want even a little measure of control over Our destiny, and if We only want to make *some* of the decisions that will determine the quality of Our lives, then We are going to have to be prepared to take the extreme measures that the maroons and other Black Nationalists of an earlier era took. In other words, We must be prepared to separate from America and govern Ourselves.

Having said that, we will discuss the abolitionists movements. We say movements because there were in fact two abolitionist movements. Both had a major weakness; instead of trying to get Black People to take their freedom, they tried to act in a manner that would force the government to give freedom to Black People. At times the two seemed like one and the same challenge to slavery and discrimination, but the attentive observer would have been able to clearly distinguish between the two. The sincere abolitionist movement, the one that should most concern Us, was the one that was spearheaded by Black People. The other abolitionist movement, the one whose leading figures students of history are so familiar with, had a questionable motive. This abolitionist movement was led by white people.

For all intents and purposes, before 1800 there was no abolitionist movement in this country other than that in the minds and hearts of the slaves and free Blacks who rebelled against the slave condition. There were whites who called themselves abolitionists, but they were more concerned about getting free Black persons out of this country than relieving the condition of Black People in bondage. In 1800, Black People began to seriously imprint the idea of abolition in the minds of white people when the slaves began organizing rebellions on a mass scale against white lives and white property. Then, some white people began to realize that slavery could lead to the destruction of their country, so they set out to keep that from happening.

The white abolitionist movement was not a moral movement. It was, instead, a racist political movement that hoped to avoid certain chaos in America by convincing the American people (white/government) to gradually eliminate the evil called slavery and to quickly remove the Black portion of the free population in America to another land. At first no Black individual could join an abolitionist society or organization of this type. This of itself indicates that the white abolitionists were not really concerned about the welfare of Black People.

However, a series of events took place among Black People that forced the white abolitionists to reassess their efforts to save America from the "wrath of God". In 1789, the Blacks of San Domingo began rebelling and took control of their own destiny at the expense of many white people's lives and the destruction of much white property. In 1800, as we just stated, slaves in this country were organizing to kill white people and destroy white property as a means of getting their freedom and the opportunity to govern themselves. Efforts by Black People such as these continued throughout the early 1800s (see earlier part of this lesson), and exploded in the minds of white people again in 1822 when a plot with these objectives was uncovered that involved thousands and thousands of slaves and free Black persons. Additionally, during the 1820s the free Black population in this country stepped up its abolitionist activities because such Blacks saw abolition as a death blow to white people's plans to colonize all free Black persons in other parts of the world (they would be sent from America. For a review of colonization, see the section concerning David Walker in this lesson.). The efforts of these free Blacks imposed pressure on the gradual freedom movement of white abolitionists, but their impact was minor when compared to the impact of events that took place in the years 1829 and 1831. In 1829, David Walker issued his Appeal, which logically appealed to Black People to violently rebel against their condition, and in 1831

Nat Turner and his comrades took David Walker's advice and attempted to take their freedom and determine their own destiny. In the process of so doing, many whites were killed and a thousand times more were panic-stricken. These events, and matters related thereto, forced white abolitionists to recognize and accept the fact that freedom for Black People was not a matter that was to be decided on and acted on by white people alone. They recognized that Black People could and would bring about this condition if whites failed to do so, and that Black People would bring it about in a way that would totally disregard the life, liberty and property of white people. In order to avoid this, the white abolitionist movement became more receptive to Black individuals being among their ranks and they became more militant. By being more militant they hoped to save America, and by being more receptive to Black participation they hoped to decrease the possibility of Black People getting together among themselves and deciding to take care of business in a hurry while using any means necessary.

As a result of this, the Black abolitionist movement and the white abolitionist movement began to merge, so much so that they almost looked like one and the same movement. But an attentive observer or participant would have recognized that that was not the case. That observer would have been aware of the attitudes white abolitionists had traditionally held about Black People, that observer would have been aware of the attitudes white people hold in general about Black People, that observer would have recognized that the factors that were motivating the white abolitionists and the Black abolitionists were fundamentally different and, at times, contradictory (opposites), and that observer would have been aware of the emerging economic aspect of white abolitionism. These factors would not prevent white abolitionists and Black abolitionists from struggling against slavery together, but they would assure that both of these groups would not benefit from that struggle. Let Us see why.

The Black abolitionist movement, the one whose motivating factor was getting the government to give freedom to the slaves and equality to all Black People, was a natural outgrowth of an enslaved and abused people's desire for freedom and equality (human equality). It was not a formally organized nor clearly defined movement, but it was one that had the potential to drastically unnerve this country because it was independent of white control. Therefore, the Black abolitionists were just as apt to encourage a slave rebellion or a riot as they were to speak at rallies and donate to anti-slavery societies and organizations. What the Black abolitionists lacked were adequate finances, adequate access to public opinion (both national and international) and the support of a respected, if not influential, element of the power structure (the system). By operating side by side with white abolitionists, Black abolitionists recognized the possibility of overcoming some, if not all, of these shortcomings.

The white abolitionist movement, as we stated earlier, was mainly concerned about the safety of white people and white property in America. They, then, were concerned about the preservation of America, not the condition of Black People. At first they thought their major obstacle to eliminating the threat of slavery to the preservation of America was the opposition of those whites who benefited from slavery and sympathized with slave owners. Later, as we just stated, they realized that Black People were an even more immediate threat to America's preservation, and they concluded that their major shortcoming was their lack of control of the Black abolitionists. By beginning to work with Black abolitionists, white abolitionists felt they would be in a position to control the more extreme tendencies of Black abolitionism. Also, white abolitionists would be able to further their own cause by using the misery experienced by former slaves and presented by former slaves to arouse the sentiments of other whites. In other words, then, the white abolitionists began to undermine the potential of the Black abolitionist movement by getting Blacks abolitionists to participate in a white movement that seemed to have the same objectives as those of the Black movement.

The merger of the two movements represented an effort on the part of Black abolitionists to overcome their weaknesses or shortcomings, and an effort by white abolitionists to increase their effectiveness and undermine the strength (Black self-control) of the Black abolitionists. It is the same type merger that exists today in so-called communist, socialist, workers and civil rights organizations. Unfortunately for Black People, today, as in the 1830s, the Black rebellers seem unaware of the objectives of the whites to undermine Black strengths. The Black rebellers also fail to realize that their strength and their potential lies not with whites who can provide finances and access to public opinion but with Black People who are not under the control or influence of white people. Finances and access to public opinion are necessary items, but they are not the necessary item or ingredient. The necessary ingredient for Us is Black People who are beyond the control and influence of white people. We must have this ingredient of self-control and maintain this ingredient. Finances and access to public opinion must grow out of this necessary ingredient. Under no circumstances should We ever view them as more important than Black self control.

As a result of the merger between the Black abolitionists and the white abolitionists, Black individuals emerged as leaders of the overall abolitionist movement. Black preachers and writers were able to promote abolition, Black speakers were able to excite the emotions of those who attended abolitionist rallies and conferences, Black individuals worked on and supported major abolitionist publications, Blacks assumed operational control of the Underground Railroad, and more than a hundred former slaves had their stories published and sold to interested persons in America and Europe. But, this merger also made it possible for white abolitionists to undermine the real strength of the

Black abolitionists. As a result of the efforts of white abolitionists, Black abolitionists became less extremist, and Black abolitionists began to consider the possibility of integrating with whites (since they picked up the impression that all whites were not anti-Black) and of making the American economic structure in the North work for Black People. By so doing, the Black abolitionists lost control of the abolitionist movement but failed to recognize this loss because they were projected as leaders of the movement and because events of the 1850s and 1860s overshadowed the abolitionist movement and rendered any talk of abolition as just that— talk and no more.

The abolitionist movement gave many white hypocrites the opportunity to run their mouths and have their egos inflated. It was supported by well educated and well-to-do white persons who were in sympathy with the efforts of northern businessmen to transform the economic basis of the South from one that used plantation slave labor to one that used wage slave labor. It was made useless when political and economic tensions between the North and South began to come to a head, but it had had its negative impact on Black People. It had ridded many of Us of Our self-control, it had introduced some of Us to the possibility of integration, it had seduced Us into thinking of Black economic survival as an arm of American economic survival, and it had left Us unable to recognize that those whites who supported the abolition of slavery were not concerned about the welfare of Black People. But, more than that, the abolitionist movement had an inborn weakness because it appealed to those in power to change the condition of Black People, instead of appealing to Black People to bring about that change. It failed to recognize that We, Black People, hold the key to Our destiny. Nonetheless, the abolitionist movement did indicate that Black People were not satisfied and were not idly accepting Our "place". We were rebelling and seeking to gain more control over Our lives. Unfortunately, in this case We did not rebel wisely.

The Underground Railroad was a route escaped slaves took to freedom (the route was not always the same). Usually these runaway slaves headed for the northern section of the country (across the Mason-Dixon Line), since the chances of them maintaining their freedom were greater in the North than in the South. The Underground Railroad became a formal part of the white abolitionist movement at an early stage in the development of white abolitionism. It provided assistance to slaves who ran away, and in so doing hoped to encourage enough slaves to run away to slightly disrupt the stability of the plantation system. Yet, before the time of Harriet Tubman, the efforts of the Underground Railroad were not worth mentioning. Very few slaves took that route to freedom because white abolitionists were not really concerned about freeing substantial numbers of slaves. They only wanted to free one here and another one there for showcase purposes, just like white organizations support certain Black causes (like the Scottsboro Brothers, the Wilmington 10,

Gary Tyler, etc.) today for showcase purposes. (They give inalert individuals the impression that they are concerned about the welfare of Black People, but in fact they are not. What they are really concerned about is what they put substantial time, effort and money behind, not what they put showcase time, effort and money behind.) However, most people fail to realize that whites are not serious until someone like a Harriet Tubman comes along and shows how active the Underground Railroad (or whatever) could really be. Then, Black People who think recognize that whites ("liberals" and "comrades") have been gaming on Us all the time, and therefore stop having anything to do with them. Like Harriet Tubman, such Blacks begin functioning for the benefit of Black People not because of the assistance they get from whites, but in spite of the assistance they get from whites (in other words, white people's help is more likely to slow Us down than help Us along).

Briefly, we will mention a fourth type of rebellion, that which had as its objective a degree of personal relief from the extreme wretchedness of slavery. These were mostly individual efforts to escape from slavery or get a break from the rigors of slavery. Individuals who functioned in this manner either did not recognize the value of group rebellion, didn't trust others or didn't think other Black persons were going to do anything (but run their mouths, for example). There were uncountable instances of this type resistance. As a matter of fact, it was undoubtedly more frequent than any other form of resistance we have mentioned. It's regularity was no indication of its effectiveness, however. Individual resistance rarely benefited the rebeller for long, and benefited Black People even less. Still, though, it indicated once again that Black People were dissatisfied with their condition and that they were attempting to do something to change their condition.

Some examples of individual resistance included the intentional breakage of equipment and tools, individual acts of sabotage such as poisoning the master's (or his wife's) food and water, running away to live in the swamps or somewhere else for short periods of time, running away with the intention of never returning (in cases such as these, Blacks frequently ran to Indian communities or tribes that were in the area), setting things on fire, including homes and crops, and spitting in white people's food, among hundreds of other things. There are a lot of individual rebellers among the Black population today. Their efforts, though condoned by more serious Black rebellers, will not help to change the condition of Black People. The type things they do might be helpful, but only if they are part of a united effort. Only a united effort, a seriously planned effort, will bring about real changes for Us. Those who are really serious about rebelling and revolution, even if they think Black People are not going to do anything or if they lack trust in Black People, should run the risk of working with an organized Black group effort anyway. Otherwise your rebellious exercises will be worthless exercises.

All responses to slavery and inequality were not rebellious responses. Many times a lot of persons submitted, and to some submission was the norm. Broadly speaking, this submission took on two shades. One we will refer to as voluntary submission, the other we will refer to as involuntary submission.

The voluntary submitters talked and acted as if white people's claims about Black People were true, and as if white people's treatment of Black People was justified and correct. They seemed to be driven by an urge to be like white people, to be liked by white people and/or to be trusted by white people. The more white people seemed pleased by their actions, the more voluntary submitters seemed to value themselves.

Voluntary submitters accepted the proposition that Black People are less human than white people (or, in other words, that white people are "better" than Black People), and viewed the destiny of Black People as one of depending on the good graces and leadership of white people. Voluntary submitters were "uncle toms" and "handkerchief heads" who spied on the Blacks and informed the master when something unusual seemed to be "in the air". Such submitters were controlled by an unacknowledged fear and the brainwashing white people had submitted Black People to. It is possible, but improbable, that they might have had misgivings about the roles they played, but it is certain that those misgivings did not prevent them from doing whatever they could to frustrate the efforts Black People made to free themselves of their wretched condition. More than likely, they did not view themselves as traitors or as the masters' "boy", but as supporters of right against wrong and good white people against good for nothing niggers.

There are a lot of voluntary submitters among the ranks of Black People today. Essentially speaking, they have the same attitudes toward Black People and white people as their forebears of more than 100 years ago. Therefore they are doing essentially the same things as their forebears were doing. In short, they are intentionally, deliberately and shamelessly doing whatever they can to keep Black People under the domination of white people. They are spying on Black organizations, informing on Black individuals who refuse to abide by this white person's "law", encouraging Black People to not trust certain Black individuals, representing white people at the United Nations and other type places, teaching Black People white lies when they have the knowledge to do otherwise, defending white people against attacks from other people, attacking people who resist being dominated by white people and planting seeds of dissension and distrust within Black organizations and among Black individuals. Voluntary submitters are doing a lot of other similar type things, all of which are crippling the efforts of Black People who want dignity, racial and self-respect and control of their destiny. Voluntary submitters, because they willingly and openly function to the detriment of Black People, do not deserve the benefit of doubt from those of Us who are serious about ending white people's domination of Black People. Whenever We get the opportunity to influence voluntary submitters, We should not attempt to educate them or rehabilitate them. We should influence them by criticizing them with prejudice and by eliminating the possibility of them ever again functioning to the detriment of Black People.

The other submitters, the involuntary submitters, were not so much influenced by the brainwashing of white people that they believed Black People were inferior to white people. Nor did they approve of what white people were doing to Black People. Nevertheless, they helped white people "get over" on Black People and abuse Black People by failing to join those who resisted white people in any substantial manner. They despised white people just as much as those Brothers and Sisters who were involved in the slave rebellions, but they were either too irresponsible or too self-centered to channel their energy in a productive pro-Black, anti-white manner. These involuntary submitters, then, are the ones who kept the Black rebellers and revolutionaries from entirely overwhelming white people during earlier slavery days. If they had been actively involved in efforts to eliminate the control white people had over Black People, even the open and direct efforts of the voluntary submitters would have been unable to preserve white power. This is because the involuntary submitters were the "silent majority" of the Black slave and free population. If they had only made some noise, Black People in this country might have pulled off a revolution that could be compared to the one the Black People in San Domingo pulled off near the end of the 18th century (the 1790s). But, they remained silent, and Black People remained wretched.

The involuntary submitters are crippling Black People in the same manner today. Those of Us who don't give a damn about white people yet function in a manner that keeps white people in a position of dominance could fill the ranks of today's Black resisters and guarantee a better future for today's generation of Black People, and a better life for coming generations of Black People. But they fail to do so by failing to participate in efforts to prepare Black People for a better future. They have funds and resources, but fail to contribute to organizations that are trying to prepare Black People for a better future. They have skills, knowledge and expertise, but fail to contribute any portion of these to the betterment of Black People. They have good paying jobs but allow the job to keep them in line instead of using the job for the benefit of their race. They talk that "whitey aint such and such" line, but their actions indicate that they are not willing to make whitey responsible to human beings, particularly Black human beings. They therefore submit; without admitting defeat they surrender because they let white people have their way and thereby make it difficult for Black People to advance to a position of dignity and respect.

However, there is one major difference between most involuntary submitters and the voluntary submitters. The difference is that the involuntary submitters might change their ways if they are made aware of their shortcomings. If they are properly educated and made to realize that their lack of resistance is really helping to maintain white power, it is probable that they will become productive Black individuals who will work toward a self-determining future for Black People. Every effort must therefore be made to urge these individuals to function in a responsible (to Black People) manner. They must be made to realize that anti-white talk and anti-white sentiments are not enough to prevent white people from abusing Us/Black People. By the same token, they must be made to realize that their "Black and Proud" declarations are not going to change the shameful condition of Black People. They must be made to recognize the importance of acting and giving force to what they say and feel. Then and only then will their rhetoric (talk) and sentiments have any real meaning.

Review history, and do it seriously. You will discover that thousands and thousands of years of human intercourse reveal that those who have power concede (give up) absolutely nothing, while those who submit concede their right to be respected and treated humanely. This is a cruel realization, but history has made it clear that cruel conditions breed cruel human beings. Today racial tensions are at an all time high, but tomorrow they will be even higher. Under such conditions, none of Us/Black People can afford to forfeit or give up one ounce of power by voluntarily or involuntarily submitting. Our motto must be "Resistance, Resistance, Resistance", Our actions must be characterized by "Resistance, Resistance, Resistance", and Our objective must be a Republic of New Afrika, a Black Nation. Nothing less will give Our children respect, and nothing less will enable Us to survive the madness that human interaction has now made inevitable/unavoidable.

LESSON 6
LESSON OUTLINE

As a result of the Civil War, the 13th, 14th and 15th Amendments and certain developments of the Reconstruction Period, Black People became confused and began seeking integration into American society as opposed to national sovereignty (a Black Nation, which was what We needed then and still need today).

I. The Civil War Period (1861-1865)
    A. Military Developments
    B. The Emancipation Proclamation
    C. The Black General Strike
    D. Black Self-Government
II. Reconstruction
    A. Economic
    1. The effort of the northern capitalist business world to gain control of and transform (change) the business/economy of the South so it would conform to northern business/capitalist interests.
    B. Political
    1. The effort by northern whites to keep southern whites from regaining control of the southern state governments (and thereby gaining control of the national government).
    2. The effort by Black People to lay the foundation for turning the country, as much as possible, into a truly democratic country.
III. White Supremacy
    A. Northern Attitudes
    B. Southern Attitudes
    C. 1877
IV. Back In Our Place
V. Meantime, In Africa
    A. Cultural, Economic, Political, Psychological Destruction
    B. Reconstruction
VI. Meantime, The Caribbean
    A. Capital Investment
    B. Political Arrogance
VII. Back Into Ourselves
    A. W.E.B. DuBois
    B. Pan-Africanism
    C. Marcus Garvey
VIII. Meantime, World Events

10 LESSONS

A. World War I
B. Bolshevik/Russian Revolution
C. Chinese Revolution

I. The Civil War Period

As a result of the Civil War, the 13th, 14th and 15th Amendments, and certain developments of the Reconstruction Period (1867-1877), Black People became confused and began seeking integration into American society as opposed to national sovereignty/Black self-government. Let Us review these events and try to understand how this process evolved (took place).

This lesson will involve Us primarily in the years between 1860 and 1885. Two important processes in American History stand out during this period. One is the American Civil War, also called the War Between the States, and the other is Reconstruction, those planned attempts to bring the states back together again that were made immediately after the Civil War ended.

We will begin by dispelling (proving false) some commonly held myths about the Civil War period. First and foremost, and loud and clear, we must emphasize that the Civil War was not fought to end slavery. Nearly all history books on the subject inform Us that the South started the War by firing on Fort Sumter. Since slavery thrived in the South, it is not logical to suppose that the South started a war that had as its aim the destruction of slavery, that is, the destruction of the South's source of labor and the destruction of its labor system.

The Civil War was a war between white businessmen in the North and white businessmen in the South over economic matters. Even though the North and the South belonged to one country, they had developed different types of economic systems. But, both of the economic systems were growing and had the potential to expand to all sections of the country. Because the North's system was more scientifically organized and had benefited more from the discoveries of the Industrial Revolution (the use of machines for production purposes), the North gained the upper hand and attempted to ensure its own market and productivity by restricting the economic growth of the South. The South resisted these restrictions because it wanted its economic system to expand throughout the country, and *the North quickly proposed a compromise. The compromise guaranteed the continuance of slavery in states where it was legal, approved of a domestic (within the United States of America) slave trade, committed the U.S. government to pay southern masters for slaves that had escaped and kept Congress from abolishing slavery in the District of Columbia. This compromise did not suit the South*, which recognized that the North would forever be attempting to impose its priorities on the South. The South therefore decided to declare itself independent and leave the Union. That way it could find an unrestricted international market for the goods it produced, it could rid itself of the restrictions imposed on the South by Congress and, above all, it could revive the African slave trade. This would put the South in control of its own economic and political destiny and cheapen the cost it would have to pay for slave laborers (the cost of buying slaves).

After having decided to leave the Union, the South decided to take control of the federal properties in its territory. This explains the attack on Fort Sumter, which marked the official beginning of the Civil War.

During the early years of the War, the South was unquestionably defeating the North. Because many northern whites mistakenly believed the War was being fought to free the slaves, they refused to enlist in the Northern army and failed to function adequately when they were drafted. Things got so bad for the North that, by the middle of 1862, it was almost certain that the War had been lost. *In order to stave off this certain defeat*, Abraham Lincoln, the President of the North, issued the Emancipation Proclamation.

The Emancipation Proclamation did not free the slaves! Since so many of Us are confused on this point, we will repeat: the Emancipation Proclamation did not free the slaves! The person who wrote it (Abraham Lincoln) was not concerned about freeing the slaves. Even if Lincoln had wanted to free the slaves, the Emancipation Proclamation could not have served the purpose because it could not be enforced in the Southern states. The Emancipation Proclamation, then, was not a moral document; it was a desperate military maneuver on the part of Abraham Lincoln. Let Us make a quick analysis of it.

The Emancipation Proclamation declared that if the rebellious states, the South, did not return to the Union by January 1, 1863, all of the slaves in the rebellious states would be free persons. We must remember that when the Emancipation Proclamation was issued two countries were in existence. Both of these countries had its own president and both made its own laws. Additionally, the laws and proclamations of one country had no authority in the other country. In spite of all this, Abraham Lincoln, President of the North, threatened to end slavery in the South on January 1, 1863, even though his laws had no authority or force in the South, even though his army was being defeated in battle by the South and even though he had not freed the slaves in his own country. To the whites in the South the Proclamation was just useless words on a piece of paper. To those people, Black and white, in the North who thought the War was being fought to free the slaves, the Emancipation Proclamation must have seemed like the words of a hypocrite (as the War seemed like the act of a hypocrite). Mr. Lincoln had not even attempted to free the slaves in the North where he had the power to do so, but here he was attempting to do so in a country that was not even affected

10 LESSONS

by his decisions. If anything is nothing, that certainly is.

The Emancipation Proclamation, then, could not have freed the slaves. The very nature of the document and the circumstances that prevailed when it was issued made this an impossibility. However, the slaves in the South saw in the Proclamation an opportunity to free themselves. Before the issuance of the Proclamation, the slaves saw no chance for freedom from either side. Of particular importance, they saw no move or commitment by the North to protect them or support them if they had escaped or organized to defy the southern slave holders. The Emancipation Proclamation, however, was viewed as a possible commitment; one that might support them if they rebelled in some way or protect them if they fled the southern plantation. Therefore, the slaves made some moves that immediately shifted the balance of power from the South to the North and, in the long run, enabled the North to militarily defeat the South and preserve the Union.

What did the slaves do? The slaves freed themselves by failing to continue working on the plantations and by leaving the plantations in large numbers in search of Northern armies (which might protect them) and the possibility of freedom. When the slaves found these armies they provided the officers with strategic military information, acted as spies, fought as soldiers and did the dirty work (like digging ditches) that makes the difference between a successful military encounter and a failure. But, more than anything else, the slaves went on a general strike (they refused to work on southern plantations) that transferred their labor from the southern camp to the northern camp. This transferal of labor meant the difference between victory and defeat for the North (and South).

As strange as it seems, the South counted on Black People as laborers to raise food and money crops that would keep the South's economy functioning and keep the South's army supplied with the food and materials it needed to efficiently carry out the War. These were denied the South when the slaves left the plantations and went to the Northern armies. As a result, the South suffered militarily in three regards: (1) it could not put as many soldiers on the battlefields because some had to remain home in an attempt to see that the work was done that slaves had been doing up to that time (2) it could not keep the soldiers it had in the fields adequately fed, clothed, armed and equipped and (3) the action of the slaves caused some of the poor whites who had been fighting to re-evaluate their condition and decide that they were no longer willing to fight a rich man's war. Clearly, these three results crippled the South to the point where it had no choice but to hold on for as long as it could (hoping for a miracle) and then surrender.

We will repeat at this point that the Civil War was not fought to free the slaves. The War was a white family feud. Unfortunately for them, it got out of hand and led to events that none of the whites who were involved had even dreamed of, the most notable one being the opportunity the slaves got to free themselves.

And We did free Ourselves. The Emancipation Proclamation did not do so, nor did Abraham Lincoln. Abraham Lincoln was a white man. He could have freed the Blacks in the North (those sections that did not rebel) but he failed to do so. It is clear then that he had no intention of freeing the slaves in the South. Lincoln's only concern was in preserving the Union. Under no circumstances would he have even conceived of or considered freeing Black People for moral reasons (morals do not "move" white people). He recognized that slavery was wrong, but he was not willing to do what was necessary to stop that wrong. Also, he recognized that Black People and white people could not live together in harmony, but he was not willing to make the sacrifices that would bring Black People adequate compensation and enable Us to settle Ourselves peacefully as self-governing People. In both these regards then, Abraham Lincoln, like all white people, was a stone racist. He was a white man who made decisions that were aimed at preserving white comforts and standards and the white way-of-life. Many of the Blacks who lived during the 1860s recognized this fact, just as many of Us in the 1970s and 1980s recognize that the "liberal" whites in similar positions are racist to the bone. Whites in the 1860s and whites in the 1970s and 1980s do not intentionally do anything that will substantially benefit Black People. If We happen to get a concession from them or make a "gain", it is because they got caught up in one of their own tricks. We must benefit from Our past by keeping this understanding in mind.

Throughout the War Black People demonstrated a preference for self-government by taking every opportunity available to govern themselves. To give proof of this preference, we will again refer to "The Republic of New Afrika: Its Development, Ideology and Objectives". This publication tells Us that Black People "flocked in large numbers to areas where northern armies had won battles, and confronted the military officers there with a situation that could only be controlled if an immediate government was established. Since whites were not available to run those governments, it was obvious that Black People would have to and had a right to. Thus, in 1864, Edwin Stanton, the white U.S. Secretary of War, and U.S. Army General William Sherman met. The result of that meeting was the issuance of Special Field Order #15, which set aside for Black People a stretch of land from Charleston, S.C. to the country bordering the St. John's River in Florida. In this area, the official order read, 'no white person whatsoever, unless military officers and soldiers detained for duty, will be permitted to reside; and the sole and exclusive management of affairs [of government] will be left to the free people [Black People] themselves.' Similar centers were established in Mississippi, where more than 70,000 Blacks established governments where all property was under Black government and control, and where all Black residents had the inalienable right to liberty. With such settlements as these, on land from South Carolina to Florida and Mississippi that had been declared Ours, We, Black People, settled down to manage Our affairs [and did a good job]." We wanted to continue managing Our affairs, too. We liked governing Ourselves. For this reason We resisted efforts made later on by the federal government to take away Our land and oftentimes only gave it up after We had been defeated in battle by army troops.

II. Reconstruction

The Reconstruction Period (1867-1877) has been very much ignored by traditionalist historians. It has been commonly defined as that period after the Civil War when efforts were being made to re-construct the country, to bring the South and other parts of the country (the North and West) back together again in harmony under one government. We will now define the Reconstruction Period from the perspective or viewpoint of a politically aware Black individual, analyze it as such and determine what lessons that period of Our history holds for Black People.

To adequately understand Reconstruction, We must view it from economic and political perspectives. From an economic perspective, Reconstruction was an effort on the part of the northern capitalist business world to gain control of and transform the business or economy of the South so it would conform to northern capitalist interests. The changes the northern businessmen were interested in, we will stress, were in the areas of control (management) and productivity. Control, naturally, implies that northern businessmen wanted to become the managers and major benefactors (profit makers) of southern business activity. They wanted to initiate changes in the productivity method that would make production more scientific and efficient. They also wanted to apply newly discovered business principles and install a method of production that would get the most out of each hour of work, and establish some manufacturing businesses when they saw the need to do so.

In order to increase the volume (amount) that was produced on the southern farms and plantations, northern businessmen felt it was necessary to release the slaves and theoretically allow them to become part of the industrial work force. This move would cheapen the cost of paid labor by increasing competition among those who were seeking employment and by ridding the businessmen of their responsibility for caring for the welfare of the laborer. Since southern slave owners had to feed, clothe and care for (in medical terms) their slaves, this expense (as minor as it was) would be eliminated.

A key to northern businessmen successfully transforming the economy of the South laid in their ability to control the political life of the South. The northern businessmen needed persons in positions of power and authority who would get laws passed that would be favorable to an industrial type economy. At all costs, they did not want persons in these positions who would be hostile toward them. Thus, the Reconstruction Period is characterized by the emergence of scalawags (northern sympathizers from the South) and carpetbaggers (northern sympathizers from the North) as leaders and respectable figures in southern localities. Such persons would be active economically and politically in order to increase the possibility that the objectives of northern businessmen would be realized.

In addition to controlling the political life of the South for economic reasons, the northern business world had to see that the South was controlled for political reasons as well. The North had fought the Civil War in order to be able to impose their preferences on the southern aristocracy. In the process of so doing, Black People had "freed" themselves. At the end of the War this fact slapped Northerners in the face when they began to realize that, because of these newly freed persons, the South would be entitled to additional representatives in the Congress once it was re-admitted into the Union. With these additional representatives the South, which had lost the War, would be in a position of power in Congress (losers usually don't end up with power) because it would be able to constitutionally dominate the legislative activity of the federal government (determine what laws would be passed and who was responsible for paying the war debts, etc.).

The Congress, which at this time (immediately after the close of the War) was composed only of Northerners and Westerners (Southerners had left the Union, remember) had to decide how to sidestep this possibility. Obviously, they could declare Black People in the South slaves again, but this would not have been a politically astute move and was not desirable anyway. Congress therefore put its stamp of approval on the segment of the Emancipation Proclamation that "freed" the slaves in the South by passing the 13th Amendment to the Constitution. This recognized the freedom of all Black People in the United States and theoretically put the South in a position to return to the Congress with more power than it had had when it left. Congress quickly kept this from happening by delaying the return of the South to the Union until circumstances had been created which were favorable to the victors in the Civil War (that is, the North).

After a couple of years of debating the issues, Congress finally decided to act. In order to counter the increase in the population of the South, and thereby counter or negate its increased representation in Congress, Congress passed the 14th Amendment. (We should mention that congressional representation is determined by the number of free persons, not the number of eligible voters.) The 14th Amendment made the Black People who had been freed by the 13th Amendment citizens of the United States, and was passed in order to make it possible for Black People to vote. With Black People as voters, northern power

10 LESSONS

holders could maintain their control of Congress even with the increased southern representation by seducing Black People into voting for northern sympathizers (Black and white). Thus, instead of more southern planters being elected to Congress, more sympathizers to the northern cause would be elected. In order to insure that southern whites would not interfere with the success of this scheme by forcefully keeping Black People from voting, Congress passed the 15th Amendment, which required the President of the Union to use all of his powers to see that each person was able to exercise his right to vote. Soon afterwards, the southern states were re-admitted into the Union, but northern troops were stationed in the South in order to make sure that political processes would unfold and go the way northern power holders and businessmen wanted them to go.

Finally, Reconstruction was an effort by Black People (who had been put in positions of power by northern businessmen and supported by the might of northern troops) to lay a foundation for turning this country into a real democracy. Up to this point, white people had given a great deal of lip service to the idea of a democratic country, but they had never seriously acted to make it a reality. They never had any intentions of doing so, but in their efforts to use Black People to control/ take away the power of southern whites, they put people in positions to make laws that were sincerely concerned about improving the condition of all persons in America. Black People, in leadership positions and as heads of state governments in the south, called for free public education that was compulsory (whites were shocked. Such had never been seriously considered before this time in the United States), they called for state provided land for the poor, attacks on race discrimination, liberal voting requirements that would drastically increase the number of eligible voters, expanded rights for women, divorce laws (which were unusual at this time), judicial reforms (including mixed juries and manners of selecting judges), wage laws, and abolishment of imprisonment because of failure to pay debts, etc., etc., etc. The northern power holders looked on in disbelief because the efforts of the Black legislators in the south would, in time, cripple the ability of the northern businessmen and politicians to manipulate the common man ("little" people). But because they had more to lose at this time with southern planters in power, they failed to substantially curtail the activities of the Blacks they had put in power. They knew it would only be a matter of time before southern wounds would be healed to the point where northern whites and southern whites could come together and see eye to eye again. Then they would quickly deal with the "niggers."

The efforts of the Black legislators indicate that they did not understand what was really going on in this country during and immediately after the Civil War. Black People seem to have come to the conclusion that a white people's moral crusade had emerged and was going strong. Indeed, there was so much

10 LESSONS   137

happening during this period that We were unaware of that the nature of Our struggle in this country changed. Up to this point We had naturally assumed that white people meant Us no good, so We naturally sought to rid Ourselves of their control by seeking self-government (in one form or another) and Black Nationhood. During the 1860s this assumption apparently went through some changes. Almost all of a sudden We began to think that white people would treat Us right after all. As a result, instead of seeking self-government and Nationhood, many of Us began to seek equality within the American economic and political structure. Our lack of understanding of the real reasons for the passage of the 13th, 14th and 15th Amendments and Our lack of understanding of the real reasons We were put in positions of power during the Reconstruction Era led Us to believe that "equality" was possible, and sent Us down a path of unfounded but magnetic hope that cripples many of Us even today.

We were thinking that white people finally wanted to treat Us right, and that they passed the 13th Amendment to prove their good intentions. We didn't know that they were approving Our "freedom" because it was good for the labor structure that an industrial/capitalist economy calls for. In other words, We didn't know they were approving Our freedom because it put white businessmen in a better position to abuse Us as laborers and increase their profits. We were also thinking that the 14th Amendment was an admission on their part that We should be and had a right to be United States citizens. If We had thought, We would have realized this wasn't true because they could have made Us citizens *immediately after* they passed the 13th Amendment— if making Us citizens had been their intention. Instead, white people waited for 2 1/2 years, and only made Us citizens then in order to use Us to help them reach their political objectives, namely their desire to control the southern planters and aristocrats. They didn't make Us citizens because they wanted to, they made Us citizens because they *had to* in order to carry out their scheme against the south. But We didn't know this, and We didn't know about the 15th Amendment either. We thought the 15th Amendment was an indication of white people's commitment to democracy and individual rights in this country. We didn't know that the 15th Amendment was needed by them to insure that their use of Our votes to bring about the ends they desired were not interfered with. These three amendments, because We were unaware of their true objectives, confused Us to no end.

And then came the roles Black People were allowed to play in the Reconstruction governments and in Reconstruction society. For the first time in American history, Black People were put in positions that are associated with political power in this country. This convinced Us beyond doubt that self-government and Black Nationhood were not necessary. "Why go through the struggle that would be needed to reach Black Nationhood when We were already participating in the governmental processes as citizens of America?"

many Blacks seemed to have asked. Why seek Black Nationhood when Black People were now recognized as governors and lieutenant-governors of states, as senators and representatives in the federal government, as state legislators (lawmakers), as judges, as jurors, as law enforcement officers, etc.? Why seek separation when Black People were now being allowed to socialize with whites, fraternize with whites and romanticize with whites on a basis of equality. Because Black People did not understand what was really behind all of these new developments, We concluded that We had made some gains and that changes had come about that no longer necessitated Us distrusting white people and making preparations to separate from and defend Ourselves against white people. Because We did not understand, Our method of responding to the historical relationship of Black People and white people in America changed from one of resistance and seeking self-determination to one of seeking to integrate. Because We were confused, We began to view mixing with white people and being accepted by white people as Our ultimate objective. If We had only known what was really going on, We would have realized that what was going on was all the more reason why We should resist, separate and go out on Our own. But We did not know, and We acted or responded the way people generally act who do not know; We acted to Our detriment (harm).

This confusion was markedly noticeable in the well-known Black figures of that time, particularly Frederick Douglass and Martin R. Delaney. Douglass, the intellectually brilliant but relatively comfortable forerunner of present-day integrationists like Vernon Jordan and the late Dr. Martin Luther King, Jr., had too much negro in him to allow his brilliance to take him past the point of militant speeches. Mixing with whites, not separating from whites, was what he desired. Delaney, early forerunner of today's militant Black capitalists, had much less negro in him than did Douglass, but he nevertheless adhered to the economic doctrines of American capitalism and proposed that Black People from America should colonize Africa in much the same manner that white people had colonized the "new world". Even though his plan did not include the extermination of the native population, it did reflect an absence of racial consciousness and a disregard for the rights of Black People that would not have been tolerated by a mature Black Nationalist. This type of confusion, at all levels of Black life, continued well into the 20th century without substantial opposition. Too much of it (confusion on the part of Black People) continues to this day.

Thus, politically, socially and otherwise, Black People were experiencing a life that had up to that point been restricted to white people. The changes were so quick and so overwhelming that We hardly had the time to analyze them in any detail. We just accepted the appearance as the thing in fact, and in so doing failed to realize that there was something insubstantial about the "changes" We had gone through and the "gains" We had made.

What was so unreal? What was it about the "changes" and "gains" that We had failed to realize? We failed to realize that, in spite of all the appearances, We were still a powerless People in the midst of hostile northern and southern white people. We failed to realize that the "gains" We had made were not based on Black strengths or Black power, but on reluctant (unwilling) handouts from white people. We failed to realize that, in spite of the appearances, We did not have any power. We had persons in positions that are associated with power (mayors, governors, congressmen, etc.), but those persons and the rest of Black People who were attempting to work through America's system did not have the power itself. As a result, We could propose a law or pass a law, but We did not have the power or ability to enforce that law. When it came to enforcement, We had to turn to white people. As long as white people (in this case northern power holders) had more to gain than to lose by allowing Black People to politicize, socialize and romanticize with white people as if We were equals, then We could continue to do these type things. Once, however, white people (northern interests) stopped benefiting from Black "equality", they could take it away from Us. They could take it away because We were not responsible for Our "equality". We were pawns, to say the least, more incidental to American political life than intentional; Our social and economic gains more ephemeral (imaginary) than substantial (real).

Thus, We were a people without power. We were soon to discover that a people without power are a people who do not have the ability to hold onto their "gains" or control their destiny. We discovered this in the 1870s, and because Our condition is basically unchanged today, We might soon discover this again (in the 1980s/1990s). Let Us then, review this process of 100 years ago and get an understanding of what it means to Black People 100 years later.

(Note: In 1980 Black People are still powerless. Yet, We are constantly talking about the gains We have made and the progress We have made. If We do not establish a base of Black Power by thinking and acting in terms of Black Nationhood, We need not get accustomed to anything better than Hell. Each decade that passes makes reality more and more race conscious and more and more competitive. Reality's message is, "Woe be unto those people (races) who cannot control their own destiny.")

III. White Supremacy

Before the Civil War white people, north and south, did not care about the welfare of Black People. During the War, white people, north and south, did not care about the welfare of Black People. After the War the same was true; white people, north and south, did not care about the welfare of Black People. White people in the north and south who were property owners had a racist outlook that was tinged by economic concerns. In other words, their racism was affected and influenced by economic considerations. White people in the north and south who had no property of note had a racist outlook that was underscored (emphasized) by their ignorance of how those whites who were in power were planning to abuse them as well as Black People. The property holders in the north, because of political and economic necessity and in spite of their racism, put the hated and despised Black People into positions of power in the south. The property holders in the south, because they wanted to regain political power, maintain control of their property and put Black People back in their place, put forces in motion that made it difficult for whites in the north to give adequate support to the Blacks they had put in power in the south. For a while the two sides wrestled with each other, and it seemed that Black People were making "gains". Northern property holders used military power to support their use of Black People in the south, while southern property holders used terrorist activities and organizations like the Ku Klux Klan and the Knights of the White Camelia to discourage Black People in the south from voting and holding public office. Whites in the north, and particularly whites in the south who owned no property of note, were dominated by their racist tendencies, and as a result either supported the efforts of the southern property holders or failed to support the efforts of the northern property holders. As the years passed, the efforts of the southern whites to remove Black People as political factors proved to be more and more productive, but the opposition of southern property holders to the new economic order that was being imposed on them by the northern property holders became less and less intense. Thus, matters were getting to the point where a compromise between the two dominant sides, northern property holders and southern property holders, was possible. By the mid 1870s, this possibility had turned into a certainty. Southern property holders were willing to give up their economic preferences in favor of the economic preferences of the north (which was what the north wanted most), and northern property holders were willing to stop supporting their Black pawns and return political power to the hands of the Southerners (which was what the south wanted most). Through their political representatives they worked on how this process was to be carried through, and took advantage of the presidential election of 1876 to give a look of legitimacy to their scheme. During that election Rutherford B. Hayes, an Ohio "southerner" seeking the presidency, was awarded questionable electoral votes that enabled him to defeat his northern opponent. His election symbolized the reemergence of the south as a politically dominant force in the affairs of the country, the emergence of a new and virtually unopposed economic order in the south and the return of Black People to a position of slavery and abject wretchedness. The year 1877 (when this compromise was consummated or finalized) then, symbolizes the end of the Reconstruction Period and the end of Black "equality" in America. What it should have symbolized also was an end to Black faith in white people and the beginning of massive efforts on the part of Black People to once again get the power We need to keep white people from playing with Us and disregarding Our rights as members of the human family.

Some historians have said that Black People were betrayed by white people in 1877. By saying this such historians mean to give Us the impression that it was the intention of northern property holders to "treat Black People right". However, we must state that Black People were not tricked in 1877. Instead, We were victimized. We were victimized by Our trust in white people and by Our ignorance of what politics is all about in the white world. We could not have been tricked because We had never established Ourselves as a base of Black political power. In fact, we had not even attempted to do so. Instead of looking to Ourselves for substantial support, We had looked to a race of people who did not even look like Us and whose interests were the exact opposite of Ours on critical issues. No, We were not tricked in 1877 because political tricks are used to undermine the efforts of those who are your political equals. During the period immediately after the Civil War, We were not consolidating Ourselves as an independent political force with objectives that revolved around Our needs, therefore We could not have been the political equals of white people. We were the political pawns of white people. As such, there was no need for them to trick Us. Their only need was to use Us, abuse Us and then feed Us to the dogs. In short, their only need was to victimize Us, and this white people did willingly and with a great deal of expertise.

Before closing, We will add that 1877 also symbolized the time when the differences between Black People and white abolitionists were made crystal clear. These differences had always been present, but they had been overlooked and/or ignored by Black freedom seekers who had not realized that the key to successfully seeking freedom lies within the group of people that has been denied its rights and privileges. Black People were sincerely seeking these rights and privileges, but the white abolitionists had other things on their minds, not the least of which were economics (identification with a new economic order and system) and personal esteem. Certainly, at that particular instance white abolitionists and Black People had what seemed like the same enemy, but a common enemy does not mean there is a common struggle (or even a basis for a common struggle). In the end the white abolitionists got what they wanted, but Black People who had struggled alongside them found themselves in virtually the same condition. At some point in the near future, Black People of the 20th century will experience this same consequence (outcome). Black People who are struggling hand in hand with white people are in for a shock. Before they know it, they will be victimized by the very same "comrades" they are struggling with (alongside) today. Before it is too late, before We suffer needlessly again, We should learn and benefit from Our history. Our generations of people and the dominant forces that motivate the people of this generation are no different in any basic way from those of an earlier period. Therefore, We have no reason to expect that, given a similar situation and a similar approach to changing that situation, a dissimilar result will come about. The result of that particular approach is already a part of Our history! To avoid pain We should learn from that and learn from all of Our history. We should stop tying Our destiny in with the destiny of white people who seem to identify with and sympathize with Us, and rely on Ourselves for salvation, regardless of how meager (small) Our resources seem. As We get Our meager resources functioning for Us they will multiply and, in time, become capable of supplying Us with all Our basic needs. Then and only then will We have a power base that We can trust. Then and only then will We have real political power, _Black_ political power.

IV. Back In Our Place

When the Southerners returned to power in the south, they continued to work toward the ends that had been sought by the Ku Klux Klan and other white terrorist organizations. Now, however, they could do so under the mask of "law and order" and they could do so without facing the opposition that the northern army had once represented. They used their now "legal" authority to forcefully keep Black People from exercising their right to vote (by way of grandfather clauses, poll taxes, reading and writing requirements, etc.) or to render the vote of Black People of no use (by gerrymandering or zoning political districts in a manner that would reduce the impact of Blacks who voted as a bloc), and they used their legal powers to complete the job of disarming the Black militias (community self-defense groups) that had developed during the Civil War years and the Reconstruction Period. These left Black People without any semblance of political rights and incapable of defending themselves against the personal attacks white people were habitually inflicting on Black People. Within a matter of months, no one was denying the fact that Black People were as bad off as they had been during slavery times. From having one white man as a master, Black men, women and children now had hundreds of white masters. Any white person, familiar or unfamiliar, could command any Black person to bow to him and take his hat off in a white person's presence. Additionally, there was no activity that a Black person could be involved in that could not be brought to question by almost any white person. Under such conditions, it got so that everybody knew that Black People had rights, but no one was quite certain what those rights were.

The integration years of the 1860s, then, were quickly replaced with the strictest form of segregation. Jim Crow, as this segregation condition was known, was no less bitter and tortuous than the practice of apartheid in South

Africa today. Jim Crow took all Black persons out of the human family and put Us in a hole that was dug by the unreal imagination of white Southerners. We were no longer personal property, the end of slavery had made that possible; but what We were (as far as whites were concerned) is difficult to pinpoint. Whatever We were, Our lives could be taken and it would not excite the conscience or regrets of white people, and injury could be inflicted on Us without an indication of empathy in the eyes or expression of white people. They certainly could not have thought of Us as animals of any degree because humans feel compassion when even the lowliest forms of animal life are injured or attacked. But no such compassion was felt for Black People. It is possible that it is because white people are not completely human. Whether that is true or not, the fact remains that they have acted and continue to act in the most inhumane manner toward Black People. From a people who were beginning to be admitted into colleges and universities in the 1840s and 1850s, white people converted Us into a people who rarely completed the early stages of an elementary education. From a people who were allowed the privilege of serving on juries, white people converted Us into a people who could not realistically accuse a white person of a crime, less still to judge that person in a court of law. From persons who could become state legislators and federal lawmakers, We became persons who could not realistically dream of obtaining anything that resembled power. From persons who had a semblance of social equality, We became persons who were castrated, ridiculed and imprisoned for looking at a white woman or being seen with a white man. There was no work available to Us that We had to be paid for (in fact) and there was no wrong that could be done Us that any person was bound to be punished for. We were, as Ralph Ellison later said, "invisible"; white people knew We were present, they knew We occupied space, had weight and could be seen, but their amazing lack of regard for Us negated all of those qualities and left Us outside of their realm of reality. This lack of esteem made it possible for them to systematically de-humanize Us, and this systematic de-humanization of Us was not to let up until the early 1960s, when Black People hit the streets with massive demonstrations, riots and revolutionary undertakings. White people, though basically unchanged, had to take note of Our plight or suffer untold losses in property and possibly lives. Since they had been caught by surprise, they had to make some quick concessions. These concessions relieved a burden that had been placed on Black People for so long that few of Us could even imagine that We had, at one time, held political positions, attended "white" colleges and intercoursed on a basis of equality with white people. They relieved a burden that had been painfully endured by Black People for so long that many of Us thought these concessions were being made for the first time. Many of Us in the 1960s thought the jobs Black People were getting and the positions We were filling were being filled by Us for the first time, and thought

10 LESSONS

therefore that they were evidence of "progress" or Black "gains". But that is not the case. As in the 1860s, the "gains" of Black People in the 1960s are temporary concessions made by white people in order to control matters until they can get in a position to put Us in Our place again. If they get the opportunity, they will certainly attempt to do just that.

Let us emphasize two points before moving on. The first of these points is that Black People have forced white people to make concessions to Us (even though they have been temporary). These concessions have never been the result of goodwill toward Us on the part of white people! We, Black People, ended plantation slavery in the 1860s and opened the door to new possibilities for Black People. White people in the 1860s did not make these new possibilities for Us. Similarly, WE emerged from the stranglehold of Jim Crow in the 1960s due to Our efforts; white people did not relieve Us of the burden of segregation. Definitely, We have forced concessions; white people have freely permitted none. Our mistake then, in flexing Our power, has been in Our failure to actually go beyond the American scheme of things. Many of Us recognize that whites have no intention of functioning on a basis of equality with Black People, but Our actions always seem to indicate that We view Our destiny as an American destiny. Even though We actually want to be beyond the influence and control of white people, Our actions seem to indicate that We view Ourselves as part and parcel of the American package. Our failure to actually function as if We are in the midst of a hostile population and Our tendency to petition them (white people) instead of organizing Ourselves leaves Us at the mercy of white people, and makes it possible for them to take away all of Our "gains" when it is to their advantage or convenience to do so. We must stop satisfying Ourselves with this combination of concessions and powerlessness. History reveals that people who turn to themselves discover their true strengths and create conditions that cannot be ignored by others. This ability to create conditions that cannot be ignored is the key to making real gains (because it is based on the strengths of the affected people); but with this ability comes the recognition that the most desirable gains must involve political and economic power and political and economic independence. These, then, are what Black People's efforts should revolve around because these will move Us beyond the bounds of white racism, inhumanity and greed.

Secondly, We should understand the circumstances under which Black People became so-called citizens of the United States of America. This will help Us understand what white people think about Us even today. Primarily, We must understand that no white people wanted Black People to be citizens of this country in the 1860s, and that Black People would not have been made citizens of this country if white people had not got caught up in one of their own tricks. Thus, a circumstance, an unexpected monkey wrench in white people's plans forced them to make an emergency adjustment. The result of that emergency adjustment was "citizenship" for Black People. If it had not been for that monkey wrench at that particular time, Black People would not have been made citizens of this country in the 1860s and probably would not be citizens of this country today. This is true for two reasons. Number one, the attitudes whites have toward Black People have not changed in any basic degree for hundreds and hundreds of years, and not one bit since the founding of the United States of America in 1776. Secondly, there has been no historical development since the 1860s that could have forced white people to view citizenship for Black People as a preferable alternative (choice). Thus, in addition to being illegal (see Lesson #7), citizenship for Black People was unintended. This should let Us know even more what white people really think of Black "equality", and end Our nonsense tendencies that are evidenced by calls for integration, equal rights and equal opportunities. Instead, We should be calling to Ourselves, organizing among Ourselves and preparing to make Ourselves the real equals of white people.

So, in the 1870s, less than 10 years after we had been in positions of state and federal authority, We, Black People, were "back in Our place." But, in fact We had been "in Our place" all the time. Even during Our glory days, We were right where white people had put Us. Our "place" was always the place reserved for those who had no political and economic power and no unquestioned human rights or social privileges. In the 1850s, Our "place" was in the cotton fields, so white people positioned Us there. In the 1860s, Our "place" was in positions vacated (left open) by discontented white people, so white people positioned Us there. In the 1870s, Our "place" was once again in the cotton fields, so white people put Us there again. Historically, Our "place" has been wherever white people wanted Us to be. Our "place", in the American scheme of things, is a place of powerlessness. As long as We abide by America's doctrines and theories, that is what Our "place" will continue to be.

V. Meantime, In Africa

During the same general period when the American Union was being re-constructed and Black People in the United States were being put "back in Our place," white people were disrupting the lives of Black People on the African continent also. Because of the rise of capitalism and industrial profiteering, the traditional manner of slavery had become outdated and the slave trade had become no longer necessary. As a result of this, slavery was abolished in most areas that were controlled by white people. It was still necessary for white people to get cheap labor if they were going to make as much profit as possible, however. Therefore, the traditional form of slavery was replaced by a more sinister form of labor exploitation and economic cold-heartedness. The effect of this transformation was felt more intensely on the

African continent than anywhere else. We will, then, briefly explore this development.

The very same economic changes that had led to the Civil War in America also brought about changes in the objectives of white people who had been exploiting Africa for slave labor purposes. Because of the discoveries of the Industrial Revolution, the center of activity of the new economic order became the factory (the old economic order had the plantation as its center of activity). Because factories made use of a substantial number of machines that did a lot of work that humans had done in previous times, it was not necessary to have such a large number of persons working in the factory itself. What became critical was that enough humans had to be working to produce raw materials that were needed at the factory. Thus, the transportation of people from one part of the world to another for labor purposes was replaced by a system of labor that called for the brutal exploitation of workers at the site where raw materials were produced/extracted, the transfer of those raw materials to the place where factories had been established, and the much less brutal exploitation of workers at the factories themselves (the factories were in white countries, and the factory workers were white).

The resources that were needed by the new economic order were most plentiful in Africa. Additionally there was a supply of cheap labor in Africa, particularly now that relatively few Blacks were being shipped away from the continent for slave labor purposes. White people quickly recognized the benefits of having a foothold in Africa, just as they had recognized the benefits of controlling the slave trade 200 years earlier. And, just as a rush followed to control the slave trade, there was a rush to control Africa. Once again, white people were about the business of taking the labor and resources of Africa and mercilessly exploiting them in order to make life comfortable for white people.

As they had done earlier (in the slave trade period), white people used superior weapons and machine power to do basically two things: (1) force Black People on the African continent to work for them and (2) rob and rape the African People of economic resources and services that white people desired. These efforts on the part of white people impoverished Black People even more than We had been impoverished by their earlier acts, and did to the Black People on the African continent what had previously only been done to the Blacks who had been transported to the Americas for slave labor purposes.

First we will discuss the theft of the African People's land. As a result of the slave trade, white people had established their control in certain parts of the continent but, as of 1876, Europeans only controlled approximately 10% of Africa (which is 10% more than they should have controlled). With the recognition of their need for raw materials, though, this percentage increased rapidly. By 1885, only nine years later, more than 25% of Africa was controlled by whites from Europe, and by 1910 whites from Europe had claimed more than 90% of Africa's greatest natural resource. Each European country that was able to do so sought more and more of Africa so rapidly and so greedily until white people had to make an agreement in 1885 to divide Africa among themselves (and thereby hoped to avoid war among themselves). This effort, as the figures indicate and as we noted earlier, was not successful (World War I was fought for control of Africa).

Thus land, the greatest natural resource and the key to all forms of wealth that we are presently familiar with, was robbed from Black People by the millions of acres and used to benefit white people. Millions and millions of acres of land were ruthlessly taken from Us without consideration for Black People and used to supply white people with gold, diamonds, cotton, cocoa, kola nuts (used to make soft drinks like Coca Cola and Pepsi), uranium (used to make atomic weapons), hevea (a source of rubber), ivory and hundreds upon hundreds of other elements and resources. Just as had been the case with the slave trade, Black People were ruthlessly seized and forced to work to produce the goods and extract (take from the ground) the raw materials white people wished for. This drive of white people was so great that, in one African country alone (the area of the Congo that was controlled by Belgium), the population was reduced from approximately 40 million Black persons to less than 8 1/2 million persons in less than 20 years. Thus, more than 30 million Black persons *in this one spot alone* died (were killed/murdered) from overwork, undercompensation and resistance to this new form of slave labor imposed on Black People by white people.

The effects of this new economic order on Black People then is the same as those outlined earlier in this Handbook (see Lesson #4, Effects of Enslavement on Africa). The minor difference is one of degrees, since the pain, suffering and political and cultural disorganization and disintegration were much worse. The major difference is that all of these changes and impositions were being forced onto Black People on the African continent itself. It was no longer directly affecting Africans away from Africa and indirectly affecting those Africans who remained on the continent. Now, the direct impact of white people was being felt all over and the damage it was causing was gnawing at the very root of Black People; at the source of Our essence, at the source of Our spiritual well-being and at the source of Our feeling of oneness with each other. Under the influence of white people at home and away from home, We were taught that We were not the same people (when We were because We are all Africans), that We were all no good, that none of Us could be trusted and depended on, that Our abilities were limited, that Our destiny was in the hands of white people, and on and on and on. Black People lost respect for Black leadership, in Africa and outside of Africa, We lost respect for Black culture, practices and values in Africa and outside of Africa, We lost respect for Black approaches to society and economics, and We developed psychological scars that will be afflicting Us even after We have wrestled Ourselves away from the physical and political domination of white people. Additionally, We had to watch Our land being taken over by white people and being turned into countries according to boundaries established by white people and in complete disregard for the Black ethnic realities that had persisted on the continent for thousands of years. In short, Africa, the land of Black People, became an outpost of Europe, and the African People were destroyed physically, psychologically and spiritually, and converted into non-beings.

Thus, We see that while the abuse and destruction of Black People in the Americas continued, the abuse of Black People on the African continent continued also. We see that during this period (1860-1885), when Black People in the Americas were being prepared for a different type of slavery and economic exploitation, the Black People on the African continent were being taken through the same type changes for the same basic reasons, and with the same basic results. It is the case now, and it has always been the case; white people benefit at Black People's expense and impoverish Black People in the process. Therefore, in addition to the Americas and Africa, we can see a similar progression in the Caribbean areas. We will now briefly review what was going on in the Caribbean during this same general period (between 1865—early 1900s), and then return to America and get an idea of how Black People here were responding to this new slavery that was being imposed on Us.

VI. Meantime, The Caribbean

Since Columbus tripped over the Americas in 1492, the history of the Caribbean (West Indies) has been overdetermined by white people's economic strivings and inhumane tendencies. It began with the extermination of the native population and continued with more or less unsuccessful attempts to make the islands prosperous for the small groups in European countries. Since big profits were not immediately realized in the beginning, the Caribbean became an area where small white farmers and white rejects could get another start in life. Then came the recognition of sugar as a money crop, the uprooting of the small white farmer, the introduction of big time capitalism (as represented by the plantation system) and the mass importation of Black People into the area to do the hard work that producing sugar cane called for. In all parts of the Caribbean one could witness different European powers establishing colonies and institutionalizing legal codes (laws) and social structures that suited them best. Because different nationalities of white people dominated different islands in the Caribbean, the people on the islands were affected by common (the same) historical developments at different times (insofar as dates and years are concerned). The one development that most interests Us right now is the abolition of slavery, particularly as it affected the lives of Black People. However, we could view this in another way. We could say Our primary interest is the change in the economic condition or prospects of white people that occurred during this general time period, and how this change (or changes) affected Black People.

The island of San Domingo was the first island in the Caribbean (also called the West Indies) where slavery was outlawed. This came about as a result of the Revolution that began in 1791 and ended, officially, in 1804, when San Domingo was proclaimed a Black Nation and renamed Haiti. After the Blacks on the island had taken their freedom, they were strangled by the white governments in Europe and the Americas. Because the Revolutionary War, the war for freedom, had damaged the island severely, the island had lost much of its productive capacity and was therefore dependent on trade with other nations if it were to prosper. This trade the whites refused to grant. Instead, the Americans and the British pressured the Blacks on the island into killing all of the French whites who still lived there, while the French themselves plotted to kill all of the Blacks on the island, re-populate the island with new Blacks from Africa and re-institute the slave system. The leaders of Haiti, mostly untrained and unlearned, were skillfully conned and seduced into competing with one another and assassinating rivals, and political problems were created that kept the Blacks in a state of constant wretchedness. Much of the political instability and economic poverty could have been avoided if whites had conducted affairs with Haiti in the manner they conducted affairs with other nations. Instead, they acted as if Haiti was a bastard nation and blatantly plotted against Haiti economically and politically. In that regard, then, whites are largely responsible for the poverty and oppressive conditions that exist in that country (Haiti) to this day.

In 1834 the British abolished slavery in all of the islands they controlled. As was to happen in the United States in the 1860s, this old type slavery was replaced by a new slavery called contract labor. Since the terms of the contract were mostly determined by those who owned property, and since the official meaning of the contract was interpreted by those who owned property, this new slavery, needless to say, adequately benefited the whites on the islands. Meanwhile, the whites in England practically ignored the plight of the Caribbean colonies (since the colonies did not fit profitably into the new economic order that had evolved) and refused to continue to invest in the economic development of the islands. Thus, the whites on the islands were able to use the powers they had to seek their own racist ends without having to answer to the "mother country". They hung onto their traditional prejudices and put up stiff opposition to any changes that even suggested Black equality. They used their laws to harass Blacks and refused to give Blacks land. This forced Black

People to work for the whites for survival (when there was work to be done). Conditions were so bad that the Blacks in some areas, particularly Jamaica, rebelled frequently. As a matter of fact, a major rebellion or revolutionary undertaking in 1865 resulted in the death of thousands of persons. All the Blacks wanted was enough land to make a living on. This the whites of the island refused to give up.

(Remember: the whites in the United States also refused to give Black People land after slavery had been abolished. Everywhere, their response to Black People has been the same. Everywhere, they have refused to recognize Us as human beings with basic human needs that have to be satisfied.)

The same basic developments took place in the French colonies (where slavery was abolished in 1848) and in the Spanish colonies (where slavery was not abolished until the 1880s). The different dates indicate that different white countries were abolishing slavery only after they were able to move into the new economic set-up or were unable to maintain the old. By the time of Spanish abolition, the United States had begun exploring the outside world for markets and other advantages. Since the European powers had begun neglecting their colonies in the Caribbean, the United States saw an opportunity to easily take advantage of the Caribbean people and readily did so. Their initial efforts were of a military concern, since they hoped to use much of the Caribbean to establish American defense bases. But economic interests were to drive the United States also. After 1898, the time of the Spanish-American War, the United States proclaimed itself as the policeman of the West Indies and used all types of excuses to interfere in the affairs of the Caribbean people. The excuses included the "manifest destiny" doctrine, which implied that the United States had a divine (God-sent) mandate to include that area in its zone of influence or national boundaries; the "natural right to expand" doctrine, which implied the same principle but suggested economic expansion as well as political expansion; and the interests of "collective civilization" doctrine, which implied that white people were spreading the gospel of real civilization and progress, and that it was in the interest of all people that this gospel be exposed to them and accepted or adopted by them— even if it meant disregarding the rights of those people who did not want white civilization and progress. The United States practically made the Dominican Republic its own, and carried out underhanded activities against the Haitians from the Dominican part of the island. The United States also purchased the Virgin Islands from the Dutch whites and turned the islands over to the United States Navy, which ruled the islands as if they were military barracks. The people of Puerto Rico, on the verge of gaining their independence from Spain, were re-colonized by the United States, and the people of Columbia saw the United States use the marines to steal part of their country and call it Panama. This theft made it possible for the United States to get the Panama Canal built. These type things were repeatedly done in complete disregard for the rights or welfare of the people on these islands (the overwhelming number of these people were/are Black). They indicate once again that white people are not concerned about the welfare of Black People, and that this lack of concern is particularly evident when white people have interests of their own to pursue.

After the turn of the 20th century, the European powers that had colonies in the Caribbean took a new interest in them. This new interest arose because World War I demonstrated how militarily strategic the islands could be. As a result, new efforts were made to insure that the politics of the islands would be consistent with the political priorities of the "mother country". This meant the selected Blacks must be trained to think white, act white, appreciate white and distrust anything Black. Such Blacks would assist and support the whites who controlled the islands. Meanwhile, the whites on the islands continued to hold their racist ideologies, while the Blacks on the islands who were not hand picked to represent the white power structure were "educated" and exposed to white priorities enough to convince them that Black People were generally no good and that Blacks in the Caribbean had no ancestral attachment whatsoever to Black People in other parts of the world, particularly Africa. In fact, the Blacks on the islands, when compared to Black People in other parts of the world, were well-educated; but it was an education that caused them to separate themselves from the rest of the Black world and consider themselves superior to other Black People. It was an education that led them to believe that they were different from Black People, that they were Europeans, and this feeling was not to undergo any major changes until after World War II. Thus, the education brought to Black People on the islands by white people (particularly the French and the British) drove a wedge between them and Black People in other parts of the world. But it was something white people were doing in general to Black People who were dominated by whites, and is all the more reason why We, Black People, should play it safe and act based on the assumption that white people are not concerned about the welfare of Black People.

The renewed interest of whites in the islands meant an increased disregard for the welfare of the Blacks on the islands. The white soldiers who were stationed on the islands were housed in certain areas, and Black People were restricted from being in these areas. Additionally, the attitudes the soldiers held toward Black People made those on the islands feel more worthless, which made it easier for them to accept the wretched economic conditions they were forced to live in. The mother countries never invested in the welfare or development of the islands themselves, but money was poured into the islands for the purpose of making the white defense bases as effective as possible. Had it not been for their military importance, then, the islands might have been ignored totally forever or forgotten by white people. Considering how this affected the lives of Black People on the islands, it probably would have been better that way.

The picture should therefore be clear to Us. Black People throughout the world were being taken through the same abusive changes at different dates, but during the same general time periods. The particular circumstances that Black People in different parts of the world had to deal with were somewhat different, but the general condition or state of affairs of Black People in all parts of the world was (and is) essentially the same. Not only that, but we can state as a fact that these conditions were brought on by white people who had dominated Black People and established a legal and social system which was forced on Black People and which was designed to keep the whites prosperous (and to keep the Blacks under control. Keeping "order" is almost synonymous with keeping Black People under "control"). Wherever there are appreciable numbers of Black People who have been dominated by white people, We can observe certain attitudes and tendencies and outlooks that have been drilled into Us by white people/white systems. For example, Black People in the United States fear the power of white people, think white people are smart, are ashamed of "niggers", are suspicious of Blacks from the Caribbean, feel superior to Blacks from Africa and have little knowledge of Black People in other parts of the world, etc. Meanwhile, Black People in the Caribbean areas fear the power of white people, think white people are smart and cultured, are ashamed of "niggers", are suspicious and distrustful of Blacks from the United States and feel superior to Blacks from Africa, etc. Essentially the same is true of Blacks from Africa who have had extensive contact with white people. Blacks in Africa fear the power of white people, think white people are smart and technologically advanced, are ashamed of their "backwardness", have mixed feelings about Blacks in the Caribbean and feel superior to Blacks in the United States, etc. These responses to racism that have been programmed into Black People all over the world by white people keep Black People unwilling to confront white people and their system, keep Black People feeling that We cannot be successful in Our undertakings without white people's input and keep Black People disunited as a Race because We remain distrustful of one another, suspicious of each other and doubtful about each other's ability to function in a responsible and efficient manner. We must overcome such attitudes and tendencies (We must make conscious efforts to keep them from determining what We do), get to know each other through direct contact (contact that produces knowledge that is not based on what white people tell Us), and develop an ideology that outlines objectives that Black People all over the world can be working toward (within the framework of each group's particular circumstances). In the process of doing these things We can effectively control the ability of white people to dominate Us and confuse Us, and enable Ourselves to build the institutions and structures which We have determined are critical to the well-being of Our race.

VII. Back Into Ourselves

Since 1860, events had taken place so quickly in the United States that few people were able to immediately realize the full impact of what had happened. For forty (40) years prior to 1860 people had had reason to expect a Civil War (or something of that nature) to break out, but few had expected the outright hostilities to last as long as the War did. In fact, it was during the Civil War that a string of quick turnabouts began that should have left most people wondering if they had ever understood the major forces operating in this country. First, the North turned certain defeat into certain victory in a matter of months. Secondly, Black People were made citizens of the United States, given the right to vote and placed in positions of power in the South. And, just as quickly, Black People were stripped of their "rights", removed from positions of power and re-enslaved (under a new type of economic system).

The first two turnabouts were totally unexpected by white people. To them America was a land of liberty, freedom and opportunity, but it went without saying that these things were intended for white people, first and foremost. Additionally, it went without saying that the misunderstandings that emerged among white people as they attempted to get "liberty, freedom and opportunity" were misunderstandings involving white people only that would be solved by white people without any real input from non-white people. Thus, after the first two years of the Civil War white people were pretty much convinced that the South, through war, had convinced the North that the South had a right to break away from the Union and govern itself. Whites were surprised then, when all of a sudden, the North took command of the War, and whites refused to recognize that Black People were responsible for this turnabout. It was inconceivable (to white people) that northern white leaders would "dishonor the race" by substantially involving Black People in white people's affairs. Whites became even more unsettled when white leaders in the North gave these same uninvolved and negligible Black People the right to vote and placed them in positions of power in the South that made it possible for Black People to control southern whites and make laws that white people had to live by. The third turnabout, the return of white people to power and the putting of Black People "back in their place", settled the concerns that had been aroused in white people by the first two turnabouts. As far as white people were concerned, this third turnabout put everything back in order. Without having really understood what had actually taken place, they felt certain, once again, that America was a "white man's land."

Without having really understood what had taken place, the final turnabout also caused Black People to feel certain, once again, that America was a "white man's land." For the most part Black People had felt this way before the Civil War, but as was stated earlier, events that took place during the Civil War and Reconstruction Period caused too many Blacks to hope and act as if this were not the case. Thus, some Blacks began to look forward to the day when they would become full-fledged Americans. As white people in this country waged war against Black People by lynching Us on tree limbs and in big pots, frying Us on woodpiles, shooting Us and castrating Us, etc., and as the United States government was systematically killing and collecting Black persons who resisted the attacks of white people in America's jails, the Black nationalist leanings of Black People began to dominate their thought patterns again. Some sincere but not well-advised Black nationalists sought peace with this country. Thus, in 1880 Henry Adams petitioned Congress for Black People's rights in the south and "for a territory to be set apart for Us [Black People] to which We could go and take Our families and live in peace and quiet. Similar peace offerings were made in the 1890s. By the 1900s, however, Black nationalists had recognized that a peaceful overture to America would not be respected (by white people). Therefore, Brothers and Sisters began to get back into their Blackness and use that as the rallying ground and the fortress of strength that would carry Us to real freedom and self-government." (quoted section taken from "The RNA: Its Development, Ideology, Objectives.)

Two of the Black individuals who struggled day-in and day-out to carry Black People to real freedom were W.E.B. DuBois and Marcus Mosiah Garvey. Early in his life, DuBois was rather confused on the issue of race relations in this country. He thought the solution to segregation and inequality was a matter of systematic investigation, that ignorance alone was the cause of race prejudice and that scientific truth could eliminate this prejudice. He was to discover, however, that intelligent white people were (and are) as prejudiced as ignorant white people, and that their prejudice remained even in the face of mountains of evidence to the contrary. DuBois therefore began to take a Black approach to the liberation of Black People. He latched onto and expanded the idea of Pan-Africanism (which was introduced by H. Sylvester Williams, a Black man from Trinidad) as a result of recognizing that the destiny of Black People must of necessity lay in the abilities, activities and determination of Black People themselves. He was the leading force in a series of Pan-African congresses (meetings) that brought Black leaders together from all parts of the globe, and he constantly ran into conflict with integrationist-minded organizations like the NAACP (even though he was editor of the NAACP's major publication, the Crisis magazine). DuBois did not hate white people and would have preferred to co-exist peacefully (live in harmony) with them, but the lessons he learned as the years passed convinced him that this was probably a little too much to hope for. To demonstrate where his true allegiance was (and to get away from the hypocrisy that characterizes white people), DuBois left America and spent the final years of his life living in Africa and working on a series of encyclopedia on the history of African/Black People. These encyclopedia, he hoped, would enable Black People to obtain an accurate view of Our history. Such information would better prepare Us to act independently of white people and function in a manner that would be beneficial to Our Race, the Black Race.

Marcus Garvey, a self-educated Black man from the Caribbean (Jamaica), brought to the African/Black People of the Americas a sense of pride in being Black. He formed two organizations, the Universal Negro Improvement Association and the African Communities League, whose combined purpose was to unite all Black People of the world into one great body which would establish a country and government absolutely their own. In his book, Philosophy and Opinions, Garvey asked himself, "Where is the Black man's government? Where is his king and kingdom? Where is his president, his country and his ambassador; his army, his navy, his men of big affairs?" He could not answer these questions affirmatively, so he decided to do all he could to make the Black man's government, king, kingdom, president and men of big affairs. In the process he taught the people he came into contact with to think big again. He reminded them that they had once been kings and rulers of great nations and would be again. His cry, "Up you mighty race, you can accomplish what you will", was a call for the Black man and woman to reclaim Our best self and re-enter the mainstream of world history.

And Black men and women, seeking nationhood and self-determination for Black People, did begin to re-enter the mainstream of world history. Though white people tried desperately to deny Us entry and left Us out of their versions of history, We were there nonetheless and We were making an impact based on the principle that Black values, Black concepts and Black self-government were just as valid as white values, concepts and government. The efforts of Marcus Garvey, W.E.B. DuBois and thousands upon thousands of other such Black persons of the early 20th century touched the very fiber of the Black masses who heard them because they encouraged the Black masses to be themselves and appreciate themselves. If more Black persons did not grab onto the teachings of such persons, it was only because they were not exposed to those teachings or because they were exposed to white propaganda that created an inaccurate image of Black nationalists and Black nationalism. In fact, white propaganda, that conspiracy of the white power structure, has far too many Black persons distrustful of so-called "radical" and "militant" Black persons and ideas. This propaganda conspiracy also has many Blacks thinking that Black objectives are unreal and unattainable. As such, it is largely responsible for many of the civil rightist, integrationist and patriotic activities of a large number of Black individuals over the years. This white propaganda conspiracy is losing its effectiveness, however. More and more Blacks are beginning to think for themselves, and as they think for themselves they recognize that the ideas of persons like Garvey and DuBois deserve the careful attention of all of Us. As We begin to think for Ourselves, We will recognize that white people have everything to gain by keeping Us within their ideological framework, and that We can benefit Ourselves in substantial (real) ways only if We go beyond their ideological framework. As a result of making these recognitions, We will have no problem accepting Blackness, Black Nationalism and Black Internationalism as the practical ideology for Black People who want real equality.

The teachings of Garvey and DuBois represent the two major trains of thought in the Black world during this (the 20th) century. Garvey's influence has been (and still is) overwhelming in the United States of America. In order to check Garvey's influence, the United States government attacked his credibility and framed him on bogus (unjust) charges in the 1920s. But before Garvey could be destroyed, Cyril V. Briggs and the African Blood Brotherhood were preaching Black nationalism too. The African Blood Brotherhood was attacked in the 1930s, but before it could be destroyed Elijah Muhammad had adapted the Black nationalist ideology and established the Nation of Islam, which was popularized among the Black masses in the 1950s and 1960s by an ex-hustler named Malcolm X. Basically the same Black nationalist objectives are being sought today, and are represented most effectively by the Republic of New Afrika. Certainly, Black People's desire for and efforts to gain self-government are two parts of Black History that white racist historians and politicians have not been able to effectively undermine or cover up.

Pan Africanism has upset the ideology and practice of white supremacy even more. DuBois' activities imposed his influence and train of thought on such later to be African leaders as Kwame Nkrumah (President of the country called Ghana), Patrice Lumumba (the Congo), Sekou Toure (Guinea), Julius Nyerere (Tanzania) and Milton Obote (Uganda), etc. Because they were sincere to the Pan-Africanist concept, Nkrumah and Lumumba put in motion a plan that would politically unify their two countries as the first phase in the development of a United States of Africa. Even more, however, is that Pan-Africanism gave many African leaders an ideological basis for their independence movements, movements that have brought about drastic changes in the white world. These movements have forced white people/governments to make concessions to Black People that have actually changed the power relationship between the two. No longer can white people/white governments indiscriminately impose their preferences and mannerisms onto Black People. When they attempt to do so, whites run up against Black People who have learned how to effectively resist them. In fact, Black People have made such giant strides that it is certain that future relationships between Black People and whites will be based on mutual (Black and white) fear/respect and real equality. How long it takes this condition of real equality to reach maturity will be determined by Black People. If We take a shaking knee, hat-in-hand approach to relating to and competing against white people and question the validity of Blackness as the basis of Our actions, We will enable white people to prolong (stretch) their period of domination. If, on the other hand, We get more into Ourselves and assert Ourselves as Black People representing a Black Ideology and viewpoint, We will quickly remove white people from their dominant position and establish Ourselves as the major factor in the economic, political, cultural and psychological destiny of Black People.

VIII. Meantime, World Events

While We were getting back into Ourselves, events were coming of age throughout the world that were to make Black People realize that Our task (self-determination, real equality) was not as difficult as many had imagined. It was a difficult task, to say the least, but things were happening that made it obvious that white people could be made to bear the responsibility for their devilish conduct. Events were taking place that convinced people of all colors that white people could be removed from positions of power and domination and that these positions could be adequately assumed by other people. Three of the events that made people aware of these possibilities were World War I, the Russian (or Bolshevik) Revolution and the Chinese Revolution.

World War I made it clear that white people are too greedy and insecure to function cohesively as a race of people. At a time when Africa was so bad off that it could not defend itself, white people were unable to totally take control of the continent because they (the white nations) were fighting among themselves (each of the white nations wanted all of Africa's "goodies"). Had the whites been able to work together as a race for only 50 years, they would probably have been able to control the destiny of the African People and determine who would benefit from the wealth of the African continent. Instead, their greedy bickering gave the African People the time Africans needed to get themselves half-way together, so much so that nowadays the Africans can be more in control of their destiny than the white superpowers are.

During the final year of World War I, the Russian Revolution exploded and shattered the myth of white unity even more. As a result of the Russian Revolution, two white oppressive economic doctrines (capitalism and "communism") actually began competing with each other for control of the world. Even more, these doctrines represented somewhat different ethnic branches of western (European) white people. Eastern Europeans, after many years of being ignored and teased by western Europeans, were now asserting themselves and expressing pride in their ethnic development. As far as western

Europeans were concerned, the eastern Europeans were rather uncultured, but after the Russian Revolution eastern Europeans had to be recognized and respected because they could seriously challenge the western Europeans for influence in newly emerging countries, countries that were rebelling against being dominated and were seeking to control their own affairs and destiny. If such countries needed economic assistance or military aid, it was now possible for them to choose the lesser of two evils or, if possible, play the two evils against each other (by getting one branch of the Europeans to help them defend themselves against the other branch, for example). Such countries no longer had to accept the terms that were offered them by western European governments and businesses. Clearly, white people were not as unified as they wanted other people to think they were. This realization gave many non-white dissidents and rebellers the faith and confidence they needed to carry out a prolonged (long-lasting) struggle against white domination.

In the early 1920s, a revolution moved into high gear in China that was to radically change the nature of the world power relationships. It enabled the Chinese people to overthrow the puppet (white-manipulated) government in China and establish a government and a social order that was based on Chinese values and needs and Chinese perceptions of politics and economics. As a result, for the first time in modern history, a non-white world power existed that took non-white approaches to aiding newly developing countries. Consequently, non-white people who were struggling against oppression had the option of not having to deal with white people at all. As a result of the Chinese Revolution, it was clear that white people were not the only people who could determine their destiny. Yellow people were doing so, and with a degree of hard work, dedication and intelligent politicking, other people of color, particularly Black People, could do the same.

Thus, the end of the 19th century was noteworthy not only because it witnessed concrete efforts on the part of Black People to get back into Ourselves (Our Blackness), but because it ushered in events that shook the foundation of white world domination. The beginning of the 20th century exposed the cracks in white people's armor and set Black People to rebelling with an intensity that had not been present since the days of the maroons and other early Black Nationalists. The confusion that had been characteristic of Black People since Reconstruction did not disappear; in fact it continued to dominate the activities of most Blacks. However, those that followed their natural tendencies, those that were exposed to persons such as Marcus Garvey and ideas such as Pan- Africanism, and those who explored Black History and analyzed the traditional relationship between Black People and white people recognized the necessity of taking a Black approach to eliminating the wretched conditions that were characteristic of Black People's lives. Such persons realized that Black People have to be concerned, first and foremost, about the welfare of Black People, and revolved their thoughts and actions around that realization.

LESSONS 7 & 8
LESSON OUTLINE

I. The U.S.A., 1870-1930: A Brief Summary
II. World History: World War II - 1970
  A. Revolution in Africa
    1. "Within a decade the African Revolution and its liberation movements have shattered the colonial empires." K. Nkrumah
  B. Counter-Revolution in Africa
    1. Destruction of Leaders
    2. Military Audacity
    3. Economic Boycotts/Destruction
  C. Rebellion in the United States
    1. "Civil Rights" rejected again by white people
    2. Emphasis on "community control"
  D. Revolution in the United States
    1. Nation of Islam
    2. Black Panther Party
    3. Republic of New Afrika
    4. Others
  E. Counter-Revolution/Rebellion in the United States
    1. Counter-Intelligence Program
    2. LEAA (Law Enforcement Assistance Acts)
    3. Government Illegalities
    4. Gun Control
    5. Other Abridgements of Rights
  F. Self-Determination in the Caribbean
    1. Cuba
    2. Jamaica
    3. Steps Toward Economic Interdependence
  G. Counter-Revolution in the Caribbean
    1. Military audacity
    2. Economic Pressure
    3. Political Underhandedness

I. The U.S.A., 1870-1930: A Brief Summary

The years immediately before the turn of the 20th century were rough on Black People. During the 1870s, white people had done all they could to put Us "back in Our place". From an economic point of view, this meant keeping Black People generally poverty stricken, while politically it meant keeping Black

People powerless, unable to legally defend Ourselves and disunited as a race of people. From a racial perspective, keeping Us in Our place meant providing ignorant and unintelligent white people with some human beings they could step on and look down on, and it meant providing poor whites with a reason for maintaining their ties to the white ruling class. Overall, keeping Black People "in their place" meant harassing and pressuring Black People to such extremely inhumane degrees that We would suffer psychologically, genetically and biologically, and eventually die off "by the 1920s," as one white editor put it.

This attack on Black People was not a helter-skelter or loosely organized affair. It was carefully planned by white people and white governments, and involved the systematic elimination of Black People as direct factors in the American political life. This meant that Black People had no legal power to control the destiny or well-being of Black People. Black People were threatened, maimed, shot and lynched into believing that Black People should not concentrate on political matters at all, and thus came to view economics as the sole key to Black survival. Since economic pursuits in any social system are determined and controlled by political policies and decisions, one can see that, politically speaking, the years immediately before the turn of the 20th century witnessed the de facto (in fact) re-enslavement of Black People by white people.

The same is true in other respects. White people, north and south, used their brute force, mob tendencies and newspapers to psychologically re-enslave Black People (it would probably be more accurate if we said white people used these things to re-enforce the psychological enslavement of Black People that had been a result of the slave years). White people strengthened and solidified their attempts to make Black People question themselves and their worth as human beings. These same white people also instituted measures that were designed to keep Black People supporting and financing the day-to-day needs of white families. Black People were forced to work sharecropping jobs which made white people rich and/or economically secure; Black People were forced to pay taxes to support governments that provided goods and services to white people but not to Black People; Black People were forced to work in factories at wages that made white people rich and/or financially secure; Black People were railroaded to prisons and forced to work on jobs that made white individuals rich and provided revenue for white governments; and so on. Black People went from slavery under one name to slavery under another name, but the name was all that changed. A Black person's life and "freedom" were still not worth a play penny, and white people took advantage of that fact to abuse, kill and maim Black People at will. Other races of people under similar circumstances might not have survived, but Black People did. Because of the mental strength and intelligence of Our Forefathers, because they were able to depend on each other and because of the shortcomings of white people and their economic system, Black People were able to stumble through the late 19th century and into the 20th. Let us touch on this process briefly.

It did not take Black People long to recognize that white people were attempting to re-enslave Black People. In every branch of the government (executive, legislative and judicial) and on all levels Black People could see white people positioning themselves to make life hell for Black People. However, because they had ignorantly put so much confidence in the federal government, Black People had failed to take some measures they should have taken during the Reconstruction years (when whites were disunited and at odds with each other) and therefore found themselves almost defenseless once the whites overcame their differences and went into action against Black People. For example, Black militias had been formed during the 1860s, but Black People waited for the government to arm and train these militias instead of making it their business to arm and train the Black militias themselves. Additionally, the Blacks who had been in positions of power during the late 1860s concentrated on laws and policies that would be beneficial to the country as a whole. This was admirable, but it failed to account for the fact that Black People needed special attention because they were in the midst of hostile white people. In all areas, along all lines Black People should have been putting into effect catch-up and contingency (emergency) measures that would have enabled Blacks to hold their own against white people under any circumstances. But, because they were confused about recent developments (we discussed these earlier-Reconstruction, the 13th, 14th and 15th Amendments) that had taken place in this country, Black People put their faith in the very same white people who had enslaved them, maimed them and ignored their welfare— and found themselves paying a dear price for doing so.

As it became clearer that white people had made it their public policy to attack, kill, maim, abuse, exploit and generally disregard the human rights of Black People, Black People had no practical choice but to fall back on their learned ability to make the best of a bad situation. In times past, while on the African continent and in the Americas, Black People had been confronted by circumstances that were beyond their immediate control, but instead of allowing such circumstances to completely overwhelm them and lead to their extermination, Black People adapted responses and mannerisms that would ensure their survival until they had gained enough stability or established a strong enough foundation to begin asserting themselves or acting in a manner that was more representative of their real sentiments and perceptions. Thus, Black People in the years immediately before the turn of the 20th century responded to white people's attacks by smiling, submitting and trying to "hide" or "fit in". Under no circumstances did Black People want to get white people upset, so Black People did all they possibly could to operate within the impossible limitations imposed on them by white people. White people did not want social equality between the two races and claimed to not want any kind of race intermingling, so Black People made it their business to be born among other Blacks, to grow up and mature among other Blacks, to succeed or fail among other Blacks and to bury each other among other Blacks. White people did not want Black People to accumulate any worthwhile property or become economically self-sufficient, so much of the economic life of Black People was marked by fishing, planting family gardens and getting robbed "on credit" while they worked on white people's farms, in white people's houses and while they did menial chores for ridiculously low wages. But, what white people failed to recognize was that Black People had become accustomed to pacifying their basic needs instead of satisfying them, so much of the little Black People did receive as earnings could be saved or used for enjoyment. The savings helped give a feeling of material achievement to those who saved, and those who could spend pennies every now and then to enjoy themselves felt a small degree of relief if not satisfaction. These feeling, coupled with the degree of spiritual contentment that regular activities such as going to church and participating in recreational activities (playing ball, singing, dancing, etc.) provided and the hopelessness that drinking liquor and hanging on street corners were evidence of, go a long way toward summing up the Black life-style and experience in this country prior to the 1900s.

What Black individuals saved was never used to invest in a business unless it was a business that catered to the Black market in those areas that were neglected by the white business establishment. Nonetheless, Black People were able to develop a fragile Black economic structure, but it was one that was a bastard child of the white economic structure. Within that structure, Black People were allowed to cut and straighten each other's hair for pay, feed each other for pay, entertain each other for pay, bury each other for pay and do various other minor things for each other for pay; but Blacks were not allowed to start any manufacturing or agricultural concern (business organization) that could provide the haircutter, hair fixers, cooks, morticians, entertainers or "jacks of all trades" with the goods and services they needed to keep their little business activity going. These goods and services, including the necessary utilities, tools and items (like clippers, scissors, cookware, etc.) had to be obtained from white people. White people therefore controlled the lifeline of the bastard Black economy, and Black People, particularly business persons, acted as if they were satisfied with this arrangement because they were too weak and vulnerable (open to attack) to act otherwise.

Above all, Black People did not seriously rebel during this period. This is not to say Black People did not reach their boiling point during this period because there were many instances of Black resistance to white atrocities, but such efforts were mostly poorly organized responses of desperation that were begging for relief rather than seeking to improve the general condition of Black

People. Black People avoided the involvement that a well-organized resistance movement would have required. After all, to put together a serious resistance effort would have caused Black People to blow their "cover"; it would have made it more difficult for Black People to "hide" or "fit in", and it would have let white people know that We/Black People were not content with Our condition and thereby make white people less comfortable around Us, more suspicious of Us and more hostile and brutal toward Us. In order to convince white people that We were not a threat to them, We shied away from any type of aggressive actions. In fact, We did such a good job of convincing white people that We were satisfied that We almost convinced Ourselves as well. But the hell white people constantly put Us through made it impossible for any of Us to honestly think such a thing. At the same time though, the fear of what white people might do to Us made it possible for Us to be more content than We should have been. The fear of what white people might do to Us forced Us to adapt attitudes of almost total submission, to emphasize the role of "the man upstairs" and the morality of "turning the other cheek", and to sincerely follow and believe in the teachings of such persons as Booker T. Washington. We became not only willing but eager to follow such persons, and this fact indicated that We had allowed emotions such as fear to interfere with Our desire to analyze Our condition and act in Our best interest. It indicates that We were forgetting why We had adapted the submissive responses in the first place, which is another way of saying We had allowed fear of what white people might do to Us to cause Us to lose sight of Our objective and Our purpose. Fortunately, individuals such as W.E.B. DuBois and Marcus Garvey began to put Us back on the right track; to remind Us of what We were supposed to be about and to establish organizations and bases of operations that would make it less difficult for Us to reach Our objectives. The impact of individuals such as these is the major difference between Black People of the late 1800s and Black People of the early years of the 20th century.

However, world events directly affected the lives of Black People in the early years of the 20th century also. World War I, which was mentioned earlier, caused Black People to have greater access into the white economic system. This access proved to be temporary (for a short time only), but it did enable Black People to work on jobs that had been traditionally reserved for white people, and resulted in economic "progress" for a few Black persons. As we stated, this was only temporary, but it established a precedent and laid the basis for greater employment for Black People in later years. In short, then, World War I had the direct affect of increasing Black People's ability to purchase goods and services. We must remember, however, that Our increased ability to purchase goods and services did not change the attitudes of white people toward Us, did not break down any of the traditional barriers that nourished racism and did not change the general condition of Black People.

Most Black People remained in the rural ("country") areas, but a large number of Us headed for "the city". Those who remained on the farms continued to barely survive by working, when possible, for racist white people and by pacifying their basic needs. Those who headed for "the city" crowded into ghettoes and barely survived by working, when possible, for racist white people and by pacifying their basic needs.

America's response to the Russian Revolution had the impact of making many Black persons anti-communist. The American government put out anti-communist propaganda, and Black People, in Our continuing efforts to convince white people in America that We were no threat to them, adapted America's anti-communist line. If We had been sensitive to Our position in America and the rest of the world, and if We had taken positions based on how events and occurrences would affect Us, We would not have taken an anti-communist nor a pro-communist stance. We would have realized that Russian communism is as much about white world domination as American democracy and American capitalism are, and that neither of them is concerned about the welfare of Black People.

Whatever affected America in general affected Black People also, but not in the same way nor to the same degree. We were always the exception to the trend (whatever the trend might be), yet never entirely unaffected by the trend. Thus, as white people speculated, schemed, robbed and got rich during the 1920s, Black People were able to get an additional crumb or two. With the coming of what is called the Great Depression, hard times hit the general white population on a massive scale. Black People felt the ripple effect of the Depression, but the Depression did not radically worsen Our condition because We had been experiencing an economic depression since the day We had been forced to come to the Americas and work as slaves. Certainly, the depression years of the 1930s did not improve the condition of Black People any; the Depression did, however, force the American government to institute measures and programs that would relieve the hard times that had suddenly fallen on the general white population. Government work projects were started, social assistance (welfare) programs were initiated, social security funds were established— in short, the white population was given a "new deal". This new deal amounted to the American government forcing the rich to share more of America's goodies (goods and services) with the common white population. Without this new deal, the whites who had been used by the white upper class probably would have lost faith in the capitalist theory of economics. With the new deal, the poor whites were allowed to share a greater portion of America's wealth, and they were convinced to maintain strong ties to an economic system and a class of people that had been parasiting off of them for decades.

The "new deal" was the American trend of the 1930s. However, as was just stated, Black People represented an exception to the trend. Put another way, there was no "new deal" for Us; there was no effort to improve the general condition of Black People. Still, Black People did feel the ripple effect of the programs that were started to help white people, so some Blacks ended up employed on work projects or receiving some other form of social assistance. Thus, the so-called Great Depression did not change the condition of Black People, but because of it some doors to economic assistance that had not even existed before were opened to some Black persons.

In conclusion, the period between 1870 and 1930 is one that casts shame and disgrace on Black People in this country. It does this in spite of the fact that We accomplished a near miracle by surviving one of the most vicious and persistent attacks ever waged against a race of people. We can, then, stand tall for surviving and even being able to make Ourselves representative of the American image, but those accomplishments are almost completely diminished when one compares them with the loss of Our will to assert Ourselves, the loss of Our manhood and womanhood due to fear, the loss of Our desire to be Black and free and Our willingness to unconditionally accept less than was due Us. During this period, We demonstrated a willingness to reject reality and let fantasy guide Us. We began to lose concept of Ourselves as a Race of People and allowed fear to almost totally control Us and push Us toward giving allegiance to the doctrine of the very people who had historically abused Us and misused Us. We allowed fear to cause Us to reject much of the native intellect that had admirably guided Our Forefathers for thousands of years, and let fear render Our ability to reason useless. Certainly, to survive was the most important intermediate step, but to allow survival to become an end in itself was not the intention of the Black People who experienced and struggled against the early years of slavery/hard times. From the earliest times of Our civilized life in Africa until the late 1800s, Black People had been concerned about governing themselves and being the masters of their own destiny first and foremost. Those of Us who lived between 1870 and 1930 seemed to have lost the desire to seek these objectives and seemed to have resigned themselves to being the defenseless doormats of the world. Present and later generations of Black People should understand why they acted as they did, and sympathize with them; but Our understanding and sympathy should not distort the fact that, during this period, Black People shamed a great Black tradition and failed to try to lay an adequate foundation for future generations of Black People. We should seek, at all costs, to avoid a similar period of shame in the years to come.

[Note: We/Black People cannot afford to downplay how Our failures contributed to Our condition during the period just discussed. After all, We were so defenseless against white people because We had failed to take Our welfare into account when We were in positions of power, because We put Our faith in a government that was controlled by white people— a government that had historically demonstrated that it was racist/anti-Black, and because We did not let Our common sense influence Us to arm Ourselves and organize Ourselves for defense purposes (in case the whites who surrounded Us intended to do Us further harm). Because of Our failures, We were not in a position to defend Ourselves adequately when white people went into action against Us; because We could not defend Ourselves adequately We were dominated by fear (that is, thoughts of what white people could do to Us or might do to Us); and because fear dominated Us We allowed submissiveness and survival to become ends in themselves as opposed to being necessary but temporary steps toward an end. Considering all factors, We were at a disadvantage, but the disadvantage would not have caused Us to respond the way We did (by letting fear control Us) if We had made some realistic preparations when We had the opportunity to do so.]

II. World History: World War II - 1970

The late 1800s witnessed the end of the transportation of Black People from Africa to other parts of the world for slave labor purposes. The money-makers who seized control of the discoveries of the Industrial Revolution determined that a new economic set-up would be more profitable for them, so they began to emphasize the transportation of resources (instead of workers) from Africa to the white world, they had slavery outlawed in countries in the white world (like Great Britain, France, the United States of America, Russia, etc.), and they introduced a treacherous form of forced labor (slavery) on the African continent itself (where the resources were located). Entire ethnic groups or tribes of Black People were enslaved on the spot and forced to work for the benefit of white people and to the detriment of Black People. The work the Blacks were forced to do consisted mainly of extracting precious metals and resources from African land. These metals and resources kept factories operating that gave employment to millions of white families; they kept food in white people's stomachs and clothes on white people's backs, they provided white people with many of the conveniences they desired, they stabilized white governments and they made "law and order" attainable in parts of the white world. However, white people have been conditioned to hoard and feel insecure (see Lesson #1), and this conditioning manifested itself during the late 1800s in spite of the fact that white people were accumulating wealth like never before. The various white nations were rapidly taking control of more and more of the African's land, but each white nation began to want what another white nation had seized control of. The different white nations began to confront one another and challenge one another for the rights to certain areas, and were on the verge of outright hostilities when, in 1885, they got together in Germany and decided to split most of Africa up amongst themselves. This theft and division of Africa, which was intended to keep the whites from going to war with each other, gave certain parts of Africa to a designated country and resulted in parts of Africa being called names such as German East Africa, British East Africa, French Congo, Belgian Congo, Spanish Guinea, etc. But, this division did not eliminate the greed, insecureness and hoard tendencies of white people. Each white nation continued to want what another white nation had; in fact, their mutual envy and greed were so great that, by 1914, they had decided to take sides and settle the issue by shooting it out. This shootout, where the winners would get the rights to all of Africa, is commonly referred to as World War I. [Note: As it was in the 1900s, so it was in the 1700s and 1800s. Review Section IV of Lesson #4.]

White people made war on each other in 1914, but they had been making war on Black People in Africa long before that time. Millions of Blacks had been physically molested and died as a result of the slave trade, and hundreds of millions had been molested in other ways as white people ruthlessly and eagerly collected Black persons and shipped them to the white world, where they were forced to work for white people. The decision by white people in the 1800s to enslave the Blacks on the African continent itself meant additional pain and suffering for a People whose life-style and civilized ways had already been practically demolished. As a result of more than 1000 years of being hunted down by whites, first eastern whites and then western whites/Europeans, Black People on the African continent had become politically disunited and suspicious of one another and economically backwards (much of the economic backwardness was due to the fact that Black People/Africans were not allowed to benefit from the discoveries of the Industrial Revolution). Their culture had been viciously assaulted and maligned but they managed to maintain rather strong allegiances to their forefathers in that regard. Unfortunately, they were forced to give up much more than they managed to hold on to, so much so that, overall, they were becoming only a little more than physical images of the People who had once dominated that part of the world.

By the late 1800s, Black People had been hunted for so long and their lives (political, economic and psychological stability) had been disrupted so much that they were virtually powerless against the calculated efforts and machines (including weapons) of white people. Black People in many parts of the continent were resisting the invasion of the whites from Europe, but their chances of succeeding were minimal because they had too many disadvantages to overcome. If the Europeans had been able to work together as a race of people against the Africans for only 50 years after the late 1800s, they probably would have gained almost complete control of that part of the world. But as we have seen, white people were unable to demonstrate that much unity, so African People were given the time they needed to get around many of their disadvantages, organize themselves politically and militarily and successfully challenge white people for control of the Black continent.

Evidence of the weakness of the African People at the turn of the 20th century is that, out of more than 50 countries on the African continent, only one was under the control of the native population. That country was Ethiopia. (Liberia was "free", but it was not under the control of the native population. As such, it was more a colony of the United States of America that was overseered by former slaves than an independent nation.) As late as World War II (1930-1945), the same was true. Black People all over the African continent were being imposed on by white people whenever white people felt like doing so. Black People were being whipped, forced to work, starved, policed, killed, raped, robbed and psychologically abused as a matter of course. Their pleas of mercy were ignored, if heard at all, by the sadistic whites who were abusing them. For all intents and purposes, the Black People on the African continent, just like the Black People in the Americas and just like the Black People in the Caribbean and just like the Blacks who happened to be in Europe, were powerless from a political point of view. But the years immediately after World War II were to bring about drastic changes in this regard. During those years, Black People in all parts of the world, but particularly in Africa, were to get together, recognize the power they had and rapidly upset the world order that had been established by white people.

The doctrine of Pan-Africanism played a profound role in the re-emergence of the Black People on the African continent. In 1945, a Pan-African congress (meeting) drew Black representatives from across the globe and signalled the beginning of co-ordinated efforts on the part of many African leaders-to-be to regain control of the African continent. Pan-Africanism, with its emphasis on Black self-determination, represented an ideology that was directly opposed to the doctrine that white people had been forcing onto Black People. Pan-Africanism was a call for Black political power, Black economic power, Black cultural stability and Black psychological stability. In short then, it was a call for total Black self-determination, and its message was so strong that many of the "uncle tom" leaders of the African continent had to either go along with it or lose face in the eyes of most people. By the mid-1950s, Pan-African forces were bringing about tangible results.

In 1955, there was still only one African country under the control of the native population. However, by 1955 five additional countries on the African continent had gained their independence. It is important to note that these five countries, all in North Africa, were under the control of eastern white people who called themselves Arabs. Thus, the Arabs were the first people to get tangible results from the ideology of Pan-Africanism. During the ten years immediately after 1955, the African Revolution/Pan-Africanism bore fruit for the African People themselves. Liberation movements, most violent but some non-violent, took root and shattered the colonial (white-controlled) empires. In 1956

Ghana got its independence. Within four years, seven other Black nations had proclaimed their independence. By 1965, twenty-one African countries were politically independent (that is, they were under the visible leadership of native Africans). In other words, between 1956 and 1965, African People who had once been at the mercy of white people got themselves together and gained independence in 29 different countries. Before the turn of the decade (1960-1969), the names of other African countries were added to that list.

We have been using the term "independence", but We must be careful and precise when We apply it to African countries during this period. More accurately, it was during this period (1950s) that Africans began occupying positions of power in their respective countries. Africans were becoming legislators and presidents of countries and were making laws that were supposed to have been respected by African People and people who had contact with African People. This African power, however, was not all that it should have been. Many of the African leaders were puppets of white businesses and white governments; as such, they granted privileges to whites that victimized the native population and they made governmental policies and decisions with the intent of pleasing whites instead of benefiting the native Black population. Additionally, many of the "leaders" had adapted the ways of the whites as best they could. They sought an education that would enable them to imitate whites, they accepted white people's brainwashing without serious analysis, they were convinced that Black People were inferior and attached themselves to the mannerisms and standards of the white world in order to emphasize their "different-ness" from the general Black population. To such leaders, "independence" meant riches and authority for themselves, so they conducted business and governmental affairs in a manner that would benefit themselves and their cohorts. Most importantly, the "independence" of African countries during this period was less than it should have been because of the destructive and disruptive capabilities of white businesses and white governments. The failure of white people to keep Black People in complete subjection (slavery) did not decrease the ability of the whites to undermine the efforts of progressive Black leaders and de-stabilize Black governments. Whites still had immense economic interests and investments in Africa, so they protected their interests and investments by supporting Black leaders who would be puppets and uncle toms and attacking Black leaders who refused to go along with the white agenda. If whites felt the necessity to do so, they could go so far as to send their armies into Black countries (since Black countries were weak militarily) and take control, or execute Black leaders who were "undesirable" and replace them with more acceptable persons (according to white standards) . So, it is true and accurate to say that African countries were gaining their independence, but We must not overlook the fact that it was an independence that was not powerful enough to force white people to respect it.

But, no one can deny that it was real because it was a definite step toward genuine Black Power. It was real because it brought about tangible results that changed the basic nature of white/Black relationships, not only on the African continent but throughout the world. Thus, African independence at this early period put an end to a white power world order that was not seriously challenged by Black People. African independence, at this early stage of its development, introduced the need of white people to negotiate with Black People for goods and services that white people had grown accustomed to getting free of charge. African independence represented the necessity of white people making concessions and bargaining with Black People for privileges whites had previously taken for granted, and it represented the recognition by white people that they would have to treat and deal with Black People as equals whether they wanted to or not. Thus, it would not be unfair to say that African independence (spurred on by the Pan-Africanist ideology) at its early stages represented a greater decrease in white power than an increase in Black Power. Power is the ability to control yourself and others, and Black People were definitely not at the point where they could control themselves or white people. A lot of building blocks would have to be laid before either of those ends, if desirable, could be realized. Nonetheless, Black People were at the point where white people were able to control them (Black People) less, and this change in itself was monumental.

This exhibit of Black Power did not resemble the "Black Power" that existed in the United States of America during the late 1860s. In fact, the two were as different as Black and white. Whereas the Blacks in the United States were in positions of power because of the military might of white Northerners, the Blacks in Africa in the 1950s were in power in spite of the military might of white people. Additionally, Black People in the United States were functioning within the confines of a white governmental structure, but the Blacks in Africa were functioning around their own structure (even though it was tainted by the influence of colonial practices). Furthermore, the Blacks in the United States were in the midst of a hostile racist white population that had the support of the state machinery, while the Blacks in Africa were among their own kind; and the Blacks in the United States failed to acquire their own land base, while the Blacks in Africa had a massive land base that was almost indisputably their own. What the Blacks in the United States experienced during the 1860s was not Black Power at all; it was a mirage, a substance-less illusion that could not possibly have brought about the ends that Black People desired. The Black People in Africa in the 1950s had much more going for them than a mirage. They were not basing their actions on the good intentions of white people nor promises from white governments. Quite to the contrary, what they were doing was determined by the needs, abilities and strengths of Black People. The most aware individuals among the African People were even going beyond independence for selected African countries and had begun actively seeking to unify the whole continent under a common political set-up called the United States of Africa. These Blacks were not concerned about integrating with white people. In fact, many of them were thinking of ways of removing white people, eastern whites and western whites, from the African continent altogether.

The fact that African People in nearly 30 countries were able, in only 10 years, to seriously cripple the oppressive structure that whites had been building for more than 80 years contained a message for white people that white people did not want to accept. It indicated that Black People were already able to effectively resist and frustrate the economic and political racism of white people on the African continent and signalled that the day was not far off when Black People would consolidate their forces and force the white world to curtail its racist and exploitative activities in all parts of the world where Black People lived. The white powers recognized that this awakening of Black People in Africa might take on proportions that could force white people to take a back seat in the international arena insofar as politics and economics were concerned. White people saw this message written in Black, and put forces in motion they hoped would stop the African Revolution before it took root in the minds and hearts of the African masses.

Because they had imposed an economic order on most of the world by seizing most of the available resources and controlled the modes of producing finished products from raw materials, white people were in a position to determine which governments/countries would be allowed to benefit from the established world economic order. As such, they were able to boycott and strangle those countries that seemed intent on furthering the African Revolution by refusing to grant them loans and machinery that would make it less difficult for such countries to support the needs of its native population. Whites would also manipulate the world market in a manner that made it difficult for progressive Black nations to receive a fair price for the products they attempted to trade, and further caused unnecessary problems by financing the sabotage activities of individuals within a country who did not support the policies of the government (for whatever reasons). This type of financing would enable individuals to start mischief and spread ideas that would bring about an anti-government response from the politically unaware people who saw no need to continue to support a government that was not relieving them of their poverty-stricken lives.

Such de-stabilizing activities had a great deal of affect because of the generally chaotic conditions that existed in most countries immediately after independence was gained. To say the least, there was very little stability in such countries, and that would continue to be the case until an adequate state machinery could be made operational. Since this state of instability worked to the advantage of white interests, it was part of white people's policy to maintain or extend the period of instability until progressive Black leaders could be overthrown or executed. Using this method, white governments successfully eliminated two of the most progressive of African leaders, Kwame Nkrumah (in Ghana) and Patrice Lumumba (in Congo, now called Zaire).

Many times, selfish and politically obtuse (dumb) African dissidents were encouraged to overthrow Black progressive governments. White businesses and governments would provide such near-sighted opportunists with the money, military training and materials they needed, and then use their propaganda powers to legitimize the dissident activities. Because of such efforts, Zaire today is ruled by the incompetent Colonel Mobutu and the relatively progressive government of Milton Obote in Uganda was overthrown by Mr. Idi Amin.

But, most of all, white businesses and white governments used uncle tom-minded leaders such as Houphouet-Boigny (Ivory Coast), Leopold Senghor (Senegal), Moise Tshombe (Congo/Katanga) and Jomo Kenyatta (Kenya), among others, to keep whites unfairly benefiting at the expense of the African masses. Such Black "leaders" attempted to hide behind their Black skin and militant talk, but were usually betrayed by their inability to act in a manner that would frustrate the desires of white people. These leaders continually apologized for the supposed shortcomings and lack of development of Black People and helped their masters spread the doctrine of white leadership, white superiority and Black weaknesses. They felt white input was essential if Black People were to "progress", and used their powers and influence to institute national policies that would keep white people in the mood to give Black governments handouts in the form of loans and technical assistance. The terms of these loans gave a boost to the white economic system and were an insult to Black People, but tom-minded leaders seemed unable to recognize that and put it in its proper perspective. Instead, they repeatedly initiated economic policies that did not fundamentally address the problem of satisfying the basic needs of the native population, and agreed to follow a political program that would allow whites to manipulate the controls from behind the curtain, so to speak. Such "leaders" were not ready or willing to challenge white people for the wrongs they were inflicting on Black People; instead they were willing to accept the abuses if it guaranteed continued contact with white culture and "civilization". These leaders, then, were ready and willing to sacrifice the blood and resources of the African People, and the ability of white people to use them to attain white objectives made such leaders uncle toms and traitors of the African Revolution.

In spite of the efforts of white people and their Negro cronies, the African Revolution continued to magnify. It did not progress as speedily as it would have if it had been left unobstructed, nor did it maintain the desired degree of ideological clarity, but it was still forceful enough to demand respect for African

People everywhere. Since, in the political arena, respect is reserved for those who can generate fear in others, the respect whites were now eager to give to African People was an admission that African People could and would harm the white world. This recognition had such an unsettling impact that the white world began to argue and bicker in public around white policies toward Africa, and the stronger white nations began to sell the weaker white nations with African interests "down the river". As the 1970s came and liberation movements swept through Mozambique, Guinea Bissau, Angola and Zimbabwe (formerly called Rhodesia), white leaders recognized that they had no viable choice but to flow with the African tide as best they could while trying to damage it from within. Nonetheless, the African Revolution is completely beyond the control of white people and their governments/businesses/institutions.

Yet, the African Revolution is not under the control of Black People, and this could have unfortunate repercussions if it remains so because white people are still willing to fight over Africa. As a matter of fact, according to white officials and persons in the know, Africa is now the only place on earth worth fighting a war over. Africa contains resources that are universally needed, so people from all corners of earth will be thinking and scheming of ways to get as much of Africa as they can. White people, today particularly, are consolidating their forces as best they can in order to keep whites in control of the Union of South Africa. White people would have a mass heart attack if Black People gained control of that highly mechanized, industrialized and technological structure, but it is a heart attack that cannot be avoided. What its impact will be, however, is uncertain because, as was just stated, African People, particularly "leaders", have not assumed control of the African Revolution. Until Black People do assume that control, there is the possibility that white people can take advantage of unfortunate occurrences or circumstances and frustrate the Revolution.

The leadership that emerged on the African continent during the late 1960s and 1970s left, in nearly every case, a lot to be desired. Mental pygmies were becoming presidents and heads of state, and such leaders had little or no idea of the implications of the African Revolution and could not imagine what they could accomplish as policy makers. If they performed any progressive act at all, it was probably because the force of the African Revolution dragged them along. Needless to repeat, consistent progressive policies and programs were beyond their scope and comprehension (understanding) and beyond their scope of reality. For this reason, they failed to attempt to adequately organize the energy that the African Revolution had generated. They failed to follow the political objectives sought by Nkrumah, Lumumba, and Sekou Toure (Guinea) in that they did not pursue the idea of a United States of Africa. As a matter of fact, they attempted the reverse by distorting the ideology of Pan-Africanism itself, making it seem like a nationalist ideology as opposed to a continental

10 LESSONS

or Black internationalist ideology. In so doing, they forfeited much of the international power of Black People and left Africans unable to compete against the white superpowers militarily.

Economically, the pygmy-minded leaders failed to take measures that would make the African People independent of the established world (white-controlled) economic order. Africa has all the resources it needs to be self-sufficient, not only from a productive (agricultural and manufacturing) standpoint but from an energy standpoint also. All the African "leaders" needed to do was initiate policies that would combine and co-ordinate economic activities, revolve their productive plans around the needs of the African People and work together to make the most of the energy reserves and sources of energy that are found in abundance throughout the continent. Such measures, apparently, were beyond the scope of reality of the leaders that were emerging. Their preference was to become part of the world economic order that had been established and was still controlled by white people. In attempting to get a footing in that world order, they kept Black People dependent on white people for goods and services (and thereby slowed down the liberation movements that were attempting to move into high gear) and put the survival of millions of Black People in the hands of white people..... and watched millions of Black People needlessly starve to death.

Additionally, subjecting Black People to the pressures and priorities of the white economic order (capitalism) is damaging to the African personality and spirit. Capitalism represents values that are directly opposite to the values that characterize the African life-style. It imposes an oppressive concept of time, production, ownership, leisure and the self onto African minds and spirits, and seriously disrupts the African psychic structure. In fact, it makes it possible for white people who were unable to defeat or destroy the African People militarily or politically to do so culturally and spiritually. Capitalism is genocidal; therefore Black People cannot afford to become capitalists (whether they have a land base or not).

In spite of white intrigue (tricks), in spite of uncle toms and pygmy-minded leadership, in spite of white military audacity, in spite of all forces operating to the contrary, the African Revolution moved on steadily to higher and higher stages of development. Each liberation movement, each inept leader, each trick carried out and each exposed contradiction has been a political education for Black People across the world, and will continue to be so until Black People have learned enough lessons to effectively grab control of the Revolution and make it realize its full potential. As We move deeper into the 1980s, the learning process continues, but the day of reckoning is much nearer than many suppose. If it does not come soon, it will not be because of the might and intelligence of white people, it will be because of the failure of today's Black People to take advantage of the opportunities that have been made possible by earlier generations of Black revolutionaries.

The period between World War II and the 1970s in the United States of America saw Black People abandoning much of the submissiveness that had largely characterized them since the 1870s. Black People in the United States began to express open dissatisfaction with the restrictions the American structure had placed on them, and in so doing realized something that the maroons (their Black nationalist ancestors) had realized 300 years earlier; they realized that Black People could boldly resist and confront white people and the white power structure without getting wiped out. Between 1870 and 1940, Black People had allowed the fear of being injured or wiped out (personally and/or as a Race) to control them, and had sat passively by as a result. In the 1950s, as they looked back, they realized that all those years of passive non-resistance and reliance on imaginary hope had been wasted. They realized that in any human confrontation it is likely that some persons will get hurt or injured, that Black People would not make any progress unless a confrontation took place, that Black People were not avoiding personal and racial injury even though they were not resisting, and that new tactics and methods of defending themselves and gaining relief were necessary. These new tactics, combined with the re-emergence of Africa in the 1950s (which made white national leaders more prone to publicly "sympathize" with the complaints of Black People and less prone to publicly abuse Black People), pushed Black People into the undisputed forefront of American history.

Simply put, Black People pushed themselves into the forefront of American history by hitting the streets in the 1950s and the 1960s. Black People wanted political power, economic redress and social equality, and the only route Black People knew of that would bring about these gains was to boldly defy the laws and norms of American life. In a manner of speaking, this was their only alternative because Black People had no systematic means of convincing white people that Black People were seriously dissatisfied, nor did Black People have organizations or vehicles of their own that could effectively promote a positive course of action for Black People. Being thus unable to stand (so to speak) in order to look white people and the white structure "in the eye", Black People forced white people and their structure to kneel. Black People demonstrated for civil rights and attacked those laws and norms that were considered unfair. Black People demanded that the federal government serve the needs of Black People as well as whites, they defied Jim Crow (segregation), they sat-in, they marched, they danced, they sang and they rioted. Black People confronted whites on the streets, they boycotted businesses, they destroyed property, etc., and in so doing made white people realize that they would either have to make some concessions to Black People or lose billions of dollars in property and production and much of their "progressive" international image. So, lunch

10 LESSONS

counters were ordered de-segregated, "separate but equal" educational opportunities were replaced with integrated public schools, equal opportunity employment objectives and quotas were established and social welfare programs and policies were reviewed. Voting rights measures were passed, congressional districts were rezoned, and "affirmative action" (white people and their structure acting in a manner that recognized the validity of the demands that were being made by Black People) was pushed. All of a sudden, in fact too suddenly, Black People got good paying jobs, became managers of businesses and were elected to political offices. Black People began to get a better "shake" from the judicial system and more protection from the abuses of authority (police, etc.). Recognizing these changes, Black People, by the late 1960s, had begun to "cool down", to terminate their street activities and to prepare themselves for the piece of the American pie they were now anticipating.

In 1980, Black People were still waiting for that piece of the American pie. As a matter of fact, they were waiting holding less of the pie than they seemed to have possessed in the late 1960s. Instead of receiving the fair share of America's economic, political and social life they had anticipated, Black People discovered that the "gains" they had made during the 1950s and 1960s were being taken from them. In the same manner that Black People in the 1860s had made "gains" and lost them, Black People 100 years later made "gains" and lost them. Let Us briefly see how this happened. (It would be to the reader's advantage to review Lesson #6, Section IV at this time.)

When Black People hit the streets in the 1960s, they caught white people by surprise. As a result, white people were not able to respond to the street activity the way they wanted to respond, but had to respond in a manner that would immediately stop the destruction of their property and productive functions and give them time to steady themselves and re-group. Thus they, like their forefathers of 100 years earlier, made concessions to Black People that were temporary in nature and that were not a true reflection of their attitude toward the aspirations of Black People. Black People, on the other hand, just as their forefathers of 100 years earlier had done, thought the concessions were changes that represented the beginnings of real equality for Black People in this country. Black People, therefore, failed to recognize the necessity of building Black bases of power that operated on the same basic principle the street activities operated on, that principle being the almost total disregard of American laws and norms (because those laws and norms were not designed to benefit Black People). In other words, Black People failed to attempt to develop a power base that would "buck the system," and instead did the exact opposite by putting their faith in the very system of laws and norms that had forced them to hit the streets in the first place. It does not make sense and it is hard to believe, but it is true. Black People recognized that America's system was one of the major problems, hit the streets and got some relief from that system, and then went right back to that system in search of additional relief and direction. In so doing, We, Black People, failed to reduce white people's ability to control Us and left Ourselves powerless. As a result, once white people had steadied themselves and re-grouped, they had little trouble doing what they had wanted to do all along— make it clear to Us where Our "place" is in the American scheme of things.

Put another way, once white people recovered from Our surprise attack and discovered that We had left Ourselves powerless, they decided to put Us "back in Our place." Just as their forefathers had done in the 1870s, they set out to do in the 1970s. The biggest thing whites had going for them in this endeavor (in the 1970s) was the fact that Black People had failed to learn from the mistakes Our forefathers had made 100 years earlier. As a result, We repeated/ retraced their moves. Instead of seeking to control Our own destiny, We sought civil rights (entry into and equal rights within the American structure). Our forefathers of 100 years earlier had made the same mistake. As a result of white resistance to civil rights for Black People, We began demanding community control of the institutions that affected Us most directly, institutions such as schools, hospitals, etc. This demand was evidence of Our lack of understanding of the American political system. That system leans toward bigness and centralized control, so much so that the federal government is constantly challenging the rights of even state governments to control their own affairs. Surely, if this system white people have created seeks to control the affairs of highly organized political bodies like state governments, it is not even going to consider allowing a vague collection of persons who call themselves a "community" to control anything. There could therefore be no control for Black People within the system unless the system were first taken through some basic, fundamental changes. Black rebellers had no program for bringing about such changes, therefore their aspirations were doomed from the "git-go."

Black People have a lot to learn from the rebellions that were carried out by Us in the 1950s and the 1960s. We can learn that a disorganized activity (a riot, for example), no matter how explosive, has little chance of maintaining itself against a well-organized opposition force. Thus, even if Black People had continued to hit the streets, the objective would not have been realized. Granted, Black People would have been more feared by white people and would have prompted white people to make more substantial concessions, but the attitudes of white people and the basic objectives of the white system would have remained unchanged. As such, Black People would have continued to be less than full-fledged citizens.

We can also learn that, between the years 1870 and 1970, there was no change in the attitude of white people toward Black People. Between 1770 and 1870, the same was true, as was the case between 1670 and 1770. We, Black

People, should therefore stop expecting white people to go through changes that will result in them looking upon Us as "equals". It is possible that they will do so at some time, but history tells Us that We should not base Our course of action around that possibility.

Additionally, We have to realize that it is not necessary that white people view Us as their equal. If they want to hold onto their prejudiced attitudes, then that should not bother Us. What has to change, however, is their disrespectful manner of relating to Black People. Once We have consolidated and organized Our forces, there is no doubt that they will relate to Us with a great deal of respect.

We can also learn that people who are born, nourished and raised on force and violence (in this case, white people) do not respond in a respectful or understanding way to non-violence resistance. The advocates of non-violent resistance who hit the streets in the 1950s and 1960s apparently did not understand this. *They did not understand that they would be mercilessly attacked simply because they were refusing to defend themselves* (either that, or they feared violence so much that it caused them to act in a manner that maximized their chances of getting physically abused or killed). In the Black community, We know all too well that the most vicious cop is the one who captures a suspect who is unarmed or has been handcuffed. If a cop realizes that a suspect is defenseless, he takes full advantage of him. Once, however, the cop realizes that the suspect is "dangerous" (able to defend himself), the cop is better able to control his savage instincts. Black People should keep this in mind whenever We are organizing Ourselves for "progress."

We cannot afford to take chances in these lessons, so we will repeat what was just said. In the American social structure, given a positive emotion, action or possibility (love or equality, for example) and a negative emotion, action or possibility (hate or racism, for example), the negative is the more powerful, the more persuasive, the more domineering. In a different type structure where positive emotions and thoughts are planted, nourished and tended, such would probably not be the case. It is important that We recognize that We do not presently live in the latter-mentioned type social structure. As such, it does little, if any, benefit at the moment to theorize or philosophize about such a structure. We should, instead, accept the fact that the reality exists and deal with the reality; the reality of the negative outweighing the positive, the reality of an oppressive economic structure, the reality of a powerful and dominant political concept and practice called racism, the reality of exploitation and discrimination, the reality of Black and white. Yes, We, Black People, must accept the reality of Black and white. We must, *in Our minds and within Our thought processes*, accept the reality of white people dominating Black People, of white people enjoying their domination of Black People, of white people doing whatever they feel is necessary to continue their domination of Black People. We must not allow a dream to interfere with Our ability to recognize this reality, *nor can We allow an emotion to interfere with Our ability to act intelligently in the face of this reality.* Visions of Black People and white people holding hands at some time in the future should not determine Our response to the racial abuse and exploitation of Black People today, and the fear of what might happen should Black People challenge the reality of racism alone (without the assistance of white people) should not cause Us to submit to that reality until white people are ready to challenge it. What is real is real, and We can only maintain what is real, change what is real or destroy what is real by first accepting the fact of its realness, its reality.

It is not logical for Black People to hope for assistance from white people in the destruction of racism. Racism placed white people on top of the world and keeps them there. Additionally, it is unreasonable for Us to expect white people to "have mercy on Us" or have a conscience simply because We protest against inequality non-violently. White people love to see Black People protest non-violently because a non-violent protest is no threat to white people's security (their lives and their property). That is the reality, Brothers and Sisters, and Black People must accept the reality if We expect to organize and operate in a manner that will be beneficial to the Black People of the world.

Not all Black activists were rebelling in the post-World War II period. Not a small number of Blacks were engaged in revolutionary activities, activities that were aimed at achieving self-determination and self-government for Black People and changing the basic nature of Black People's relationship to white people (and vice versa). These Black men and women, the direct spiritual and political descendants of earlier Black nationalists like Gabriel Prosser, Denmark Vezey and Nat Turner, etc. (See Lesson #5, Section II), recognized the futility of expecting white people to act in a manner that would be beneficial to Black People, particularly since white people have historically been able to make advances at the expense of Black People. These Black revolutionaries also recognized the necessity of Black People establishing Black bases of power that are independent of the influence of white people and white systems. Unfortunately, many of the Black revolutionaries were either not ideologically sound or did not fully understand how their ideology was supposed to manifest itself in practice, so they tended to make demands, participate in activities and form alliances that were not consistent with their analysis of the struggle of Black People. Nonetheless, they set out to make Black People aware of Our basic needs and established organizational structures that could develop independent Black institutions that would liberate Black People if they were properly supported by Black People. Let us briefly mention a few of these organizations.

We have already mentioned the Nation of Islam. Popularly known as the Black Muslims, the Nation of Islam appeared in the 1930s under the leadership of Elijah Muhammad. The political principles of the Nation, summarized in a 10 point program entitled "What The Muslims Want," was largely consistent with the teachings of Brother Marcus Garvey. The religious aspect of the Nation, specifically its emphasis on Islam, was based on the recognition that religion is a basic element of Black People's being; an element that must be present if an organization aspires to represent the totality of Black People's experiences and aspirations. Since Christianity was known to be foul and hypocritical, Mr. Muhammad chose Islam (which he learned about from Wali Fard Muhammad) as the religion Black People should be introduced to. He adapted the principles and practices of Islam to the needs and realities of Black People in America, and went about the business of making the Nation of Islam known to the masses of Black People.

The Nation of Islam called for the separation of the Black and white races. Point 4 of the Muslim program states, "We want Our people in America whose parents or grandparents were descendants from slaves, to be allowed to establish a separate state or territory of their own - either on this continent or elsewhere. We believe that Our former slave masters are obligated to provide such land and that the area must be fertile and minerally rich. We believe that Our former slave masters are obligated to maintain and supply Our needs in this separate territory for the next 20 to 25 years - until We are able to produce and supply Our own needs." Point 7 states, "As long as We are not allowed to establish a state or territory of Our own, We demand not only equal justice under the laws of the United States, but equal employment opportunities NOW." "We want the government of the United States to exempt Our people from ALL taxation..." (Point 8), "We want equal education..." (Point 9) and "We believe that intermarriage or race mixing should be prohibited" (Point 10). The Nation stressed that white people are "devils" because of their evil ways, and urged Black People to "do for self" and prepare for the War of Armageddon, the inevitable war for control of the earth between the forces of good (Black People) and the forces of evil (white people).

The Nation of Islam took its message to the Black man and woman in the street, but probably its most productive move was toward the Brothers and Sisters who had been caught in white people's legal traps. Such persons, commonly called criminals, are in fact prisoners of war, and in many regards represent the finer elements of Blackness because they refuse to take a submissive, hat-in-hand approach to the economic abuse of Black People by white people. Mr. Muhammad, who himself had spent time in prison, recognized that the Brothers and Sisters in prison, in addition to being relatively desperate, were also intelligent and aggressive enough to go beyond talk and attempt to do those things that needed to be done. He therefore attempted to educate such persons, to politicize them and to get them to organize their intelligence and aggressiveness in a manner that could bring about basic changes in the condition of all Black People. He taught them to take pride in their Blackness and to take pride in themselves and what they do. In so doing, Mr. Muhammad transformed many persons with a so-called "criminal mentality" into progressive leaders of the Black community and leaders of the revolutionary activities of Black People throughout the world.

One of the reactionary prisoners-of-war the Nation of Islam helped transform was Brother Malcolm X. Malcolm X studied and learned intensely while he was in jail, but unlike many of today's prisoners-of-war, Malcolm remained true to what he had learned and maintained a strong commitment to the struggle of Black People after he got back on the streets. While in jail, he joined the Nation of Islam. After being released he became a very popular leader in the Black community and the most articulate spokesman of the Nation of Islam itself. He made it clear to Black People that white people had been running a "heads they win, tails We lose" game on Us, and insisted that it was time for Black People to stop being a participant in that game. He urged Black People to get economic and political power "by any means necessary", and insisted that We had a right to defend Ourselves against anybody who attacked Us or tried to keep Us from getting what We had a right to have. And, very importantly, he made it clear that the cards were not stacked up against Black People in the manner We had become accustomed to thinking. He internationalized Our way of thinking by informing Us that We were not outnumbered; that in fact, white people represented the smallest portion of the world's population. Additionally, he kept the examples of other struggling peoples before the consciousness of Black People in this country, particularly that of the Vietnamese, who with heart (serious dedication) and a "bowl of rice", had been able to militarily defeat one of the most advanced armies in the world (the United States Army). If these handful of overexploited and undernourished people could overcome the "might" of the United States of America, then surely Black People could do likewise.

During the last months of his life, Malcolm X's ideology seemed to waver somewhat. He seemed to change his attitude toward some white people and his plan of attack for Black People. This was primarily because Malcolm did not have the time to fully analyze and digest all of the information he was being exposed to. He was becoming knowledgeable of too much too rapidly, and he was unable to place all that he learned in its proper perspective (with his time as compressed as it was). Early in his political life, this was not the case because Malcolm had had the time to analyze theories and philosophies and see where they stood in relation to the struggle of Black People. As a result, the early foundation on which he stood was a solid one. Later, as he became caught up in the leadership aspect of the Black struggle and in the personal struggle to keep himself from being assassinated, the wealth of information he was being introduced to invaded him (in a manner of speaking)

10 LESSONS

and began to control him somewhat; so much so that he began to appear uncertain as to where he stood on several vital issues.

Perhaps many of Us can learn a lesson from that simple explanation. That lesson is that information is valuable and worthwhile to you only so long as you are able to control the influence of that information on you, particularly in a world dominated by politics (the power game). You must know exactly where you stand in the scheme of things and where you want to be. Black People have to realize that Our response to all information must be determined by the fact that no one is going to give priority to the welfare of Black People but Black People. Others might sympathize with Our cause and form alliances with Us, and others might say that they are prepared to make a supreme sacrifice for Us, but We must not allow such declarations to result in Us compromising the Black struggle in favor of a more general struggle (like a "class" struggle or a "third world" struggle, for examples). We are Black, and until fundamental changes have affected the social make-up of the known world, We should be concerned about improving the condition of Black People first and foremost. It is unfortunate that We have to take a stance such as this because it removes some of the universalist aspects from Our list of priorities. But, as unfortunate as it is , it must be because it is necessary. History, filled with examples of non-Black people betraying their Black "brethren" and "comrades", has been teaching Us this lesson for generations. It is time for Us to take heed of it.

The shortcomings and contradictions within the ideology of the Nation of Islam are clear. All of Us know that, in spite of what ought to be, the United States people nor government has no intention of giving Black People land. Therefore, one must wonder if the Nation of Islam was serious about Black Nationhood. It made no mention of preparing Black People to take control of the land We have a right to occupy. Additionally, the Nation seemed to expect the United States government to help the Black Nation survive. If not, the Nation's solution was to demand equality and separation of the races (but, within the present system). It is beyond doubt that the Nation of Islam was sincere when it spoke of land for Black People, but it is questionable if the leadership (with the exception of Malcolm X, if he can be considered part of the leadership), ever gave this question the attention it should have been given. The land issue and the issue of Black Nationhood indicate that the political ideology of the Nation of Islam was not as well thought out as it should have been.

The religious aspect of the Nation of Islam went astray as soon as Islam was chosen as the religion Black People should be taught to adhere to. Certainly, if the founder of the Nation had seriously checked into the history of Islam he would have discovered that Islam is just another white religion whose advocates and followers have traditionally slaughtered Black People,

10 LESSONS   183

enslaved Black People and benefited at the expense of Black People. Islam, like Christianity, is based on concepts and principles of the Ancient Blacks, and like Christianity, Islam had changed and distorted those principles and concepts so they conform with and cater to the white way of doing things. Thus, leaving Christianity for Islam is like running from one slick fox to another slick fox. Instead of adapting a religion that is controlled by white people, Mr. Muhammad should have checked into the traditional religious practices of the African People/Black People themselves. In the African tradition he would have discovered the principles that naturally appeal to and are consistent with the essence of Black People everywhere.

One of the reasons more attention was not given to the question of land and Black Nationhood might have been because of the ideology of Islam, which is anti-Black Nationalism. Additionally, the almost total dependence of Muslims on Allah might have left them less willing to deal with the land question, or incapable of realizing that Black People would have to take Our land even if it rightfully belongs to Us. Black People, whether they are religious or not, have to constantly keep in mind that what is "right" is not necessarily what is real.

Islam, like Christianity and all other non-Black religions, is a monkey in Black People's minds.

Another revolutionary Black organization was the Black Panther Party. The Black Panther Party was also primarily concerned about self-determination for Black People. Point 10 of the Black Panther Party Platform and Program declares, "We want land, bread, housing, education, clothing, justice and peace. And as our major political objective, a United Nations supervised plebiscite [vote] to be held throughout the Black colony [the United States of America] in which only Black colonial subjects [Black People] will be allowed to participate, for the purpose of determining the will of Black People as to their national destiny."

Founded by Huey P. Newton and Bobby Seale, the Black Panther Party emerged in the Bay area of California in the 1960s. It was, as much as anything else, a reaction to the tendency of Black People to waste away as a consequence of being continually abused by white people's system and representatives of that system. It is not surprising, then, that two areas of concentration of the Black Panther Party were on drug and alcohol use and police brutality. The rules of the Black Panther Party addressed the issue of drug use repeatedly, and the policy of the Party addressed the issue of reducing (if not eliminating) police brutality and police terrorism in the Black community. Party members decided on a course of action to control police brutality that involved policing the police and advising criminal suspects of their rights. Party members, in groups with a legal handbook in one hand and guns strapped around their shoulders, would follow police who were patrolling sections of the Black community. If the cops stopped a Brother or Sister, the

184   10 LESSONS

Panthers on patrol would be there to see that no one was brutalized and to advise the Black person of his or her rights.

As a result of their policing program, the Black Panther Party drew a lot of attention. However, one must understand that the policing program was only one aspect of one of the most active organizations to ever emerge from the Black community. In keeping in line with Black People's tradition of communalism (sharing/community ownership) and extended family-hood, the Black Panthers organized a host of services called "survival programs" that were available to members of the Black community free of charge. The survival programs included free food programs, free education facilities called liberation schools, free legal assistance, free busing programs, free clothing programs, free medical programs and free youth programs, among a host of others. These programs were used to politicize Black People to the necessity of Us acting in an organized and positive manner if We expected to progress in essential and substantial ways. They were used to mentally and psychologically prepare Black People to take on the task of taking Our destiny into Our own hands. All such programs in the Black community should serve that purpose because, until We take on that responsibility We will continue to be abused and exploited by white people and the capitalistic system. The Panthers constantly delivered that message to the Black community.

The Black Panther Party was also active in organizing Brothers and Sisters in prisons. The Panthers recognized what the Nation of Islam had recognized; that much of the best of Black People have been railroaded and stored in white people's detention centers. The prison activities of the Panthers produced some of their more dedicated supporters and advocates, and brought the Panthers into contact with Brother George Jackson. George Jackson was to emerge as a legend among prisoners and an inspiration to revolutionary forces across the country. Brother George was not given the opportunity to function on the streets though; he was murdered by prison authorities as part of the United States government's co-intelpro (counter-intelligence program) operations. (More on co-intelpro later.)

More than anything else, the Black Panther Party pushed an active self-defense program. Unlike the Nation of Islam, the leadership of the Panthers during the late 1960s was young and aggressive— and eager to do battle with "pigs" (cops) and other reactionary (non-progressive) elements of the white social structure. They were daring, as the policing program proved, and this daring trait unsettled white people, particularly the leaders of this country. The daring, coupled with the very numerous and effective programs the Panthers were carrying out in the Black community (that were making it clear to everyone that Black People did not have to remain in Our wretched condition), convinced the leaders of the country that the Black Panther Party had to be eliminated. As a result, an intensive murdering program was instituted by police and FBI

(Federal Bureau of Investigation) agents against the Panther Party membership.

But an even more sinister response of the federal government to the Black Panther Party in particular and the activities of revolutionary organizations in general was the push toward gun control legislation. White people hoped to convince Black People that it was to Our advantage to give up Our right to carry weapons because such a move would lead to a decrease in major street crimes, but the fact of the matter is that white people wanted to underhandedly disarm Black People in order to reduce the threat Black People posed to white people's "security" and in order to render Black People less capable of defending Ourselves against the attacks of the white government agencies and representatives. Think about it! If weapons are manufactured, the so-called street criminal is going to get them whether it is legal or not, so gun control will not benefit the Black community in that regard. And, the white argument is nonsense anyway because We all know that white people do not care if Black individuals get injured, robbed or killed. But, whites are concerned about the destruction of white property and white lives (in that order). Gun control, they think, will disarm the mass of Black People and maintain the rule of those in power.

Since many individuals do not use weapons properly, the use of arms needs to be controlled, but the right of Black People to bear arms need not be taken away in order to achieve this end— particularly since the gun abusers in America are relatively few in number (when compared to the number of gun users who do not use weapons improperly). More important, though, are two other considerations: (1) the government's misuse of weapons is greater than the community's misuse of weapons, and (2) most persons in the Black community who misuse weapons would not do so if this white system did not make life hell for Black People as a matter of course. Thus, gun control could become a reality without taking away one of the people's basic rights (self defense) if fundamental changes were made in the present system itself. As long as the present system refuses to make those fundamental changes, Black People should refuse to give up their/Our arms.

The effectiveness of the Black Panther Party in the Black community drew the attention of a lot of negative forces, including representatives of Marxism, the "communist" party and the "working class." Such representatives expressed an interest in allying with the Black Panther Party. Their major objective, which they failed to reveal but which should have been known to the Panthers anyway, was to infiltrate the Party and destroy its Black appeal by convincing the Party to emphasize an integrated struggle and de-emphasize the race question. All along, the Black Panther Party leadership had stressed revolution and espoused Marxist/Leninist/Maoist ideas, but neither the leadership nor the Party membership was interested in integrating the revolutionary Black struggle with a reactionary white struggle. The Panthers were interested in waging a

10 LESSONS

struggle that would result in progress for all oppressed peoples, but they did not want to ally with whites because they knew that white people, regardless of what they say, are up to no good. George Jackson was particularly skeptical of them; because of that he took great pains to keep Angela Davis from joining a Marxist/communist/working class party or organization.

Nonetheless, the Panther Party fell victim to integration (the "class" struggle). After Huey Newton, the theoretician of the Black Panther Party, was imprisoned, the leadership of the Party fell into unwise hands. What had happened in Ancient Egypt more than 5000 years earlier was about to repeat itself in the United States of America. A strong, vibrant, Black movement was about to be handed over to white "liberals" and white protestors by mini-minded Black individuals who had stars in their eyes and personal hang-ups. As white hippies, yippies and communists tried to push the Black Panther Party into the vanguard (front) of white people's struggle against the government, the Party itself suffered. Discontentment, disillusionment, disgust and petty power seekers resulted in defections and a split in the Party, a split that seriously hampered the efforts of the Party from that point on.

After the people had forced Huey Newton's release from prison, he attempted to get the Black Panther Party back on the right track. The role of whites was de-emphasized, as was the ideology of the whites, and more energy was expended in Black community-oriented programs. But the killing and imprisonment efforts of the FBI and the police against the Panthers and the effects of the split were dictating that the Party make some adjustments in its methodology, at least until it had regained some of its lost strength. Thus, the Party began to concentrate on working through the system as a revolutionary tactic. The programs and tactics the Party had traditionally followed were not given up, but other tactics were added in order to make the Party more appealing to skilled Blacks, educated Blacks with common sense and white voters in the Bay area, and less prone to be attacked by police. In other words, the Black Panther Party stopped ignoring traditional party politics as a possible avenue to change. The Party attempted to get a revolutionary footing in the American system by running some of its members for public office. The biggest push was toward getting Bobby Seale elected mayor of Oakland in the mid 1970s. Seale lost, and it is well that he did. He could not have functioned as a revolutionary officeholder in a country as intricately reactionary as America is. With his defeat, the Black Panther Party faded.

It is important that We take note of several points. To begin with, the Black Panther Party's chief objective was a Black Nationalist objective. The Party itself was formed to carry out the principles that had been advocated by Malcolm X. Malcolm X had been the most effective person in the Nation of Islam, which had been founded by Elijah Muhammad, who based much of his political ideology on the teachings of Marcus Garvey. These persons and organizations used different words, but what they all said had one major objective in common— self-determination for Black People. The drive for self-determination has therefore been unbroken since the early 1900s, and continues today. It has yet to reach the level of intensity that was present in the early 1700s and 1800s, but the fact that it has maintained itself in spite of all obstacles and devilish schemes is proof that Black People who are presently in America will govern themselves at some point in the future.

Secondly, even after the Black Panther Party had faded, the "authorities" continued to harass and pressure Huey P. Newton. This is because whites realize that Newton personifies the objectives of the Party and he will be about making the objectives a reality whether the Party itself exists or not. He is not going to give up because a grand attempt failed to realize its total objective. Consciousness and self-determination have transcended Huey Newton's being; therefore he will always be a threat to white people's "security." Whites recognize this and do all they can to neutralize that threat.

Any person in the Black community who is a real Black Nationalist will get the same treatment from "the authorities" once his or her activities have drawn their attention. Others, those who play or experiment with revolution for a few months or a few years, fade back into the establishment mode after a while and are left alone. Those whose consciousness has transcended their being get no peace nor any concessions. Think about that when you think about yourself and keep that in mind when you analyze the sincerity of others.

Third, it is not enough to stress the necessity of arming Ourselves and defending Ourselves. A major tenet of the Black Panther Party was the armed resistance of Black People to oppression, but the Panthers apparently were not able to cultivate the personal discipline that would have reduced their chances of being caught off guard or seriously out of position. This discipline is essential to an adequate self-defense program. Additionally, the Black Panther Party did not establish sound self-defense principles or techniques. Perhaps this was due to their youth or them being necessarily pre-occupied with other matters; regardless, these two factors made the job of FBI and police murderers less difficult. Of all the organizations that functioned during this period, none suffered as many casualties as the Black Panther Party (rarely did any of the attackers get killed. By comparison, the RNA, which we will discuss soon, was frequently attacked by the same forces, but the RNA always got the better of the deal.). We admit, the Panthers drew more of the wrath and anger of the governments (federal, state and local) than other organizations, but the same tactics that were employed against the Panthers were used against other organizations, but with a lesser degree of effectiveness.

Discipline is an essential element of any program, from teaching a class to learning how to protect yourself. It can mean the difference between being able to react effectively and being caught totally by surprise.

Finally, We should _know_ two things by now. We should know that white people are not concerned about the welfare of Black People; that white "liberals" and "communists", etc., contribute more to the destruction of Black progressive movements than they do to the destruction of the government they say they want to overthrow. A review of white involvement in the Black movement during the 1960s and 1970s will probably reveal the role they played as one of the major contributing factors to the downfall of healthy Black organizations. Also, We should know that We cannot bring about real changes in the condition of Black People by working through the system that is inherently programmed to abuse Us. A lot of sincere individuals believe this can be done but history tells Us it can _not_ be done. Working through the system can bring about cosmetic (seeming) changes, but it cannot bring about the basic changes that convert one thing into an entirely different thing. It is natural for an organism or a system to automatically function in a manner that will preserve itself and maintain its ties to its roots. To change such an organism, one would first have to destroy it; and to destroy it with you a part of it is to destroy yourself. Since Black People should fight, at all costs, to maintain as much of Our essence as We possibly can (We have already lost so much!), We should not unnecessarily allow any of it to slip away from Us or be destroyed.

We, Black People, have to _build_ a system that reflects what We are about. We cannot convert a system and expect it to adequately represent Us, particularly if that system is based on the opposite of what We are about.

In the late 1960s, a convention of Black delegates met in Detroit, Michigan and proclaimed that Black People in the United States were in fact a Nation of People separate from the American people. This convention of delegates, including Imari Obadele (who was later elected president of the Black Nation) gave that Nation of People a name, the Republic of New Afrika.

The Republic of New Afrika took the concept of Black Nationalism to its ultimate stage when, in 1968, it declared Black People to be free and independent of the United States government. The Republic of New Afrika declared Black People's independence because it "believes that Black People in Amerikkka make up a nation of people, a people separate and apart from the Amerikkkan people. The RNA also believes that as a nation of people, We are entitled to all of the rights of a nation, including the right to land and self-determination. The RNA further believes that all the land in Amerikkka, upon which Black People have lived for a long time, worked and made rich as slaves, and fought to survive on is land that belongs to Us as a People, and it is land We must gain control of because, as Malcolm X said, land is the basis of independence, freedom, justice and equality. We cannot talk about self-determination without discussing it within the context of land. Therefore, the RNA [identified the five states of Mississippi, Louisiana, Alabama, Georgia and South Carolina as Black People's land and] believes that gaining control of Our land is the fundamental struggle facing Black People. Without land, Black Power, rights and freedom have no substance.

"The RNA asserts that Black People in Amerikkka are not legally U.S. citizens. History is quite clear on this point. In 1865, the 13th Amendment [to the U.S. Constitution] "freed" the New Afrikan (Black People) and left Us as a political entity rightfully settled on land that was claimed by the U.S. Along with freedom, according to international law, came four choices as to what Our political destiny would be. Number one, *if We wanted to*, We could seek admission to citizenship in the Amerikkkan community. Number two, if We so desired and if We could afford to, We could return home to Afrika. Number three, if We so desired, We could emigrate to (re-locate in) another country where We preferred to live if that country did not object. And, number four, if We so desired, *We could and had a right to set up an independent state [Nation] of Our own, and could legally do so on land claimed by the United States* because We had lived here long enough, worked here long enough and fought here long enough to satisfy the requirements laid out by international law. Additionally, establishing an independent nation where We were was Our most logical choice because (1) We had experienced self-government in this land before, (2) We could not trust Our welfare and government to the people who had enslaved Us and dreadfully exploited Us, and (3) most New Afrikans [Black People] were unwilling and/or unable as a practical matter to emigrate to another land or return to Afrika. Land in this country where the ex-slave had already contributed his labor and blood, all as a result of wrongful kidnapping, wrongful transport and wrongful exploitation was the only logical and practical option left.

"The RNA believes, and historical records verify [prove], that the U.S. government was aware of the options We had, and U.S. presidents Andrew Johnson and Abraham Lincoln talked about voluntary emigration and colonization as solutions, since neither wanted Black People to be citizens and neither wanted Black People to claim land that We, by now, had a legal right to have. But, *the Amerikkkan government and community, because it needed Black labor and Black political pawns, decided to take away three of the options We had [and forced] U.S. citizenship upon Us.* Thus it was that, 2 1/2 years after We were "freed" We were made citizens of the U.S. without Our consultation or consent. In order to keep from giving Us land in the North, South or West *that We legally had a right to*, the U.S. treated Us as slaves [even though We were free] and *told* Us that We were going to be citizens of the United States of Amerikkka.

"At no time were the former slaves provided information as to Our rights under international law or permitted in any referendum or plebiscite to make an informed choice from among the four natural choices open to Us. (A referendum is a vote on a proposed law, like the 14th Amendment. A plebiscite is a vote on a choice of government. We had, and still have, a right to vote on whether We want U.S. citizenship or land for Our own government.) This constitutes fraud on the part of the U.S. government, and makes the 14th Amendment illegal and non-binding upon Us, New Afrikans. This massive fraud, continuing today, is almost certainly the most infamous such fraud and rape of the rights of free People in all history.

"The RNA believes that the passage of the 14th Amendment was, in fact, a declaration of war by whites and their government against Black People and the governments We had established during the Civil War. White military expeditions against and invasions of all the Black governments were begun, meetings and conventions of the New Afrikans [Black People] were terrorized and harassed, and widespread white violence which led to lynchings and burnings of Black People was granted the general approval and support of the white government (since white governments punished Blacks who resisted white violence by putting them in jail). The RNA believes that, despite these attacks and illegalities by whites, Black People continued to seek land and self-government because they preferred it, and still do so today.

"Thus, independent land for Black People is the cornerstone of the ideology of the Republic of New Afrika. This quest for independent land is accompanied by two other major principles. They are (1) We must internationalize Our struggle for land, and (2) We must defend Ourselves.

"According to the Republic of New Afrika, internationalizing Our struggle...means clearly declaring to the world bodies that We are not Amerikkkan citizens, but colonized and oppressed citizens of New Afrika. Internationalizing Our struggle means aligning and allying Ourselves with other nations of the world and opening up diplomatic channels and relations with those countries. By internationalizing Our struggle, according to the RNA, We become international citizens and open Our struggle to the review of the world.

"International law guarantees Us certain rights if We declare Ourselves as an oppressed Nation of People. If We do not declare that, if We do not declare that Our goal is for land and sovereignty/self-government, then other nations of the world have no right to speak out in Our behalf or provide other support for Us. If We do not declare that Our struggle is for land and self-determination/self-government, then Our struggle becomes a domestic matter, one that involves a conflict between citizens of a nation who are treated right and those who are treated wrong. As such a matter, Our struggle can be rightfully or legally suppressed by Amerikkkan forces (military, police, judicial, etc.) as a strictly internal matter. We can be murdered, stored in prison for no legitimate cause, disarmed (gun control), forced to work without just compensation, and experimented on....and have no body to complain to other than the very same people who damaged Us in the first place.

"Finally, if We internationalize Our struggle, according to the RNA, We put

Ourselves in a position to take Amerikkka to court, so to speak. We can demand that the world force Amerikkka to pay Us reparations (money, machinery, etc.) for the wrongs that have been inflicted on Us for 400 years, reparations that can be used to benefit New Afrikans after We have gained control of Our land and assured Our independence.

"Events and expedience (necessity) have steered the RNA toward the concept of a People's Army. The primary role of a People's Army is a defensive one, since its stated purpose is to ward off unlawful attacks by whites who attempt to keep New Afrikans from doing the work We have a right to do. Also, Our experiences in Amerikkka have proved to Us that We cannot live side by side with white people without them attempting to dominate and harm Black People. And, needless to say, we need a People's Army in order to keep white people from interfering with Our efforts to separate from them, in order to gain control over the land that is rightfully Ours, and in order to maintain control over the land We acquire by defending the integrity of the New Afrikan People and the government that represents New Afrikans.

"The concept of the People's Army technically includes all New Afrikan citizens. It recognizes that defense should be a primary function of all New Afrikans, and it therefore stresses the value of mass military training. The concept of a People's Army does not rule out other types of security forces, nor does it downplay the value of tactical offensive warfare. It simply recognizes that, at this stage, a People's Army properly organized and maintained is an adequate arm of self defense for the Republic.

"[The objectives of the Republic of New Afrika have been clearly laid out.] According to international law, Black People in Amerikkka have a legal right to establish independent governments in the urban areas of the north and in several of the southern states because We have lived in these areas, worked in them and defended them against attacks for hundreds of years. We also have a right to build a Black government in the west because We (Our ancestors) were kidnapped and illegally transported to this land from Our native home (Africa). Because we have a right to choose where We want to establish Our government in Amerikkka, the conveners and establishers of the Provisional Government of the RNA identified an area in the South that is presently divided into five Amerikkkan states (South Carolina, Georgia, Alabama, Louisiana and Mississippi) as the homeland of New Afrikans. The basic thrust of the Republic's Provisional Government, then, is to develop cadres (working groups) that will go to each of these areas, inform Black People of their rights, educate them to what the RNA is all about and hold an election (plebiscite) by which the Black People of these areas would choose between being U.S. citizens or citizens of the Republic of New Afrika. If the majority of the Black People in these areas vote to be citizens of the Republic of New Afrika, then the land and the People will be declared independent and New Afrikan governments will be established. The governments would carry out the function of institutionalizing new military, economic, governmental. political, social and international arrangements that will be aimed at strengthening and benefiting New Afrikans and New Afrika.

"(Black People in other parts of Amerikkka will be encouraged to come to New Afrika to live, but will not be required to do so. It will be possible for them to remain in Amerikkka- if they are not expelled by the U.S. government- and maintain their New Afrikan citizenship if they desire to do so)" [Quoted material taken from "The Republic of New Afrika: Its Development, Ideology and Objectives". Italics added.]

Other revolutionary organizations began functioning during this period. Two of the others were the All-African People's Revolutionary Party, which views the liberation of Africa as a necessary first step toward the liberation of Black People in the United States, and the Black Liberation Army, a concept that focused on self defense and armed revolutionary activities. But, more important than either of these collectives and more important than either of the organizations we have mentioned were the thousands of local community organizations that evolved during this period and took on a militant posture even though most of them failed to concentrate on Black self-defense measures. These organizations became branches of the national structures, continually kept in contact with local Blacks and educated them, and thereby made Black People more leery of white people and their systems and more receptive to the more largely organized concepts like the Republic of New Afrika, etc. The larger structures got the attention and the recognition, but the substantial groundwork was laid by these thousands of relatively unknown Black community organizations. It is important to note that these organizations functioned independently of the established governmental structures.

In response to the rebellious and revolutionary activities of Black People during the 1950s and 1960s, an anti-Black counter-intelligence program was financed and carried out by United States government agencies. Its aims, outlined quite clearly in FBI documents, included:

(1) Preventing the coalition of militant Black Nationalist groups;

(2) Preventing the rise of a messiah among Black People who could unify and electrify the Black Nationalist movement;

(3) Preventing militant Black Nationalist groups from gaining respectability in the Black Community by discrediting them; and

(4) *Preventing the long range growth of militant Black Nationalist organizations, especially among the young Blacks.* ["The RNA...."]

Under this anti-Black campaign, the U.S. government was able to systematically attack Black organizations and individuals across the country. Under this program, Fred Hampton and Mark Clark, two Black Panthers, were brutally murdered in Chicago, Illinois, and nearly 30 more Panthers were brutally and sneakingly murdered in other parts of the country. Even more Panthers were railroaded to prison after murder attempts by FBI and police agents had failed. "Under this program, antagonisms between the Black Panther Party and United Slaves (US, Inc.) were created that led to several shootouts between the two Black organizations. Under this program, the Nation of Islam was attacked in city after city. Under this program, SNCC (Student Non-Violent Co-ordinating Committee) was virtually destroyed. Because of this anti-Black program, agents/spies began to appear in every Black organization across the country. Their job was to stir up controversies, to provide authorities with information that could be distorted and used to discourage other Blacks from joining or supporting these organizations, and to provide the authorities with "excuses" for attacking Black organizations in military-like manner. Under the influence of this anti-Black campaign, the Law Enforcement Assistance Administration (LEAA) received millions of dollars in grants, and terrorist teams such as SWAT (Special Weapons and Tactics) began to get a reputation for eliminating Blacks who did not agree with the racist practices of this governmental structure.

"Because of this *government financed anti-Black campaign*, a healthy Black movement that had breathed new life during the late 1950s and early 1960s was seriously hampered. Well known Black activists such as Huey Newton, Bobby Seale, Angela Davis, Rap Brown, Ericka Huggins, Benjamin Chavis and T.J. Reddy were illegally imprisoned and detained. *Because of this anti-Black campaign, Black People* [who did not understand what was actually happening] *became disenchanted with the Black movement* and began to act in an irresponsible manner that could get Us exterminated in the long run. Because of this anti-Black campaign, 'Black is Beautiful' faded into the past, and blue eyes became the objective of [too many Black persons'] activities.

"In attempting to destroy [the forces of Black progress], the FBI and its support agencies used every dirty trick an insane mind could think of... Letters were put out that accused the President of the RNA of stealing funds, and other letters were put out that intended to create friction between the RNA and the Black Panther Party. Rumors were started that were intended to discredit members of [Black organizations], and in general rumors were put out that were intended to disrupt the family life of Black activists. All of these activities, coupled with the ignorance of the Black masses and of many Black leaders, almost ripped the Black movement to shreds.

"But these anti-Black campaigns were destined to fail. History has been quite clear on this point. From day one, Freedom, Independence, Self-Government and Self-Defense had been sought by Black People who had been illegally and ruthlessly brought to this land. In 1526, We rebelled and sought a better way-of-life. Throughout the 1600s, We did the same thing, and began establishing Our own governments in the form of maroon villages. In the 1700s, We continued to rebel and set up self-governing establishments and villages. The same was true of the 1800s, which were marked by rebellions that involved thousands and thousands of early Black Nationalists. During the period immediately after the Civil War We were somewhat confused for a while, but We still struggled for the rights We felt were Ours by nature. During the late 1800s and early 1900s, We began to get back on Our nationalist trail. The twenties and thirties witnessed Marcus Garvey and the African Blood Brotherhood. The forties and fifties witnessed the Nation of Islam and the rise of Malcolm X. The sixties witnessed SNCC, the riots, the Black Panther Party and the Organization of Afro-American Unity. Throughout these developments, the U.S. government and its citizens did everything imaginable to stop Our process of growth and development. The maroons were attacked, Black men and women were imprisoned, lynched, burned and castrated, and Black men and women were hanged/executed for planning rebellious activities. But the process went on, always to higher and higher stages of ideological and practical development. And, the process will continue to go on.

"The attacks on the RNA in the 1970s were recent attempts to stop Our nationalistic development, but they were no more effective in achieving this end than were the attacks on the Black maroons in the 1700s. Black People were on the road to self-government and Nationhood in the 1700s, and We have continued to follow that road. In spite of all obstacles, We will continue to follow that road until We "FREE THE LAND". And We will FREE THE LAND that rightfully belongs to Us, Brothers and Sisters. Black People will win this struggle if We struggle seriously; there is no doubt about that. A Republic of New Afrika will prevail. History is quite clear on that point." [Quoted, "The RNA: Its Development, Ideology and Objectives"]

As might have been said earlier, to adequately cover the Caribbean area, one would have to review the area island by island or country by country. It is not the purpose of these Lessons to be that exhaustive. Without doing much damage, we feel We can get an adequate idea of what was happening on each island by following the trends that were common to nearly all of the islands. We will therefore use this approach in covering the Caribbean area of the world during the post-World War II time period.

Just like Black People in Africa and just like Black People in the United States, the Black People in the Caribbean area were moving toward self-determination also. The moves of the Blacks in the Caribbean toward self-determination were less definite and self-definitive (or more European-inclined) than that of the Blacks in Africa, and less explosive and defiant than that of the Blacks in the United States, but there were factors in their favor that made "independence" not only a realistic goal, but a very realizable one. The move toward "independence" began with the recognition by the Blacks in the Caribbean that they were part of the Black world and not part of the European (white) world. That Black People in the Caribbean considered themselves part of the European world is a well-accepted theory, since the educated and industrious (achievement-oriented) Blacks in the Caribbean imitated and championed the culture and society of Europe with all their heart. Even the masses felt more left out than Black, and tended to view local economics and the class system (rather than international racism) as the issue in their lives. However, once they were brought face-to-face with the fact of their Blackness, it was possible for them to re-evaluate the factors that were largely determining the quality of their lives and their ability to survive. This re-evaluation did not cause the Caribbean Blacks to de-emphasize the class factor, but it did make them aware of the fact that they were part of the victims in a world-wide scheme against Black People and that, as Black People, they should concern themselves with upsetting that scheme.

Black People in the Caribbean, until the 1930s and 1940s, recognized they were not white but were firmly convinced that they were not Black either. They knew they had Black skins, but felt certain they did not belong to the race of Black People. They were better than Black People, did not want to be associated with Black People and were offended if they were accidentally put in that category. However, in the 1930s and 1940s events began to take place that would in time change their views. The first of these events was the return of Marcus Garvey to Jamaica. Garvey, who had been expelled from the United States by white people, brought back to Jamaicans and other Islanders the same message he had delivered to Blacks in the United States. He encouraged the Blacks in the Caribbean to take pride in themselves, their color and their racial heritage, and started organizing people with this message as one of his standard bearers. A few years later, Aime Cesaire began passing on the same message, although not as aggressively as Garvey, in the French-controlled islands, particularly in Martinique, Cesaire's home. "It is all right to be Black," Cesaire said, and even though most of the Blacks who heard him thought he had lost some of his marbles, the thought had been introduced to their minds nonetheless. Later, when Caribbean Blacks were constantly exposed to white people who declared their superiority and made no attempt to disguise their racism, the ideas of "Black is Beautiful" and "Black Pride" became less and less disturbing. In fact, such ideas as these became more and more acceptable, so much so that by the 1950s, Black People in the Caribbean were doing all they could to emphasize their identity with the Black world, particularly with Africa.

The development of pride in being Black led to consciousness on their part of color/race as a factor in the political and economic condition of a group of people. As the Blacks in the Caribbean recognized this, race became more of

10 LESSONS

a factor in local politics (even though it might not have been explicitly mentioned regularly), but it did not come close to challenging the class factor that was mentioned earlier. However, it introduced a perspective of seeing things and defining events and conditions that was the opposite of the colonial or white perspective. This emerging perspective was clearly a Black perspective, but one that was only beginning to develop. As such, it was trying to find itself, it was uncertain in its Blackness and it was unclear about its objectives, but it was having an impact nonetheless. It strongly influenced the positions that were taken by the political parties that developed in the Caribbean in the 1940s and 1950s. As a matter of fact, the political parties were so strongly influenced by this new perspective that they were proof that the Caribbean people were beginning to view themselves as different from white people. Though subtle, this was a tremendous development.

As the Caribbean people began to view themselves as different from the colonial powers, they began to demand changes in the political relationship of the islands to the colonial powers. There was open dissatisfaction with the traditional system that amounted to indirect rule by the colonial powers, and demands for more representative forms of government were made. At first, these demands were made with the understanding that the colonial system would be kept in tact. Later, they were expressed in the form of political independence for the Caribbean colonies. As a result of these demands, nearly every colony in the Caribbean was granted nationhood during the 1960s.

In nearly every case, the independence that was achieved during these years did not require violence or military-like operations. This was mostly due to the role the Caribbean island played in white people's economic scheme of things. With the exception of sugar, there was little about the Caribbean that fitted the tastes of modern capitalism, and the large businesses and multinational corporations had only a small amount of money and resources invested in the Caribbean area. Thus, the demands for independence by the Caribbean people did not noticeably threaten white people's pocket books and therefore were not fiercely resisted by the white governments. However, measures were taken by the white governments to control the political atmosphere of the islands and to keep the islands dependent on and of service to the capitalist economic system, but there was not the steep resistance that had occurred on the African continent. In fact, many of the white governments considered their Caribbean possessions as burdens, so when the representatives of the Caribbean people said they wanted independence, independence was granted.

In order to strengthen themselves and improve their economic condition, the Caribbean "leaders" spoke in terms of economic interdependency and political federation of the Caribbean countries. The efforts toward economic interdependence were intended to reduce the control the white western powers had over the economic affairs and viability of the Caribbean nations. The purpose of the steps toward political federation were made in order to render the Caribbean nations more capable of defending themselves and more powerful as a force in world affairs. It would cause them to get more respect from other countries of the world and enable them to influence the policies other countries held toward the Caribbean nations. For practically all intents and purposes, both of these efforts failed.

To explain why they failed is to address one of the major weaknesses of the Caribbean countries— leadership. For the most part, the leadership in the Caribbean preferred to maintain economic ties to the white western powers. In spite of their rhetoric (talk) and in spite of all the evidence to the contrary, they thought and felt that maintaining those ties was the best thing to do. As such, their efforts toward economic interdependence were not true to the cause that had inspired the call for economic interdependence. Their efforts, instead of being inspired by a "We must be economically independent of Europe" attitude, was inspired by a "We Caribbean countries can work together for economic progress if my country stands to benefit" attitude. With this attitude motivating them, they were unable to seek economic interdependence. Since economic interdependence was not sincerely sought, it was not achieved.

The steps toward federation failed for the same basic reason. The Caribbean leaders did not like the fact that the Americans and British (and other white powers) could militarily occupy their country (and thereby dictate political policy) at any time. They wanted to develop a power base and a force that would discourage these type actions on the part of whites, but they were not willing to give up their personal power in favor of establishing a Caribbean power base. Their decision to move toward federation instead of unification is in itself proof of this. Logical analysis and sincere dedication to the Caribbean people would have told them that unification was desirable and necessary because one government can function to the benefit of the Caribbean people better than several independent governments can. One government in that area is all that is needed. Additionally, one government would be appropriate because the Caribbean area is overwhelmingly populated by Black People who live close to each other (in geographical regards), who speak common languages, who practice a common religion and represent a common cultural heritage. One government would carry more weight in the international political arena, could co-ordinate the economic development of the entire area and could best develop a military force that could defend the Caribbean people and the integrity of the Caribbean government. But the "leaders" in the Caribbean recognized that most of them would have to give up their power and authority if the Caribbean area were united under only one government. To avoid giving up their power, they sought a solution that would centralize certain functions in the Caribbean yet allow each country to retain its autonomy (self rule). That

10 LESSONS

way, all of the leaders would be able to hold onto their power and seek "Caribbean unity" at the same time.

But unity could not be achieved that way. Progress that would really benefit the Caribbean people could not be obtained that way. White people knew that, and therefore encouraged the Caribbean leaders to federate. The whites knew that if each country had its own decision makers and maintained self-rule, then that country was not required to go along with the policies established by the central government. If a policy was to a particular country's favor, that country might support it. If a policy was not to a particular country's favor, that country could refuse to go along with it. The probability of internal fluctuations such as this are not favorable to the realization of substantial economic, social, political nor military objectives.

Thus, the lack of adequate leaders was a major obstacle to progress in the Caribbean. It was not the only obstacle, however. Probably just as important were the psycho-social make-up of the Caribbean people (Caribs were highly Europeanized) and the impact of the world economic system on the economic pursuits and priorities of the Caribbean governments. The Europeanization of the Caribbean people made them appreciate white images and desire the contact of white culture, which in turn made them less capable of radically confronting the white establishment. As for the latter factor, the impact of the world economic system (which was controlled by whites), it has been discussed previously in this Handbook. Therefore, we will not go into any more discussion of that system. Let it suffice to say that white people manipulated that system in a way that would strangle Caribbean countries and impoverish Caribbean countries whenever they felt it was desirable to do so.

The strength of the Caribbean lies in its Black masses. These are the persons who, even when politically ignorant, push the political parties and "leaders" toward objectives that have the potential of actually benefiting the Caribbean population. The Black masses are the least Europeanized, and therefore have the least amount of respect for white people and white systems. Consequently, they are more capable of attacking the system and destroying that system. The Black masses, even though ignorant in many regards, are the strength of the Caribbean because of their native intelligence and natural tendency to relate to persons in other parts of the world who look like them and experience the injustices they experience. The Black masses are the ones who sincerely listen to men like Marcus Garvey and sincerely long for extensive contact with Mother Africa (once they have been taught the truth). They make the "leaders" aware of what little power and authority they (the leaders) actually have: the Black masses can demonstrate, and the "leaders" tremble with fear; the Black masses can riot, and the "leaders" run to Europe for help or sit by while European/American troops attempt to put down the riot (most of the time without checking with the "leaders" beforehand); and the Black masses can refuse to do the lowly and seasonal work they are expected to do, and the economies of Caribbean countries would collapse. Certainly, the Black masses are the strength of the Caribbean. With them is the hope that a better tomorrow will materialize. Because of them the Caribbean will unify and become part of a Black international power network that will oversee the well-being of Black People in all parts of the world. It is with that in mind that We must struggle and continue to struggle.

LESSON 9
LESSON OUTLINE

I. World History Today
   A. Revolution, Self-Determination, Destruction of Neo-Colonialist Structures and Policies
   B. Counter-Revolution, Political/Military Extremism (Repression)
   C. Confusion
   D. Race War
II. The Future: Will Black People Be Prepared?
   A. Political Immaturity
   B. Political Irresponsibility
   C. The Hangover Effects of Our Cosmogeny
   1. The whites have ordered a world that We have not adequately adjusted Ourselves to.

I. World History Today

The trend that started among Black People and took root in the 1940s and 1950s continues to this day (more than 30 years later), and indications are that such will be the case for quite some time to come. When Black People began to break out of the mental programming that had been run on Us by white people, We began to see all types of possibilities for Us as a race and for people of the world in general. We began by dealing as best We could with the problems that were most obvious and most immediate, but as We struggled to eliminate or control these obvious problems, We discovered a host of other problems that had to be resolved also. Let us sum up some of these, first in Africa, then in the Caribbean and, finally, in the United States of America.

The movement that took root recently in Africa and resulted in independence for a number of African countries had the objective of eliminating European white people and their oppressive economic system as disproportionate factors in the lives of Black People. That movement, though deterred by the petty-minded, brainwashed African "leaders", is still going strong today and will not come to an end until every country on the continent has achieved "independence" (the first step toward self-determination). The fall of the apartheid (Jim Crow) regime in South Africa and the placement of Blacks in control of the political processes of that country will probably signify the completion of the initial stages of this process, but it will in no way signal the completion of the African Revolution. That is because the African Revolution is much more than a political process with cosmetic objectives. The African Revolution is much more than a series of events that seeks to put Black persons in positions of power. The African Revolution is a process that seeks self-determination, economic and psychological well-being and justice for African People. It represents a preference of life, a harmonious role for man (people) in the natural scheme of things, a set of values and principles, an interpretation of the world; and its force cannot be fully understood nor appreciated in a purely political context. After the white government in South Africa falls, other processes, many of them intangible, will have to mature, and the African People are very much aware of this. These processes will re-develop the African man and woman and resurrect the African genius and spirit. They will remove much of the psychological and spiritual damage that has been inflicted on Black People in recent centuries and restore Black People, real Black People, to their/ Our proper position in the natural order of things.

As political strides against the Europeans are made this process comes closer and closer to maturity. Yet, there are still many battles to be fought in the political arena. As African People come closer and closer to expelling European whites, they become more and more sensitive to the plight of the Brothers and Sisters in North Africa and they become more and more convinced that another group of foreign whites (the Arabs) will have to be expelled also. Because this other group of foreign whites is very well-entrenched (they have been in Africa for over 1000 years), African People realize that it will be difficult to eliminate them in the same manner the European has been eliminated. However, at practically all costs, these whites must be forced to give up control of the areas they claim; they must be forced to return ownership of the land they have stolen to the African People, and they must either accept a secondary role in the affairs of North Africa or leave the area altogether. Let Us briefly peek at this impending struggle that will be waged by African People to regain control of North Africa.

In very early times, when Black People were in control of North Africa, the people who were to become known as the Arabs hovered around the North African seacoasts. The Arabs-to-be plotted against the native Black population and learned much of the culture and life-style of the African People. Whenever there was a political crisis among the Blacks, the Arabs secured themselves by taking land and by playing "buddy-buddy" with selected Black individuals. When the African People had become so disunited and weak that foreigners were able to militarily invade the land, the Arabs played friend to the invaders and endeared themselves in the process. Throughout the rule of all of the invading whites (beginning with the Assyrians and ending with the Romans), particularly in that section of Africa called Egypt (the United Arab Republic) today, the invading whites attacked the Blacks relentlessly but did little harm to the Arabs (who were so pitiable that they could be ignored by the invading whites with no risk). After the Romans were forced to pull out of North Africa in the 600s C.E., the Arabs began to assume control because the Blacks had been entirely devastated. With the consolidation of Islam approximately 50 years later, the Arabs were able to politically unite themselves as the dominant power in North Africa.

Today nearly all of North Africa is controlled by the Arabs. The United Arab Republic, Libya, Algeria, Mauretania, Tunisia, Morocco and Sudan are countries that fall into this category. These countries are all clearly part of the African continent and belong to Black People. As such, Black People are justified in wanting to regain control of these areas, and the desire to do just that will increase as Black People successfully struggle against exploitation on other fronts. In the Sudan today, a civil war is being fought between the Blacks in the south and the Arabs in the north. This Sudanese War represents two things at once; it represents the final stages of a struggle Black People seem to have lost, and it represents the beginning of a struggle Black People believe they can win. On the first count, the Sudanese War is a continuation of the resistance to Arabic infiltration that has been put up by Blacks in Africa since the Arabs first began to become dominant in the area. With the rise of Islam and the political wars (for land) that were fought in the name of Allah, the Arab people were able to overcome this resistance and steadily move further and further south into Africa. The fact that Arabs now control practically all of North Africa indicates that Black People failed in their attempts to keep this from happening. But the Black People in Sudan did not give up. They continued to struggle, and indications are that the pendulum there has begun moving in another direction. The Arabs have taken control of north Sudan, but have been unable to move any further. This indicates that they have taken as much African land as they can.

Thus, the resistance in Sudan represents the end of the Arabic infiltration in Africa. But, because the Sudanese People are intensifying their resistance and because of the increasing awareness among other African Blacks that the North African situation represents an African problem, the Sudanese War represents the beginning of African efforts to get back what the Arabs have illegally assumed control of. The Arabs must be forced to realize that North Africa is not their home, and a change must be brought about in North Africa that reflects this recognition. Whether the Arabs can be de-emphasized or eliminated to the same degree that has been done to the European is doubtful, but there is no doubt that their power must be broken in each of the countries they control. In order to do this the African People will bring extreme pressure on the Arabs on at least three fronts; the diplomatic front, the economic front and the military front. Diplomatically, Black People will use their recently realized and ever-expanding powers in international organizations such as the United Nations and the Organization of African Unity to condemn and isolate the Arabic people. This will put the Arabs in much the same position that the Zionist Jews and Afrikaaners (South African whites) are in today. Economically, Black People will calculatedly use their position as provider of many of the world's necessary resources to get the major powers of the world to impose sanctions against the Arabs and manipulate the world economic market in a manner that will possibly cripple the Arabic economies. For example, Black People in the central parts of Africa could disrupt the agricultural and commercial life of the United Arab Republic. Militarily, African People in Arabic controlled areas will rise up in rebellion and African People from other areas will fight a united battle against Arabic governments. The Arabic governments and militaries will discover that they are too weak to withstand the combined effects of these measures. They will eventually have to give up the goodies they have come to regard as their own and relinquish control of the governments to the African People who rightfully belong there.

In the beginning, some African "leaders", educated persons and misinformed humanitarians will not understand this issue and will react accordingly, but they will soon be brought into line. The African Revolution will politicize them to a higher level of ideological development and sweep them along, and African justice will reign not just in the southern parts of Africa, but throughout the continent.

The real test of the African Revolution will lie in its ability to eliminate reactionary and near-sighted leaders of African governments. This needs to be done in order to clearly emphasize the African Revolution as a Pan-Africanist movement. Being Pan-Africanist, the African Revolution will move toward Black internationalism instead of Black nationalism. It is important that African People and leaders think in terms of an international governmental structure because such a structure will best equip African People to compete effectively in tomorrow's world. An international state will be the result of the unification of the African nations that presently exist. The results of this unification, in economic, political and psycho-social terms, would be essentially the same as a similar move would have in the Caribbean (which was just mentioned. Review final section of previous Lesson). However, an outstanding additional advantage that the unification of Africa would have is that it would eliminate all of the internal conflicts and bickering that are presently being aired among African countries. African unification would eliminate the territorial disputes that presently keep several African countries at war with each other (Somalia and Ethiopia, for examples), and it would eliminate liberation movements such as those that took place in Biafra (Nigeria), Katanga (Congo/Zaire) and, presently, Eritrea (Ethiopia). In short, it would eliminate much of the cause of internal discord on the African continent and thereby enable the African People to give their time, attention and energy to other matters.

But, before this can happen, African leaders must be willing to give up their positions of power, authority and prestige. Presidents and Prime Ministers of countries must be willing to become simple representatives or just everyday private citizens. How this will happen is yet to be seen, but it will happen, it must happen; or African People will pay the price.

He/She who is qualified to lead is also willing to follow. This criteria can help the African People recognize who the sincere leaders are on the African continent once unification becomes a pressing issue. This criteria can also help the forces of the African Revolution determine who should be divested of power or eliminated in the name of revolutionary progress.

Much of what needs to be said about the Caribbean has already been stated. Just for the sake of emphasis we will do some repeating.

Black People in the Caribbean are more vulnerable to abuse than are Black People in Africa. The location and size of the Caribbean and the lack of a Black world power that Caribbean governments can identify with and look to for support have a lot to do with this. Nonetheless, the Caribbean People will create a secure future for themselves if they move in the direction of a United States of the Caribbean. The factors in favor of this and the economic and political advantages of such a move have already been mentioned.

As in Africa, the key to unification of the Caribbean is the elimination of those weak-minded "leaders" who consider their personal status and prestige to be more desirable than economic progress and political stability for all Caribbean people. However, in addition to this, the Caribbean people must be mentally strong enough to withstand the efforts of outsiders to keep them from unifying. They must be dedicated enough to stand tall in the face of military attacks and occupation by the white powers, and they must intelligently resist these military moves when it is wise to do so. The Caribbean people must also understand enough to resist the efforts of the white powers to strangulate them economically. They must not let immediate economic concerns, particularly unemployment and the threat of poverty, seduce them into adopting a counter-progressive or capitalistic approach to producing and sharing goods and services. And, the Caribbean people must be able to withstand the propaganda the white powers will pour on them. They must be so well aware politically that they see through the lies, distortions and half-truths of white-controlled information centers and sources. Military, economic and propaganda pressures can be brought on the Caribbean people in degrees far greater than they can be brought on Black People in Africa. Therefore, the ideological resistance of the Caribbean people must be exceptional.

The African Revolution will succeed in the Caribbean. The genius, intelligence and functional abilities of Black People in the Caribbean will see to that.

Black People in the United States of America are in trouble. We recognize that white people have been giving Us hell and have more hell in store for Us, but because We have been so sold on American lies, ideals and speeches about democracy, equality and the Constitution, etc., We have a difficult time accepting the fact that hell is all We will ever get from these white people. As a result, We do not accept the responsibility of taking Our welfare into Our own hands. We hope white people will "act right", We pray that the American dream will become real, but we refuse to take Our welfare, the welfare of Black children, women and men, into Our own hands.

Black People in the United States of America are in big trouble. We are economically dependent on white people and, on the whole, are making no efforts to reduce this dependency. We are medically dependent on white people and, on the whole, are making no efforts to reduce this dependency. We depend on white people to educate and socialize Our children and, on the whole, are doing nothing to reduce this dependency. We depend on white people to protect Our lives and property and, on the whole, are doing nothing to reduce this dependency. We also depend on white people to organize Our social, work and recreational activities; and depend on them for clothes, shelter, food, cosmetic conveniences, toilet paper and everything else. In fact, We are so attached to white ideals and ideas that we look to their political and economic system for solutions to the problems white people cause in the first place. Because We are so attached to and dependent on them, white people can cripple Us at any time in a variety of ways.

Black People in the United States are surrounded by a powerful and hostile enemy. They are governed by a political system that has encouraged white people to make war on Black People for more than 400 years. Black People are governed by a system that has allowed white people to systematically wage a race war against Black People since 1865. Black People are in the midst of a group of people whose racism is so powerful that it interferes with their intelligence. We are bound by the laws, rules and regulations of these racists. Anything We do, from singing in public to criticizing the government's treatment of Black People can be made illegal and punishable by law. Anything We do naturally that white people don't do can be made into a crime, and any misfortune that befalls Us as a race can be systematically manipulated to further Our suffering. Considering all of these factors, We should be working overtime to gain control of Our own destiny, but too many of Us are not so occupied.

Black People in the United States of America are more vulnerable (open to attack) than Black People in Africa and the Caribbean because We have been thoroughly brainwashed and psychologically duped, We have no liberated land base, We do not have the ability to produce goods, We are economically dependent, We have no legal political institutions through which We may express Our dissatisfactions and realistically hope for redress and We have

10 LESSONS

no means of legally preparing to defend Ourselves in an organized manner. Many of Us have been robbed of even the will to defend Ourselves or attempt to improve Our lot. But, in the days to come, in spite of Our tendency to wait and be patient, the masses of Black People will begin to resist white people's madness in an organized manner because white people will intensify their racist attacks and wage war against Us more viciously. Already an overwhelming number of Us are convinced that integration will not work (because white people will not allow it to work), so Our train of thought will be more and more receptive to more extreme yet logical solutions to Our woes. First, We will become more apt to reduce Our dependency on white people in minor but important ways. We will want to teach Our own and politicize Our own, e.g. Then We will begin to re-direct Our voluntary services so that Black-oriented organizations and programs receive Our time free of charge. We will begin to financially support those efforts that are Black-oriented and recognize the need to take on the responsibility of feeding Ourselves, caring for Ourselves and defending Ourselves, for example. These changes in attitude and activities will not go unnoticed by white people, and they will respond by giving Us more hell. This response on their part will help convince Us that We cannot adequately provide for Black People as long as white people and their government can legally interfere with Our efforts. More and more, We will recognize the need to be politically independent of them. That way, they would have no legal basis for interfering with Us, and We would have a legal basis for defending Ourselves whenever they do interfere with Us.

In future years, Black People in the United States of America will recognize that the best thing we can do is prepare to govern Ourselves and establish institutions that will be beneficial to Us. We will let go of the American dream and face up to the American nightmare that exists for Black People. When We do this, much of Our confusion/brainwashing will eliminate itself and We will understand exactly where We stand insofar as national and international politics are concerned. As a result, the race war that has been waged against Us for more than 100 years will become a two way battle. For white people the war will emerge as the final move to get rid of "them niggers". For Black People the war will represent a move to defend Ourselves against racist attacks and develop into a struggle for national liberation and national sovereignty. It will be a series of bloody confrontations for self-government, self-determination and land, and it will be fought in the streets of America until Black and white heads have cooled down enough to appreciate a less vicious solution to America's woes. That war will not be a civil war, but one involving colonized people (Black People) versus colonizers (white people), and it will not be participated in by all Black persons nor all white persons in this country. But, it will benefit Us tremendously because it will force white people to respect Us and negotiate with Us as equals, it will result in self-determination for Black

People in this part of the world, and it will make it more difficult for Americans to effectively interfere with the forces of the African Revolution in the Caribbean and Africa.

Additionally, the race war will develop within Us a greater affinity for and desire to identify with Black People in other parts of the world. It will serve to make Us practical citizens of the Black world and increase interaction and interdependency between Us and Black People everywhere. It will make Us actual Pan-Africanists and part of the international Black Power movement. This development might well be the most significant outcome of Our confrontation with white people in the United States of America.

Because Black People in the United States have a somewhat thorough understanding of what is actually happening in the world (which makes Our lack of commitment all the more unbelievable), proper leadership should not emerge as a problem once we decide to take Our destiny into Our own hands. Already, the persons who are projected as Our leaders, the Vernon Jordans and Jesse Jacksons, for example, are largely ignored by the masses of Us. Such "leaders" will be completely de-emphasized once We join the African Revolution full force, and the modern day versions of the Marcus Garveys, Malcolm Xs, Imari Obadeles and Huey Newtons will draw Our attention. Such persons will give Us the leadership We need because they will sincerely represent Our will and aspirations, and because they will look to Our priorities, sympathies and actions to guide them.

Black People in the United States must be very aware of the image We are projecting to people in other parts of the world. Because We have been Americanized and because We have a tendency to let whites use Us, people in other parts of the world who are oppressed are developing a tendency to associate Us with white people. They see Us as white people's friends who get a share of the loot when white people take advantage of other groups of people. They have good reason for developing that tendency because We represent white people in the United Nations, We fight for white people in all parts of the world and We defend the actions of white governments when We vacation in foreign lands. However, We must begin to take pains to express Our discord with whites to people in all parts of the world. We must let the struggling and oppressed peoples of the world know that We are not the allies of these international hoodlums and thieves. By so doing, We will establish Ourselves as a revolutionary force and enjoy the trust and confidence of people who are playing a part in the re-shaping of the international hierarchy. Slowly but surely, America and white world power are sinking. We don't want to sink with them, so We must make it clear to the revolutionary forces of the world that We are revolutionary also. To fail to do so would be to leave Us with a handicap that will seriously cripple Us and the African Revolution.

We mentioned the re-shaping of the international hierarchy (the power

10 LESSONS

relationship of one country to other countries). For years this hierarchy has been characterized by white countries at the top (playing the bully role) and other countries below (being dominated by the white countries). Nowadays, people all over the world who have been historically dominated by the white powers are rebelling against their oppressors and taking control of their own economic and political destiny. For a long time oppressed people (because they were weak militarily) let fear of the white powers keep them in line, but now they have realized that as long as they let their fear control them the white powers will mercilessly dominate them and take advantage of them. As a result, oppressed peoples have resolved to resist the superpowers, and in so doing have realized that their will power is greater than the military might of the superpowers. This realization, of itself, set the wheels in motion that have shaken the international status quo because it made people realize that they could not be defeated by foreign invaders and gave even the tiniest nation of people the courage to insist on either economic and political justice and self-determination or total annihilation. In the face of such courage the superpowers, even with their advanced bombs and arsenals, have discovered that they cannot exploit people in the manner they want to exploit them. The superpowers have discovered that they can be forced to make concessions to even the smallest country, and they will readily make the necessary concessions in future years or suffer the consequences.

Of course, the superpowers can always choose to flex their muscles, but this will mean little to people who are ready to die if necessary. The superpowers can massacre large numbers of people and destroy virtually at will, but these type responses will not get the superpowers what they want. To destroy without the hope of economic gain is to waste time, materials, energy, money and lives, and lose international prestige. It is therefore as undesirable as it is hopeless.

But, such a response cannot be passed off as unlikely or an impossibility. Human beings have a strong capacity for acting unreasonably, and this is particularly true of white people whose economic demands have been steadfastly challenged. Instead of yielding to the demands of oppressed people from the beginning, some white countries will try to use force to get their way. If they try so against people who are committed to determining their own destiny, the white powers will get the same treatment the Vietnamese people recently gave to the French and the Americans.

This is the dawning of a revolutionary age. Already, the initial stages of this revolutionary age have been put into motion. The liberation movements in Africa, Asia, South America and other parts of the world have changed national governments and the relationship of these governments to each other. Soon this revolutionary process will move upward to a higher stage because it will concern itself with re-defining the relationship between national governments and the masses of the people they are supposed to represent. The revolutionary process that is presently taking root goes beyond the European concept of revolution. It represents a world order the European will have to learn about and adapt to. In short, it represents a world order the European is not capable of leading. For the sake of progress then, white people will have to be forced to take a back seat so non-white people, people who understand what is developing, can direct humanity to a different method and level of social intercourse.

A new world order is emerging. The masses, particularly people of color, are no longer satisfying themselves with only talking about those things that need to be done and doing those things that only need to be talked about. The masses are getting involved (and learning to stay involved) in the critical issues, and in the process are re-defining what power is. Power is no longer a strictly military (political and economic) phenomenon. Power is now psychological and spiritual as well. Power is a frame of mind. It is an ability, unquestionably: to influence others, to control others, to frustrate others and to not be co-erced or manipulated by others; but the limited and traditional means of demonstrating that ability are no longer accepted as valid. In that regard, they are indicative of the white world in general. It, the white world (its standards, etc.), is no longer accepted as valid by people of color. A new set of international standards and relationships is impending.

II. The Future: Will Black People Be Prepared?

A new world order is in store, but those who are accustomed to and satisfied with the old world order will subtly and openly fight the newly developing order at every turn. Additionally, the governments that are reshaping the international hierarchy are prompted by nationalist interests, and are therefore prone to ignore the interests of others in favor of themselves. Thus it is wise that We, Black People, peek into the future. Throughout this Handbook We have been made aware of what Our strengths are, what is in store for Us and what the possibilities are. In order to secure Ourselves, We must be clear about what shortcomings are likely to hinder Us most and be conscious of what We have to do to limit the negative impact of these shortcomings.

In 1981, Black People in all parts of the world are politically immature. We have not yet come to understand what politics is really all about. We have not yet realized that politics is about relentless, unrelenting warfare; psychological slaughter, economic strangulation, spiritual havoc, social disease and physical destruction. Politics assumes that the negative tendencies of people will dominate their conduct, and politicians therefore aim to incapacitate people (their enemies) by crippling, maiming and eliminating them. There is no room for sentiments and chances in white people's political scheme of things, nor is there room for trust outside of your own race or interest ·group. The assumption, if one is to survive, must always be, "either we act in our interest or allow others to act in a manner that will be harmful to us."

Black People must realize that politics is a dirty, dog-eat-dog business. Under no circumstances should We take on a political attitude toward each other, but We must assume a political attitude and mode of conduct toward white people. We cannot consider their humane possibilities because such considerations will make Us vulnerable (leave Us open to attack). We must assume that every move of others is geared toward taking advantage of Us in some way, and gear Our actions toward minimizing the possible affects others can have on Us. We cannot be overly concerned about doing what is right or just when We are confronted by Our enemies, but concern Ourselves with doing what will best protect Us and contribute to Our survival. We must mature in the political sense of the word, and in white people's scheme of things political maturity is characterized by the ability to be coldly calculating, prejudicial, detached and efficient. We must forget about and totally reject white ideologies and white trains of thought, concentrate on "Blackness" and let white people know that We can be just as cunning and destructive as they can be— — and demonstrate the same when We are confronted by them.

We, Black People, must mature politically in order to avoid a lot of unnecessary suffering at the hands of Our enemies in the future. We must adapt the premise that _the only chance a civilized people have in a world dominated by barbarians lies in their ability to consciously and continually manipulate others._ Sometimes this manipulation lies in convincing the barbarians that they, the civilized people, can be just as barbaric and primitive as everyone else. In order to do this effectively, We must control Our emotions and sentiments and allow practical analysis to direct the way We act.

Black People are also politically irresponsible. A brief quotation from "The People's Newsletter" will introduce Us to one aspect of this irresponsibleness:

Nobody [Black person] wants to help— to be "involved"; to become a member of a Black organization. And this is at a time when white persons are becoming members of the Ku Klux Klan in record numbers; when Jews are re-enforcing themselves; and when Nazis in America are re-enforcing themselves. Everybody or group that has traditionally slaughtered Black People and generally "screwed" Us is getting its racist and insane things going full speed again, but most of Us, for the wildest of reasons, refuse to help get Black People's thing together. At a time when the KKK is getting ready to yank you off the street, at a time when the Jews are getting ready to strangle you in the name of Jehovah, and at a time when the Nazis are getting ready to use you for target practice, you [Black People] decide to not prepare to defend yourself. We cannot understand your rationale (if that terms applies here)!!!

All of Us know what white people are running down on Us. All of Us cannot break the process down ideologically, but in the face of what Our eyes see, ears hear and noses smell, no ideological breakdown is needed to convince Us that We should be making moves to take control of Our own destiny. But far too many of Us, for the wildest of reasons, refuse to act with that objective in mind. We will do almost anything before We will function consistently and establish institutions that will rid Black People of white people's control. We will party, We will buy and steal clothes and other "goodies", We will ride around in circles in big and little cars, We will get "high" and drunk, We will look at television and listen to the radio, etc.; but We will not donate money to, steal for, support or participate in the activities of a Black-oriented organization *on a consistent basis*. We will seek almost any excuse to not function as We should politically; We will talk about losing Our job, We will stress Our personal problems (even though all of Our "personal" problems are in fact social/group, the results of racist and economic exploitation and pressure), We will talk about the power of white people and We will insist that Black People "ain't gonna do nothing." Still others of Us will "turn off" at the mere thought of supporting or participating in Black organizations and Black-oriented efforts. This type political irresponsibleness must be overcome because white people are serious about their politics. They will scientifically use every one of Our shortcomings to their advantage and against Us. If then, they are politically responsible and We are not, they will keep the power to determine what We eat, if We can dress and where We can take shelter. Whites should not be able to make those type decisions for Us, but We must eliminate Our irresponsibleness before We can keep them from making those type decisions for Us.

Unfortunately, Black persons who are aware of the intricacies of politics and of the need for Black People to function in an organized, responsible manner are themselves politically irresponsible. They fall prey to many of the shortcomings We just mentioned, but cause more immediate danger because they often work with community organizations which are supposed to be in the vanguard (front) of Black People's struggle for liberation. Being politically active, yet irresponsible, such persons project an image to the Black masses that is contradictory and reactionary (counter-progressive), and not at all representative of the sincere Black progressive person or organization. Such persons place particular organizational objectives ahead of community objectives, capitalize at the expense of the Black persons who seek an alternative life-style and set of values and alienate themselves from the Blacks who have been most victimized by white people and their political/economic system. Such aware Black persons are simply clones of many of the "leaders" we referred to recently. They turn the masses off and make the masses suspicious of persons and organizations that are truly nationalist and revolutionary. For that reason, they must overcome their irresponsibleness quickly. If not, the irresponsible "leaders' and community activists must voluntarily lay low or be forced to do so.

Much of Our political irresponsibleness is due to the brainwashing We have undergone and the historical role We have been forced to play for 1000 years or more. The brainwashing has left Us with a tendency to automatically skip the subject when serious thoughts begin to enter Our minds, and the role We have played historically has left Us accustomed to dealing with trivial matters only. It has discouraged Us from taking on serious tasks and left Us feeling comfortable letting "someone else" handle those type matters. As a result of being so, we really don't do anything as a race of people, particularly in the Americas. We look after Our personal selves in personal ways as best We can, but when it comes to Us as a race or group, We cannot practically conceive of anything to do. Black People all over the world need to be educated, but we cannot conceive of Us actually educating each other. Black People all over the world need to be fed, but We cannot conceive of Us actually putting the wheels in motion that will get Us fed. Black People all over the world need clothes and medical care, but We cannot conceive of Us actually attending to those matters. Not only do We not conceive of taking care of those matters on an international level, We don't even conceive of doing those things on a national or local level. Especially is this true of Black People in the United States of America. In spite of Our advanced level of education, in spite of Our management and supervisory positions and in spite of Our income of far more than 100 billion dollars a year, We prefer to let white people decide for and provide Us with basic needs and services. Too many of Us get the urge to spit on or harm a Black person who "has the nerve" to talk about a national system of education and economic sustenance (among other things) for Black People that is supported by Black People. Such persons will quickly tell you that they pay taxes to the United States government, that the government is therefore responsible for dealing with those type matters, and that they need what they have left over after taxes to support themselves. The fact that the U. S. government does not use Black People's taxes to benefit Black People does not bother such persons at all. What does bother them is the thought of having to buy bricks and books for a Black school instead of gas and oil for a second car. It's a pity and a shame that We are so irresponsible, but it's true.

Nonetheless, regardless of what has contributed to Our lack of responsibleness, regardless of why We are like We are, the fact of the matter is that We have to overcome that shortcoming. We must begin to take the same attitude of survival and independence that We hold for Our individual selves and apply it to Black People in general. Such an attitude will give Us something worthwhile to do, make Our lives less hectic and very fulfilling, and render Us capable of minimizing the control white people have over Us. In Our days of grandeur, We did not have a political attitude (such an attitude was foreign to Us because We believed in the goodness of people) but We were responsible to each other. That feeling of responsibleness must be reacquired and allowed to assert itself.

Finally, Black People must overcome the hangover effects of Our cosmogeny that have contributed to Our failure to adequately represent Ourselves in the world white people have ordered. The term cosmogeny refers to the manner in which a certain group of people developed its view of the universe. It refers to the attitudes, mannerisms and ways of doing things that became a part of a certain people's being and largely determined how that people (or race) related to the world around them, to objects (property) and to each other. The term also refers to the subconscious or underlying attitudes and feelings people have about economics, psychology, society, sex, war, work, pleasure, authority and responsibility, etc., and how these attitudes and feelings project themselves or motivate the people they are a part of. Do they cause a people to take a casual, "if not now then later" approach to social functions and social processes or a calculated, urgent, "do-or-die" approach? In the world that has been ordered by white people, a calculated, urgent, "do-or-die" approach is necessary. Black People have largely failed to adapt this approach, and this failure is victimizing Us in serious ways.

The broader aspects of Our cosmogeny are just as valid today as they were 6000 years ago. The theories and practices Our forefathers developed concerning economics, the social structure, work, pleasure, authority and responsibility, etc., are just as valid as (and more beneficial to people than) those white people developed. The technology Black People developed during the early years is more fundamentally sound than that which is flaunted by white people today, and the same can be said about Our ways of relating to each other, to objects and to the world around Us. Thus, it was (and is) to Our advantage to hold onto these broader aspects of Our cosmogeny because Our strengths, the keys to Our survival and liberation, are found therein. However, the underlying/subconscious attitudes and feelings We developed have been a hindrance to Us since white people gained dominance over Us. These subconscious attitudes and feelings have kept Us from making some minor adjustments that could bring about some major changes in Our ability to adequately represent Ourselves in a white-dominated world and in Our ability to become a dominant force in world affairs.

In short, We have to control Our casual, "if not now, then later" tendencies

10 LESSONS

and enable a calculated, urgent, "do-or-die" attitude to motivate Us. We do not have to change any of the broader aspects of Our cosmogeny— as was just stated, those elements are more than adequate and can serve Us well; but We must make little changes here and little changes there. Little considerations and adjustments can make big accomplishments probable, and this single adjustment in Our attitude and feelings would impel Us to take on a different perspective insofar as the use of time is concerned, the waging of war (declared and undeclared) is concerned, insofar as Our expectations from humanity are concerned and insofar as being precise is concerned.

Of all these, the different perspective of time would be most beneficial. A casual approach to the use of time manifests itself as a weakness in today's world. We must stop functioning according to "colored people's time" (which would be okay under different circumstances) and start making effective use of the clock. We cannot compete effectively nor exert Ourselves effectively if We insist on not being prompt (on time) and not doing things when they are supposed to be done. We must begin to make use of every second, and in so doing make the most productive use of each day. We cannot afford to let time "slip away" when We are supposed to be functioning. We have a lot of building to do and obstacles to overcome, and We must apply an advantageous perspective of time to the broader aspects of Our cosmogeny if We hope to exert Ourselves in meaningful, substantial ways.

Secondly, We must recognize the importance of being precise about what we say and what we do, particularly in this highly political international arena. We must get into the habit of saying what we mean, meaning what we say (being sincere about what we say) and doing what We say We are going to do (taking care of Our responsibilities). We have to be precise when we make plans, and each of Us must be committed enough to follow through on his or her role in those plans. We cannot promise 100% and come up with less than 100% when it's time for action. We have to be precise. That way, other persons will know what to expect from everybody else and plans can be made which compensate for those who are not able to function or participate fully.

Thirdly, We must realize that war is a deadly matter in this type environment. To Our forefathers war was a serious matter because it indicated a lack of harmony that mediation and negotiation could not settle. But to white people, and in the world white people have ordered, war is more than a serious matter; it is a deadly matter. It is a destructive method of forcing one people's will on another group of people, and it seeks to destroy people psychologically and spiritually as well as physically and biologically.

In the world white people have ordered, war is a condition. In Our world, war was a circumstance, a temporary clash that was characterized by brief skirmishes, few injuries and a relatively quick cessation of hostilities. The hostilities are ever-present in the white world, so "the enemy" is always being scoped out and plotted against. Black People must recognize this reality because it will help Us defend Ourselves and wage war against Our enemies effectively. We must recognize that We must defend Ourselves and attack Our enemies even when there are no bombs being dropped or shots being fired. We must be aware of and willing to wage economic warfare, psychological warfare and spiritual warfare as well as physical and biological warfare, and We must be mentally prepared to do so for extended periods of time. In order to build a world that will be more respectful of and beneficial to Us, We are going to have to prove to those who love war that We can be just as destructive as they can. Our civilized attitude toward war is no good to Us in this type environment. Therefore, We have to control that attitude and allow one to motivate Us that is better suited for the occasion.

Finally, We must realize that the humanitarian tendencies of people in this type environment are not as strong as those of people who are accustomed to less threatening conditions and circumstances. People in this type environment will talk about justice and what ought to be, but their energy and concern run out at that point. Rarely will they act in a manner that can bring about justice. We should recognize this and stop expecting certain persons to sincerely assist Us or function in a manner that Our ethical orientation would consider proper. People in this type structure are motivated more by economics than humane considerations, so We should stop expecting them to do what civilized people feel obligated to do. Instead, We must recognize their humanity as a farce and concentrate Our spiritual energies on generating good feelings among Ourselves, about Ourselves. We must get more into Ourselves, and as a result of so doing better enable Ourselves to organize effectively and build the type power base that will force those fake humanitarians to stop abusing Us and give up what they have that rightfully belongs to Us.

Humanitarianism is no more than a notion to white people. We cannot maximize Our advances if any of Our energy is being used to appeal to a notion. (To understand more about these points, review Lesson #1.)

Because of Our cosmogeny, We developed attitudes, practices and habits that make Us vulnerable in a world dominated by white people; We are not inclined to be as cruel as they. Because of Our cosmogeny, We respond to certain needs and wants and react to threats to Our survival in ways that are inadequate and inefficient (in a white-dominated world); We are not as insecure as they are (psychologically speaking). Because of Our cosmogeny, We possess many of the traits that contributed to the failure of the native American (the so-called Indian) to resist the bloody march of white people across this continent (Review Lesson #2). In order to insure Our survival, liberate Ourselves and effectively compete with other people, We will have to control many of Our tendencies that are ill-fitted for this white-ordered world, adapt many of the elements that are advantageous in a structure such as this, and apply those elements to the broader aspects of Our cosmogeny.

Will Black People be prepared for future events? Probably not. In future days Black People will endure a great deal of unnecessary suffering in spite of the fact that We are quite aware of what is to come. We will continue to procrastinate (waste valuable time), We will continue to make excuses and rationalize, We will continue to hope things will turn out all right (there is no sound basis for this), We will continue to shun Our responsibility to Ourselves, Our loved ones and future generations of Black People, and We will fail to overcome the hangover effects of Our cosmogeny (that were just mentioned) quickly enough. However, We will survive, and We will eventually make the necessary adjustments that will enable Us to free Ourselves and become a dominant force in the world. We will do this because of Our advanced state of civilized development and because of Our ability to apply Our intelligence to practical situations during a crisis; but more than anything else, We will do so because white people will force Us to do so. They (white people) are going to be putting Us through so much extreme hell and slaughtering Us in such large numbers that We will have no other choice. It is unfortunate that We have to suffer that way before We do what We should be doing anyway, but it seems that, as unfortunate as it is, it is real.

So, Black People will not be prepared in time (the very person who is reading this Handbook will probably be partly to blame), but We will survive. Because of Ourselves and in spite of Ourselves We will survive; We will react without adequate pre-planning, We will make adjustments in the midst of chaos, We will become self-determining and, step by step, We will regain Our proper place in the natural order of things.

I. Synopsis
II. Excerpts

I. SYNOPSIS

A proper study of history reveals the development of two extreme approaches to life and principles related thereto. One approach was molded into Black People who developed under natural conditions that were rough but conducive to humane considerations and feelings of economic security. The principle related thereto will be called the pleasure principle. The other approach was molded into white people who developed under natural conditions that made economic security a near impossibility and contact with others for sociable reasons an exceptional (infrequent) event. The principle related thereto will be called the business principle. Neither principle is more or less valid than the other and neither represents a superior or inferior degree of intelligence. Both are simply human responses to conditions that greatly influenced a particular people's quest to survive. No more or less, insofar as relative merit is concerned, need be said.

Whether human activities, human intercourse and the social order will revolve around life as a rewarding, enjoyable experience or life as a struggle to survive is the basic question addressed by each of these principles. Those who developed and functioned according to the pleasure principle were able to view life as an experience that should be enjoyed. They recognized that certain social functions (economic, governmental, judicial, etc.) had to be organized, that rules of conduct and responsibility had to be established and that certain roles had to be defined, etc., but their basic contention was that these functions could be carried out adequately without taking the joy out of life. Those who developed and functioned according to the business principle did not have the opportunity to experience and develop a real appreciation for life as an enjoyable experience. To them life was a struggle to survive first and foremost, therefore the social functions that were recognized as necessary and the roles that had to be defined were done so with survival in mind. There was little, if any, time for fun, play and relaxation, and no room for a casual attitude. Life was primarily business, and those who failed to keep busy struggling to survive would certainly meet up with disaster.

Whether human activities, human intercourse and the social order will revolve around life as a rewarding, enjoyable experience or life as a struggle to survive is the basic question upon which Black People and white people differ today. It is the issue upon which the two have differed from the beginning, and white people's efforts to reduce their feelings of insecurity by imposing their solution to this question onto other peoples of the world has forced them to develop strategies and theories that justify white approaches to life and ridicule all other approaches. White people's inability to "hang loose" even in the midst of plenty and their insistence on organizing the productive energies of the world's peoples for the benefit of white people have led them to rotate much of their educational system around "scholarly" teachings and doctrines that are not consistent with nor supported by an objective interpretation of human history. For white people, the purpose of education is not to report the facts in order to develop minds properly, but to present information that will mold a train of thought that justifies what white people do. Thus, persons who have been directly or indirectly educated by white people have a distorted view of history and a distorted view of the people white people have taken advantage of (particularly Black People).

These distortions make it difficult for people to tell right from wrong and keep people from accurately evaluating history. The failure to accurately evaluate history keeps people moving three steps forward and two steps backward, then two steps forward and three steps backward; that is, seemingly making progress but actually never doing so. The failure to accurately evaluate history also keeps people holding onto narrow prejudices that have no validity outside of a certain set of circumstances. Inasmuch as this is the case, it keeps the different peoples of the world from accepting each other as equals and sincerely working toward a world order that systematically discriminates against nobody.

All told, these distortions serve the purpose of prolonging the economic and psychological domination of the world by white people. However, that period of domination has been stretched to its limit, and strides are being made by people of color that are tearing the basis of white world power apart. Many of the people of color who are changing the world order are not advocates of the pleasure principle; they have adapted many of the ways of white people in order to compete with whites effectively. But, the advances that are being made by Black People are definitely strides toward an efficient and humane but enjoyable way-of-life. Because other people of color are less inclined to take the business approach that white people take, other people of color will adapt the pleasure principle approach to life as Black People become more influential and white people less so.

A gigantic task rests upon the minds, spirits and bodies of Black People. That task involves the perpetuation of human forces that will steer humankind in the direction of the pleasure principle. We must make it possible for people to realize that life is supposed to be a joyful process, and make it possible for people to reject ideas and innovations that are not consistent with this principle. As was stated earlier, this principle does not assume that life is a period of irresponsible fun and play; it simply contends that the social functions, rules of conduct and areas of responsibility can be efficiently carried out without taking the joy out of life. Since white people have imposed conditions that make life a struggle, and since this in itself is unnatural, it is necessary that a group or race end this living hell and create conditions that will allow people to live and function according to Nature's scheme of things (in peaceful co-existence and harmony with all of Nature's constituents). Black People are best equipped to so do.

But, We must deal with first things first. The reality of today's world is that governments and the people they supposedly represent are not concerned about all of humanity. Particularly in white countries, the tendency is for a given group of people to go all for themselves as single units or as part of a power bloc. As a result, in order for Black People to effectively represent Our interests, We will have to be able to defend Ourselves against white people and people who have seriously adapted the white principle of life.

In other words, We must concentrate on making Ourselves powerful before We can afford to function for the benefit of humankind. Black People all over the world must work toward becoming part of an international Black Power bloc that adheres to a philosophy of international Black Power first and foremost. Conditions necessitate that We become Black-centric and remain so until the basic needs of Black People are righteously and systematically satisfied. If such a course brings on cries of reverse racism or whatever, then so be it. Hopefully, We have matured enough by this time to not be concerned about accusations made by Our enemies and people who fail to think objectively or intelligently.

The future of Black People lies in the hands of Black People. What WE do or fail to do will be the determining factor in Our immediate condition and Our long range condition. If life once again becomes a joyful process (relatively free of mental, spiritual and psychological stress and strain), We will need to look no further than Ourselves for the reason why. If life continues to be a living hell, We will need to look no further than Ourselves for the reason why.

II. EXCERPTS

Brothers and Sisters, if you are sincerely concerned about the well-being and future of Black People, you must begin to analyze events seriously and from a Black perspective. To get a clear understanding of where you stand historically (and otherwise), read the books listed in the Introduction of this Handbook at least twice (if you can get copies of them), read other information that revolves around Black People and get involved in the work of the independent Black community organizations in your area (local and national). We must be in control of the forces that determine the quality of Our lives before We can claim to be "equal", but We can never be in control of those forces if Black individuals like yourself (the reader) fail to be responsible to the Black Community at large.

We will close by citing excerpts of two articles from "The People's Newsletter." The first is geared to those of Us who are just being introduced to the concept of Black Power and real equality. The second is geared to those who profess to be politically aware and committed to the liberation and self-determination of Black People. Pay close attention to each of them.

(1) "HAVE BLACK PEOPLE MADE IT?"

Black People have made it to the suburbs, where We live next door to white people in houses and apartments and stand in line with white people in department stores and quick food restaurants. Black People have made it to white schools, where We learn to speak white languages and tell white lies just like white people do. Black People have made it to the beauty parlors, where We straighten Our hair, squeeze Our noses and make Our thick lips thin so We can look like white people look. And, Black People have made it away from the used car lots; now We can buy a brand new car and make it to the Capital Centre (a place of recreation) in style. If these things are what equality is all about, then Black People have certainly made it.

But, do Black People have independent land of Our own where We can grow food Black People need in order to survive? No, We don't, but white people do. Do Black People have a government of Our own that makes the laws that Black People live by? No, We don't, but white people do. Do Black People have an army of Our own that will defend Us against foreigners who attack Us? No, We don't, but white people do. Do Black People have an economy of Our own, one which focuses on the economic well-being of Black People? No, We don't, but white people do. And, do Black People have a social structure of Our own, one that will direct Us in Our personal and interpersonal relationships. No, We don't, but white people do. It follows then, that if these things are what equality is all about, Black People certainly have not made it.

(2) [TIME AND VISION]

Time is the factor that separates the revolutionaries from the reactionaries. Time reveals who is serious about Nationhood and who is not. Time exposes those of Us who are "for real" about Our Blackness, and segregates those who rant and rave and use Blackness as a platform aimed at relieving their individual frustrations and anxieties. Time, Brothers and Sisters, Time. Time will tell.

Vision is necessary if We are to stand the test of time. Vision enables Us to peek into the future, to see where We are going, and to prepare for the obstacles which are temporarily going to hold Us back. If We can't see these things (obstacles and victories) beforehand, We will become disenchanted and use any setback as proof of the hopelessness of Our efforts, and thereby excuse Ourselves from any further involvement.

You can't see into the future with your eyes, Brothers and Sisters. You have to use your mind. But your mind must first be developed. Anyone can see from one day to the next, or from one week to the next, but this short vision won't prepare you to deal with a struggle that spans generations. To do this you have to understand, to the core, what has happened and what is happening.

10 LESSONS